MW00573668

Teachers' Roles in Second Language Learning

Classroom Applications of Sociocultural Theory

A Volume in
Research in Second Language Learning

Series Editor:
JoAnn Hammadou Sullivan, *University of Rhode Island*

Research in Second Language Learning

JoAnn Hammadou Sullivan, Series Editor

Teachers' Roles in Second Language Learning

Classroom Applications of Sociocultural Theory

edited by

Bogum Yoon
State University of New York at Binghamton

and

Hoe Kyeung Kim
Cleveland State University

Information Age Publishing, Inc.
Charlotte, North Carolina • www.infoagepub.com

Library of Congress Cataloging-in-Publication Data

Teachers' roles in second language learning : classroom applications of
sociocultural theory / edited by Bogum Yoon and Hoe Kyeung Kim.
p. cm. -- (Research in second language learning)
Includes bibliographical references.
ISBN 978-1-61735-847-0 (pbk.) -- ISBN 978-1-61735-848-7 (hardcover) --
ISBN 978-1-61735-849-4 (ebook) 1. English--Study and teaching--Foreign
speakers. 2. Language and languages--Study and teaching--Social aspects. 3.
Education, Bilingual. 4. Code switching (Linguistics) I. Yoon, Bogum. II.
Kim, Hoe Kyeung.
PE1128.A2T384 2012
428.0071--dc23

2012011838

Copyright © 2012 IAP–Information Age Publishing, Inc.

All rights reserved. No part of this publication may be reproduced, stored in a retrieval system, or transmitted in any form or by any electronic or mechanical means, or by photocopying, microfilming, recording or otherwise without written permission from the publisher.

Printed in the United States of America

CONTENTS

FOREWORD

Leo van Lier

This collection contains a number of valuable studies on the many different roles that teachers enact in language classrooms. The contributions relate these roles to principles and practices that underlie them, united by a sociocultural theory (SCT) perspective. It is both necessary and illuminating to see so many studies that are firmly situated in language classrooms, yet illustrate a wealth of different settings. Despite the variety, all the studies illustrate one or more of the fundamental principles and practices of SCT: mediation, meaning making in interaction, the relationships between gestures and language to create meaning, the combined force of different languages in bilingual and multicultural classrooms, drawing on funds of knowledge, intercultural processes, collaborative interaction and engagement, and more.

What is also worthy of note is that SCT theory and pedagogical practices are fully integrated in these studies; theoretical ideas and practical experiences inform one another, as aspects of dynamic classroom interaction are illustrated and analyzed. In this brief foreword I will make some comments on the theoretical side of SCT, and then conclude with some practical observations.

Sociocultural theory (SCT) has become increasingly influential in the field of second language learning and research since its first appearance in the 1980s. Before that, there is no doubt that many of the ideas and promises of Vygotskyan thinking had already been much discussed in educational circles (e.g., through the work of Jerome Bruner, Urie Bronfenbrenner and many others—see van Lier, 2004), as well as in language teaching contexts. However, it was not until translated versions of

Teachers' Roles in Second Language Learning:
Classroom Applications of Sociocultural Theory, pp. vii–x
Copyright © 2012 by Information Age Publishing
All rights of reproduction in any form reserved.

Vygotsky's work became widely available in the late 1970s and early 1980s that the core ideas of SCT began to be applied to language education.

To begin with, much of the attention of the field was devoted to coming to grips with the theoretical ramifications of SCT, and how these related to other theories within SLA and applied linguistics. Having said that, as early as 1994 two collections were published that contained a number of practical studies as well: Lantolf and Appel (1994), and a special issue of the *Modern Language Journal*, edited by Jim Lantolf. Among the contributions that are still very influential to this day were Aljaafreh and Lantolf (1994), Donato (1994), and Coughlan and Duff (1994).

Theoretical research is very important, and so of course are theoretical advances. SCT has provided a number of closely argued and carefully supported areas of relevance of Vygotsky's ideas for language education and development, relying also on Vygotskyan scholars in general education and social psychology, such as Jim Wertsch, René van der Veer, Jaan Valsiner, Michael Cole, Luis Moll, and Yrjo Engeström, among many others (for an authoritative exposition, see Lantolf & Thorne, 2006; for references to these authors' work see the chapters in this volume). There is little doubt that, as a result of these endeavors, SCT now has a solid footing among theories of SLA. At the more practical and pedagogical level, in addition to the two 1994 collections mentioned above, the more recent collection edited by Lantolf and Poehner (2008) also includes a number of classroom-oriented studies.

At this point in time, then, it is safe to say that SCT has, over the last three or four decades, matured and that it now exerts a significant amount of influence on SLA, both in the theoretical and in the practical realm. In addition, SCT has become what I would call "a family member" of a variety of approaches of theory, research, and practice that have many principles and practices in common. These include situated learning (Lave & Wenger, 1991), conversation analysis-for-SLA (Kasper & Wagner, 2011), complexity theory and developmental systems theory (Ellis & Larsen-Freeman, 2009), the ecology of learning (van Lier 2004), and a several other approaches that extend the traditional concerns of SLA. Many of these approaches are influenced, directly or indirectly, by Vygotskyan ideas.

I do not claim that SCT can be the be-all and end-all of SLA theories. I do not think for example, that it makes any sense to see it as a new orthodoxy replacing an older one that is sometimes called, rather unhelpfully in my view, "traditional" SLA. What we do see is an increased diversity of perspectives that, according to some critics, amounts to an unhealthy proliferation of different theories and outlooks, thus diminishing the likelihood for concerted progress in our fledgling field of SLA. I personally do not think that theoretical diversity has a detrimental effect on a field's progress. However, I do think as well that open-minded dialogue and frank debate have a place in an open arena for argument and discussion. From this perspective there is much to be learned from the variety of theoretical and practical presentations and colloquia that we see nowadays at the major international conferences, and also at the increasing number of specialized gatherings worldwide.

The present collection focuses on teachers' roles in creating proximal contexts in the classroom, that is, contexts in which collaborative learning opportunities are created jointly by teachers and learners. In particular, the chapters focus on ways in which teachers can promote conditions in which learners are supported in their growing sense of agency and self-efficacy.

This is an important topic. One often hears that it is easier to teach beginning and in-service teachers how to design lessons and activities, than to teach them the moment-to-moment interactional decisions that they have to make: how to respond to a learner's remark or question on the spot, how to encourage learners to take the next step, and so on. These aspects of the mindfulness of the teacher are far more difficult to teach. A distinction that is relevant here is the one drawn by Lee Shulman between *subject matter knowledge* and *pedagogical subject matter knowledge* (1987). One may be well versed in the former without necessarily be able to enact the latter. The relationships between teacher knowledge and teacher expertise are well illustrated in several of the contributions to this volume.

The variety of classrooms studied in this volume ranges from kindergarten to college level, and include some settings outside the U.S. as well as English as a Foreign Language (EFL), English as a Second Language (ESL), bilingual and multicultural, content-based and mainstream classrooms. In these contexts a number of key teaching practices are illustrated, including exploratory talk, the use of gestures, code alternation, scaffolded interaction, and in many ways, the management of learners' peer interaction. While I noted above that it is difficult to teach teachers the delicate skills involved in contingent, responsive and co-constructive discourse at the micro level, the studies here show that these skills rest upon solid foundations in the core principles underlying SCT, namely, the realization that higher-level academic and linguistic skills to be developed are built on a foundation of social processes, that a teacher's contributions should promote learners' agency and engagement, and that meaningful talk itself is the "engine" of transformative, interfunctional systems, as Vygotsky powerfully argued almost a century ago. The understanding of these fundamental principles of SCT can assist teachers in developing the interactional skills that can bring the promises of Vygotsky's vision to fruition. This volume provides many useful models and examples that can help teachers and teacher educators to bridge the gap between "knowing" and "doing."

REFERENCES

Aljaafreh, A., & Lantolf, J. P. (1994). Negative feedback as regulation and second language learning in the zone of proximal development. *Modern Language Journal, 78*(4), 465-483.

Coughlan, P., & Duff, P. (1994). Same task, different activities: analysis of SLA from an activity theory perspective. In J. Lantolf & G. Appel, (Eds.), *Vygotskian approaches to second language research* (pp. 173–194). Norwood, NJ: Ablex

Donato, R. (1994). Collective scaffolding in second language learning. In J. P. Lantolf & G. Appel (Eds.), *Vygotskian approaches to second language research* (pp. 33-56). Norwood, NJ: Ablex.

Kasper, G., & Wagner, J. (2011). A Conversation-analytic Approach to Second Language Acquisition. In J. Atkinson (Ed.), *Alternative approaches to Second Language Acquisition* (pp. 117-142). London: Routledge.

Lantolf, J. P. (Ed.). (1994). Special issue: Sociocultural theory and second language learning. *The Modern Language Journal, 78*, 4.

Lantolf, J. P., & Appel, G. (Eds.). (1994). *Vygotskyan approaches to second language acquisition*. Norwood, NJ: Ablex.

Lantolf, J. P., & Poehner, M. E. (Eds.). (2008). *Sociocultural theory and the teaching of second languages*. London: Equinox.

Lantolf, J. P., & Thorne, S. (2006). *Sociocultural theory and the genesis of second language development*. Oxford, England: Oxford University Press.

Lave, J., & Wenger, E. (1991). *Situated learning: Legitimate peripheral participation*. Cambridge, England: Cambridge University Press.

Shulman, L. (1987). Knowledge and teaching: Foundations of the new reform. *Harvard Educational Review, 57*, 114-135.

van Lier, L. (2004). *The ecology and semiotics of language learning: A sociocultural perspective*. Boston, MA: Kluwer Academic.

ACKNOWLEDGMENTS

We are grateful to series editor, JoAnn Hammadou Sullivan, for her support throughout the entire process. She recognized the importance of our project when we submitted the proposal and invited us to work on this edited book. Special acknowledgment must be made to Leo van Lier who wrote the Foreword for our book despite his busy schedule. We would also like to acknowledge all contributing authors to this volume. This book would not have been possible without their dedication to excellence and passion for sociocultural theory. Special thanks is extended to our reviewers who read the chapters, provided invaluable comments to the authors, and made this book successful. The reviewers include: Gulbahar Beckett, University of Cincinnati, Cynthia Brock, University of Nevada, Reno, Francine Falk-Ross, Pace University, Keonghee Tao Han, University of Wyoming, Namsook Kim, University at Buffalo, Wen Ma, Le Moyne College, Paul Chamness Miller, Purdue University North Central, Cynthia Reyes, University of Vermont, Jennifer Moon Ro, State University of New York at Fredonia, Cynthia Rodriguez, University of North Texas Dallas, Anne Simpson, Texas Woman's University, Erin Washburn, State University of New York at Binghamton, Carol Wickstrom, University of North Texas, Joan Williams, Sam Houston University, Lee Wilberschield, Cleveland State University. Finally, we would thank George Johnson and other editorial staff at Information Age Publishing for their consistent support, and Marianne Lawson and Jerome Amaechi at Binghamton University for their editorial assistance.

Teachers' Roles in Second Language Learning:
Classroom Applications of Sociocultural Theory, pp. xi–xi
Copyright © 2012 by Information Age Publishing
All rights of reproduction in any form reserved.

INTRODUCTION

Sociocultural Theory as a Theoretical Framework for Understanding Teachers' Roles in Second Language Learning

Bogum Yoon and Hoe Kyeung Kim

Sociocultural theory has been one of the most important learning and development theories. Its contribution to the field of second language and literacy is immensely informative; it provides new theoretical lens of cultural, historical, and social contexts in teaching and learning. To the second language and literacy field, which has been often dominated by the behaviorist approach, sociocultural theory avails insightful lens by shifting the focus to learners' active role to (re)construct the context for their own learning. Sociocultural theory's orientation is constructivism, which has been developed and expanded by Lev. S. Vygotsky (1962, 1971, 1978). Vygotsky views human learning and development as relational, rather than individual. Both Piaget (1926) and Vygotsky (1962) espoused learning and developmental theories based on the constructivist ideas that position the learner as an active participant. However, Vygotsky focuses more on human interactions. He emphasizes that the mediation of learning involves a social interaction between the more capable members and the less informed members of a community. If human interaction is important for learning, what are the teacher's roles to second language learners' (SLLs) language and literacy development?

[handwritten margin note: constructivist approach]

Teachers' Roles in Second Language Learning:
Classroom Applications of Sociocultural Theory, pp. xiii–xxix
Copyright © 2012 by Information Age Publishing
All rights of reproduction in any form reserved.

This question prompted Hoe Kyeung (second editor) and me (first editor), who are in the field of second language and literacy education respectively, to start this edited book project. We read most literature that we could locate on the relevant topic on sociocultural perspectives. We were excited and impressed by the numerous books and articles that talk about the influence of sociocultural theory on the second language field in the U.S. context. However, we were also concerned that there is little that provides specific examples of teachers' roles in a classroom setting where they interact with SLLs. In this respect, sociocultural theory seems separate rather than unified in practice. That is when we came up with the idea of this edited collection, a volume series of *Research in Second Language Learning*. This edited book is our attempt to make a close link between theory and practice. The title of this book: *Teachers' Roles in Second Language Learning: Classroom Applications of Sociocultural Theory* reflects the attempt. We hope that this book responds to educators' needs, who intend to see vivid and specific examples of teachers' roles in second language learning based on sociocultural framework.

In the remainder of this chapter, we provide an overarching framework of Vygotskian sociocultural perspectives for the reader's appreciation of the chapters that were selected for this edited book. The main idea that we intend to address through the book is how Vygotskian sociocultural theory frames teachers' roles in second language learning. It is mutually inclusive to discuss the influence of Vygotsky on the educational field in general and the reason why his theory matters to second language learning in particular. Vygotsky's key concepts—the zone of proximal development (ZPD) and language as mediation—are the backdrop of this work and will be reviewed in the context of teachers' roles in second language learning.

VYGOTSKY AND KEY CONCEPTS OF SOCIOCULTURAL THEORY

Vygotsky and His Influence

Few scholars might question the influence of Lev. S. Vygotsky (1896-1934) and his colleagues and students (e.g., Luria and Leont'ev), who developed and expanded sociocultural theory, to inform educational practices of learning and teaching. Notably, Vygotsky was intellectually energized by fellow contemporaries including Piaget, Watson, Skinner, and Freud. As theories are consistently contextualized, we believe that Vygotsky's work is much influenced by these contemporaries whose theoretical framework is based on constructivism, behaviorism, or psychoanalysis. Vygotsky studied these theorists and reacted to them with his new and extended perspectives on human learning and development.

Vygotsky's main focus was the mind and the tool for thought processes. He argued that, unlike animals, humans know how to appropriate the psychological tools for their learning. To Vygotsky, language was considered as the main mediational tool in mental development. These ideas particularly garnered the attention of western psychologists in the 1960s when his work *Thought and Language* (1962) was translated in English (Bodrova & Leong, 2006). With the translation of *Mind in Society* (1978), Vygotsky's ideas became more popular and known to western countries in the 1980s. Many scholars in the United States were eager to introduce and discuss his cultural and historical aspects of human learning. Based on our review of literature focusing on U.S contexts, the beginning of the 1990s was the periods that his ideas flourished, and this is shown by the number of books that include "Vygotsky" in their titles such as: Kozulin's (1990) *Vygotsky's Psychology: A Bibliography of Ideas*, Moll's (1990) *Vygotsky and Education: Instructional Implications and Applications of Sociohistorical Psychology*, and van der Veer & Valsiner's (1991) *Understanding Vygotsky: A Quest for Synthesis*.

It is evident that there was a pattern to introduce Vygotskian perspectives in the United States. Although all disciplines are interconnected in some ways, the introduction of his ideas first started with the psychology field as shown in the several books of Jerome Bruner (1986) and James Wertsch (1991). These scholars of psychology worked rigorously to deepen educators' understanding of Vygotsky's thoughts. It caught the scholarly interest of educational researchers, who then applied it in such areas as literacy education. These educational researchers include Rogoff (1990), Tharp and Gilmore (1988), and Lee and Smagorinski (2000). Their work indicates that Vygotsky's sociocultural theory is relevant in and out of classroom settings. Researchers in the linguistic field like Lantolf (2000), Donato (1994), van Lier (1996), and others employed sociocultural perspectives to frame their studies on second language teaching and learning. Although Vygotsky did not specifically discuss second language learning, these scholars and researchers interpreted and expanded on his perspectives to help educators broaden their understanding of SLLs by focusing on linguistic, cultural, and social aspects of learning and development.

The account so far indicates the impact of Vygotskian perspectives on the different fields and the characteristics of applicability of his theory to the various educational areas. His theory's applicability was also confirmed by our review of the manuscripts for this book. Although we editors recognize that Vygotskian theory is applicable across academic disciplines, we did not realize the intense level of interest until we received the manuscripts from the second language and literacy researchers for this edited book. When we sent out a call for chapter proposals via several professional organizations such as American Educational Research Association, and International Linguistics Community Online, we were excited to hear about many second language researchers' enthusiastic interest in contributing their work to our edited book. They were from geographically diverse areas including Australia, China, Hong Kong, Japan, Korea, New Zealand, and Sweden. Not only are they geographically diverse, the researchers' topics of studies were various across the grade, pre-K-16. As researchers who are familiar with U.S educational contexts and have little understanding of how researchers in other countries employ sociocultural theory, it was a new and refreshing finding and observation.

The diversity of the contributing authors of this work compounds the evidence of the Vygotskian influence and theoretical contribution to the educational field. It is interesting, though, that the Russian educational psychologist, Vygotsky, might not have realized during his short lifetime (38 years) how widely his cultural and social perspectives of learning and development could have been used in the educational field by western scholars and researchers. Given that Vygotsky's work was originally written in Russian and much work was translated in other languages including English, it is impressive that this did not hinder the widespread influence of his ideas into the western world. However, we also recognize that during the translation process, Vygotsky's meaning might have been changed, lost, or interpreted in different ways. His theory on human learning and development needs to be closely and carefully examined by focusing on major concepts that he attempted to present to the educational field.

Having broadly addressed Vygotsky's perspectives above, we now concentrate on his theory's implications on second language learning which is the main purpose and focus of this edited book. Among others, the concepts of the zone of proximal development and language as mediation are closely relevant to the issue of the teacher's roles in language and literacy education.

Zone of Proximal Development

Vygotsky's notion of the zone of proximal development is particularly insightful to guide teachers' roles in second language learning. No concept might be more widely discussed in the educational field than the ZPD that Vygotsky used to explain children's learning and adults' teaching. In Chapter 6 in his book, *Mind in Society*, Vygotsky (1978) discussed the ZPD in detail along with the definition: "*It is the distance between the actual developmental level as determined by independent problem solving and the level of potential development as determined through problem solving under adult guidance or in collaboration with more capable peers*" (p. 86, emphasis in original). This definition provides important ideas that learning and development are continuous interactive processes between the teacher and the student. Several authors from this edited book also employed this symbolic concept as the theoretical framework of their studies (e.g., see Smiley & Antón, and Yoon, in this volume). Based on the chapters that are presented in this book, the principles of this concept are summarized in three different ways with regard to teachers' roles in second language learning. We direct the reader to the specific chapters when the relevant concepts are introduced.

First, the ZPD focuses on SLLs' current state and level that teachers need to be aware of to promote their learning and development. In the classroom where the zone is constructed, the teacher's understanding of the student's current independent level is important, which Moll (1992) and his colleagues including González Moll, and Amanti (2005) conceptualized as "funds of knowledge." This notion is aligned with the ZPD since teachers should know what background knowledge that students bring to the classroom. The students' psychological tool (cultural, historical, linguistic, and social knowledge) is a crucial resource that teachers can utilize to assist and mediate their learning (see Kim & Lee, and Bezdicek & García, in this volume).

Second, the ZPD consists of flexibility and possibility. The zone is created and moving, rather than fixed and stable. What students can accomplish with the assistance of teachers (the potential development level) and what they can do independently (actual developmental level) are not fixed. The processes of the developmental levels are continuously changing and evolving so that the students' potential development level transitions into actual developmental level. This concept illustrates its focus on future learning and development of SLLs. As Vygotsky (1978) noted, development is a qualitative transformation from one stage to another. The teacher's role is to help SLLs to achieve this possibility, to construct their own zones, and to develop their language and literacy learning. The teacher's role to promote peer interaction is another way to create "third space" (Gutiérrez, 2008), which is an expanded concept of ZPD. The zone can be continuously created and recreated through the interaction of SLLs and native English-speaking peers and through the facilitation of the teacher (see de Jong, in this volume).

Third, the ZPD implies that individual students' difference exists, which requires the teacher's differentiated and tailored guidance. Compared to Piaget who emphasizes the developmental stage of children's learning, Vygotsky focuses on the dynamic nature of human development through the ZPD concept. This notion provides teachers with insights that they need to modify their instruction based on individual students' current level and their needs. Since every individual student's level and cultural knowledge that they bring to the classroom is different, it is important for teachers to consider how they can adjust their instructional approaches based on the students' different level and status (see Kim, and Akrofi, Janisch, Zebidi, & Lewis, in this volume).

The concept of the ZPD has been criticized due to the emphasis on the specific task that students can complete rather than viewing them as a whole (Chaiklin, 2003). However, this criticism might be challenged through the chapters in this book since most of them discuss the teacher's role from a holistic perspective rather than focusing on specific tasks. Through our literature review, we also noticed that the ZPD has been criticized due to the strong emphasis on the adult's role for the child's learning (Bodrova & Leong, 2006). Based on the chapters that we present in this book, however, we believe that it provides balanced roles between teachers and students since meaning is co-constructed and reconstructed in the zone through joint activity between teachers and students. Given that the notion of the ZPD implies that teachers gradually release their responsibility to help students take ownership of learning by creating their own zones, we can argue that it does not impose the teacher's dominant role. Through the chapters in this book that describe peer interactions between SLLs and their advanced peers, readers might better understand how the teacher plays a role to facilitate the interactions. The teacher's role of assisting SLLs is extended to create an inclusive classroom where the advanced peers partake in the activity of learning (see Yoon, in this volume). In short, it is the view that the teacher's role of assistance is to position the learner as active. The assisted teacher's role manifested through the ZPD is connected to the concept of mediation, which we will describe below.

Language as Mediation

Another important concept that provides insights to the field of second language education is language as mediation. According to Vygotsky (1978), mediation has a special meaning which can be applied to human learning and development given that individuals' mental and social activities are formed by tools and signs. These tools and signs are culturally, linguistically, socially, and historically situated entities that have been transmitted and transformed from generation to generation (Wertsch, 2007). Individuals think and learn through these tools and signs including language. Vygotsky particularly emphasized the role of language among other mediated signs. Several chapters, particularly chapters 1 through 6 in this book, include this concept as their main framework of study. Vygotsky's concept of language as mediation seems to be expanded by current researchers who include non-verbal language such as gesture as an important mediation (see Rosborough, in this volume). The teacher's role as a mediator is to help SLLs move from assisted to independent performance. The frequent use of teacher as a facilitator in the second language field might be stemmed from this concept. Like the ZPD, the Vygotskian notion of mediation represents well the teachers' roles in three different ways.

Teacher's role

First, the teacher mediates and supports SLLs' learning by using language as the main linguistic tool. The concept of scaffolding (Bruner, 1975) manifests the teacher's assisted role in this respect. To help SLLs transfer their learning from interpsychological plane (social) to intrapsychological plane (individual), the teacher who is considered more experienced scaffolds and appropriates her language to facilitate the students' learning. In this scaffolding process, the teacher's form of repetition, expansion, or question is an example of using language as a mediational tool for SLLs' learning (see Herazo & Donato, in this volume). The teacher's employment of different strategies within and beyond these forms is also considered as an important scaffolding approach (see Kim, in this volume).

Scaffolding language

Second, the teacher promotes interaction by utilizing language as a social and political tool. Language does not include only linguistic components, but it includes ideological concepts. The teacher might intentionally or unintentionally deliver certain messages through language. The teacher might position SLLs as powerful or powerless through classroom activities. One of the examples is EFL teachers' code choice which shows the reasons behind their decision of using L1 and L2 (see Beers Fägersten, in this volume). Teachers' use of language as a social and political tool is shown through the way they share authority with students. It is expected for students to generate discovery and exploratory conversation when they are placed in interactive authority (see Boyd, in this volume). As Vygotsky (1978) pointed out, internalization is "the internal reconstruction of an external operation" (p. 56). SLLs' internalization might occur and is promoted when the teacher shares authority and implements certain activities and approaches as external operation, assisting the students to construct meaning internally. In this respect, the sociocultural perspectives of language as a tool are extended to social, critical, and political perspectives to help SLLs develop their critical thinking (see Handsfield, in this volume).

Sharing authority role

Third, the teacher assists SLLs to develop their learning through the meaningful activities of language and literacy in context. Teacher's assist-

Meaningful, authentic learning experiences.

ing discourse could inspire and advance students' learning through meaning-making activities (see Martin-Beltrán, in this volume). The meaningful activities are not only for the development of SLLs' oral language. Often, Vygotskian sociocultural theory was used to discuss oral language as a mediation tool. However, modern applications include written language as well (see Carbone, in this volume). Although it is hard to observe students' inner speech that Vygotsky mentioned as a key mediating tool for learning, the activities of inner speech also need to be considered when we discuss the teacher's assisted role.

In sum, Vygotsky's concepts of the ZPD and language as an important mediation provide educators with insights to help students engage in language and literacy activities. We hope the chapters we specifically pointed out are helpful and useful for the reader to better understand these sociocultural concepts with regard to the teacher's role to mediate SLLs' learning and development.

UNIQUE FEATURES OF THE BOOK

The uniqueness of this book is summarized in four different features. First, all of the 14 chapters are based on the studies that the authors conducted in classroom settings, pre-K-16. Often, edited books consist of nonempirical conceptual papers, but our book includes actual studies that took the process of multiple data collections and rigorous analysis. Although the authors used their own organization, each chapter followed the "traditional" research format due to the characteristic of this book which focuses on the clear connection between sociocultural theory and practice.

Second, all of the authors employed qualitative methods for their studies. Although we did not limit the research method during the selection of the manuscripts, we believed that their research questions guided them to select their method. Based on our review, we noticed that the authors utilized qualitative design due to the nature of their studies which focus on the details of teachers' roles to support SLLs' language and literacy learning. We believe that the purpose of the qualitative study is to gain insights, rather than generalization, and the authors' choice of the method is appropriate to show the classroom dynamics.

Third, all the authors used sociocultural theory as their theoretical framework. Vygotsky's sociocultural perspectives are expanded and applied through their studies. Although their research topics and questions are different, their theoretical underpinnings to analyze their data are all based on sociocultural theory. When they employed this theory, each author used the term "second language learners" interchangeably with "English language learners" or L2 learners. We respect their inter-changeable applications of the term rather than suggesting the use of one consistent term, second language learners, for our book. We understand that certain topics and contexts fit the choice of one over the other and we value their position.

Finally, the 14 chapters showed the dynamic classroom interactions between teachers and students and students among themselves across the grade level. Due to the fact that Vygotsky's perspectives lean heavily on the learning and development of younger children, readers might expect his theory to be more applicable in the pre-K and elementary setting. However, we found that contemporary researchers' discussion bearing on teacher's role from a sociocultural lens moves beyond the younger grade levels to address this issue in the middle, high, and college level. Since the purpose of this edited book is to illustrate the classroom application of sociocultural theory to educators, it was evident that all the contributing authors attempted to show the dynamic classroom interaction between teachers and SLLs across all levels.

Through the concept of human learning as a culturally and socially sit-uated practice, Vygotsky emphasized social interaction between adults and children. The 14 articles in this edited book reflect these key concepts of Vygotsky by focusing on teachers' roles for SLLs. Through this book, we intend our readers to "see" the teachers' roles in the classroom in their attempt to implement Vygotsky's (1978, 1987) sociocultural theory while working with SLLs. As Kozulin (2003) pointed out, the popularity of Vygotskian theory among American educators might be for the reason that it "offers us answers to the questions that were not asked earlier" (p. 15). We anticipate that this book will provide educators and research-ers with opportunities to continue to pose questions and to further develop sociocultural theories.

ORGANIZATION OF THE BOOK

As seen through the key concepts of sociocultural theory, teachers are to promote and mediate students' learning linguistically, culturally, and socially. Our book is divided into three main sections in order to reflect these aspects. Although these concepts might overlap and intersect with each other, we believe that their categorization into distinctive groups will be helpful for the readers who might want to look at certain concepts more closely.

More specifically, in Part I, we include six chapters, which show how teachers mediate the use of language as a semiotic tool and how teachers provide linguistic scaffolding using teacher talk, gesture or code switching in the classroom. In Chapter 1, Maureen P. Boyd discusses her research on a fourth and fifth grade pull-out ELL classroom. Considering the importance of promoting student talk in SLA, she examined how purposeful teacher-talk guided exploratory student-talk. From the data collected through 6 weeks of instructional unit on children' literature, she illustrated how ELL teacher's use of contingent questions, positioning ELL students in interpretive authority and using the reasoning words promoted exploratory student talks. Boyd concluded that the resulting exploratory student talk was due to a classroom culture where both teacher and her ELL students were willing to take risks and stressed the role of the teacher in creating a collective, reciprocal, and supportive classroom environment.

In Chapter 2, José David Herazo and Richard Donato begin the article with an explanation of unique EFL conditions in language education and the complicated roles of EFL teachers, especially their mediational role. Teachers mediate learners' oral participation using eliciting strategies, such as questions and attention to the content of learners' utterances. Their study, which was conducted in Colombia, compared two EFL teachers' mediation of their students' meaning-making participation during teacher-student interaction. Through the comparison of a trained teacher and a teacher without training, they examined the effectiveness of the Colombian National Bilingualism Program training. The corpus of 46 episodes collected through observations was analyzed. In coding a process, they focused on the three perspectives of mediation and their subcategories: focus (meaning, affect, language), time (proactive, ongoing, reactive), and tools (11 different strategies). In the finding, they presented the variability and patterns of mediation of two teachers. While the trained teacher focused on form and reactive strategy, the teacher without training focused on meaning and proactive in mediation. To support their findings, Herazo and Donato provided a summary of the distribution of mediation moves by two teachers in the finding section. They concluded that mediation was not a unitary activity, and recommended the refinement and elaboration of the concept of mediation to be a useful tool for teachers to improve their instruction. They further stressed the importance of understanding sociocultural factors in implementing an educational reform and designing teacher education.

In Chapter 3, Lara J. Handsfield reports her case study on a fourth grade bilingual teacher's mediation of ELL students' language and the teacher's linguistic scaffolding. Handsfield collected the data through class observations on the bilingual teacher's science unit and interviews with the teacher. The data were analyzed using critical sociocultural theory and microethnographic discourse analysis to examine how the bilingual teacher negotiated her curricular approaches and blended various discourse patterns accordingly. In this study, Handsfield employed critical sociocultural theory to further examine the power relations which influenced discourse patterns in classrooms. She viewed that two of the challenges that the teacher faced were negotiating opposing curricular (such as sociocultural and standardized assessment-focused approaches) and balancing the ideologies reflecting the different discourse patterns (such as Initiate-Response-Evaluate (IRE) and Responsive Collaborative Discourses (RCD). The findings of her study highlighted the teachers' multiple roles through learning events as examples of her way of negotiating different curricula ideologies and expectations in her classroom. Drawn from a 2-year study on two teachers' study group, her article presented illustrative examples of linguistic scaffolding, such as teaching cognate strategies and encouraging the use of L1 in supporting her ELL students. Especially during an oral true/false test activity, the teacher shifted her roles as a critic and facilitator to participant depending on phases of the activity. The teacher demonstrated how this knowledge transmission assessment could provide an opportunity for rich language scaffolding, contextualized and socially constructed learning, which facilitates high standards for academic language and content knowledge.

In Chapter 4, Alessandro Rosborough presents his study on the second grade teacher's use of gesture in assisting ELLs' learning. From ecosocial linguistic perspective, his study demonstrated how gesture was an important affordance in assisting ELLs' meaning making of their spelling words. The data were collected from a second grade ESL classroom where 19 students had different linguistic and cultural backgrounds. Rosborough analyzed and categorized gesture functions in a theme-based matrix. The findings demonstrated how the ESL teacher used gesture as a part of the ecosocial space to co-construct the meaning of the words in a spelling and phonemic awareness task. One of the examples presented is the opportunity of the ESL teacher created to use gesture as an embodied form for learning a word, "crab." Most importantly, the use of gesture provided joint-attention and shared meaning-making between the teacher and the students. He stressed the important role of gesture in the second language learning process and raised teachers' awareness of gesture use.

In Chapter 5, Kristy Beers Fägersten presents her study on a teacher's code-choice in a seventh grade Swedish EFL classroom. Based on a yearlong ethnography study, Beers Fägersten argued that language function and code choice in EFL classroom needed to be understood from a sociocultural perspective. Her chapter illustrated how the EFL teacher's code choice was influenced by the sociocultural setting and institutional context, using Vygotsky's concept of language as a social semiotic tool. She defined English as an unmarked code, the default code of instruction, and Swedish as a marked code given the fact that English was widespread in Sweden. Interestingly, the findings of her study revealed that the teacher's code switching did not indicate a topic-switch, but an affective, socializing, or repetitive function. Code switching contributed directly to establishing the sociocultural norms of classroom behaviors and classroom discourses. Thus, the teacher's code choice and the established practice of code-switching did not bear any subject instruction but served to redirect the students' focus, either to engaging in English learning, or to behaving according to the institutional context.

In Chapter 6, Melinda Martin-Beltrán reports her study on three veteran teachers of fifth grade in a dual language (Spanish/English) class. With a sociocultural theoretical lens, her study examined the teacher's roles, especially how the teachers' discourse and instructional decisions influenced the students' opportunities for language learning. The data were collected through recorded and videotaped classroom discussions and analyzed focusing on Language Related Episodes (LRE) as opportunities or contexts for potential language learning. Drawing from data during a year-long ethnographic study, Martin-Beltrán found that joint writing activities resulted in most dialogic interaction between the teachers and the students. The teachers were key mediators in the language learning process in terms of creating context, providing modeling, and offering intervention. Her chapter presented classroom examples to illustrate how the teachers modeled languaging and how teachers decided when and how to intervene productively in peer interactions. In the examples provided, the teachers encouraged students to use their linguistic knowledge, that is, using Spanish to engage in a metalinguistic analysis and inspiring students to expand their thinking about word choice. Martin-Beltrán presented a summary of the categorized patterns and features of teaching practices that created affordances for languaging. The findings of the study could encourage both teachers and students to become more aware of the opportunities for language learning afforded during dialogic interactions.

Part II presents four chapters based on the cultural perspectives of sociocultural theory. Specifically, these chapters discuss how classroom teachers employed students' cultural and linguistic knowledge, connected with everyday literacy practices, valued students' heritages, and worked with family coordinators in their teaching practice and home visits.

In Chapter 7, Hoe Kyeung Kim and Soyoung Lee present their study on a Canadian EFL college instructor in South Korea. They provided a brief trend of English education in the country: a big emphasis on improving oral communication skills and a growing number of native speakers of English teachers. Some of these foreign-born teachers were experiencing difficulties in working with their Korean students due to their lack of understanding in students' culture, language, and learning styles. The purpose of the study was to examine the case of an exemplary language teacher who was praised by his Korean students. Grounded in the frame of funds of knowledge, the study was conducted throughout one semester and the data were collected through videotaped classroom observations and interviews with the teacher as well as students. The findings suggested that the teacher used both his own funds of knowledge and his students' funds of knowledge as scaffolding to support students' participation and engagement. The findings demonstrated the teacher's use of both linguistic and cultural knowledge of students and his own funds of knowledge in his instruction to promote his Korean students' participation and engagement.

In Chapter 8, Paula M. Carbone reports her study on academic writing instruction for Generation 1.5 students' writing process in a high school class. The data were collected from 20 working class Latino students who enrolled in a 10th grade remedial English class in an urban school. Carbone defined Generation 1.5 students as those who were bilingual and bicultural but maintained their heritage language. She claimed that little attention had been paid to their academic trajectories in secondary school. Although there is enough evidence that valuing students' cultural and social funds of knowledge promotes academic performance, there is a lack of understanding of teacher's role in identifying and analyzing students' everyday literacy practices and utilizing them for writing instruction. The findings showed the teacher's role as actively identifying and leveraging students' funds of knowledge created an important context for writing instruction. This chapter demonstrated how the teacher's use of students' everyday literacy practices on MySpace and other technology could explain the expectations of academic writing effectively and the use of students' own real issue could guide the students to develop a topic in writing a persuasive essay. The findings of the study showed a way to meet expectations of academic writing that is the teacher's role as actively identifying and valuing students' funds of knowledge and understanding their lived experiences for leveraging.

In Chapter 9, Bogum Yoon discusses her study on a sixth grade regular classroom teacher's instructional approaches to the ELLs in ELA/Reading/Social Studies class. The data was collected through interviews, classroom observations, and artifacts focusing on the mainstream teacher and the two ELLs. Yoon pointed out how the teacher's cultural inclusivity approach promoted the two ELLs' class participation and resulted in native English speaking peers' positive attitude toward the students. The findings of her study demonstrated the teacher's awareness of ELLs' status, acknowledgement of ELLs' culture, and use of multicultural literature in the teaching practice. Yoon's study also suggested that the teacher's awareness of ELLs' cultural and social needs, cultural inclusivity approach, and utilization of ELLs as a cultural resource contributed to the students' learning. Her study might provide a significant implication for regular classroom teachers who work with ELLs in the mainstream classroom.

In Chapter 10, Joyce Bezdicek and Georgia Earnest García present a study on a monolingual preschool teacher's instructional support to multilingual and multicultural ELLs in classroom. This chapter illustrates how preschool classrooms can create a learning space which supports sociocultural theory. The data was collected throughout one academic year and analyzed following activity setting theory. The findings of their study showed how a monolingual English-speaking teacher collaborated with family coordinators to validate her ELLs' home languages and cultures. Bezdicek and García reported the process of hiring bilingual community members as family coordinators and elaborated their roles in family conferences and home visits. Their chapter illustrated classroom projects that the teacher developed to support her students' languages and cultures as part of multicultural curriculum. Furthermore, the chapter presented how the teacher supported her students' language learning using multiple modalities and techniques.

Part III is devoted to research on social interaction including peer interaction, collaborative group work, learner engagement, and ZPD. The four chapters included demonstrate how teachers support students' social interaction in the classroom to promote students' interaction and learning. Each chapter focuses on teacher's scaffolding strategies, developing learners' discourse and strategy competence, teacher's roles in discursive strategies, and supporting learner's ZPD.

In Chapter 11, Ester J. de Jong presents her study on two first grade teachers' intervention during peer interaction in a two-way immersion program. Her study examined how the two teachers structured their instruction to enable pair work between native and nonnative speakers of the instructional languages, Spanish and English. de Jong analyzed twenty lessons from the two teachers' classes focusing on teacher-structured pair work segments, such as Think-Pair-Share (TPS). The findings showed that the teachers enacted four important roles: (1) helping students negotiate the activity, (2) providing access to the content, (3) providing access to language, and (4) encouraging students to extend their language production. She reported that the strategies for scaffolding the activity, the content, and the language demands were more teacher-fronted in nature whereas the strategies that encouraged student language use were responsive to students and interactional needs. de Jong provided a summary table of the teachers' roles on each TPS phases to help readers understand the dynamic teachers' intervention strategies. As a conclusion, she stressed the importance of teacher's balancing macro and micro scaffolding strategies in linguistically heterogeneous classrooms.

In Chapter 12, Eun-Jeong Kim reports her study on an ESL instructor's instructional scaffolding in a college speaking and listening class. She believed that ELLs should develop discourse and strategic competence, which needed to be taught explicitly by their teacher. Her study examined the ways in which the teacher's instruction promoted students' communicative interaction and ways that students learned as a result of scaffolded instruction. The data were collected through classroom observations, interviews, field-notes, and class artifacts. The findings indicated that the teacher mediated students' interaction by constructing a collaborative learning community climate where students worked in groups interdependently while he positioned himself as co-learner. Another strategy the teacher used was to promote academic competence through focused listening and higher-order thinking skills using "wh"-questions. The findings of the study also showed how students took up of the teacher's instruction strategies and used the "Because Clause" in their discourse appropriately. Based on the findings, Kim stressed the appropriate teacher education for guiding and developing teachers' scaffolding practices.

In Chapter 13, Jennifer Smiley and Marta Antón present their study on the teacher's role in high school Spanish classrooms. This study is unique in that it focuses on teaching Spanish as a foreign language for English speakers and compares two classes with different proficiency levels. Smiley and Antón report on a case study on a stellar teacher's Spanish classes and his roles enacted through discourses. The data were collected for one semester from level 2 and level 4 Spanish classes taught by the same teacher with 31 English-speaking students. A mixed-method approach was employed, but in the present chapter they presented only four excerpts demonstrating the teacher's roles explicitly. Following ethnographic techniques, the study investigated what teachers' roles were apparent in classroom interactions and how the teacher enacted his roles through discursive strategies. The findings presented four teacher's roles: providing linguistic models, providing assistance, creating a participatory environment, and creating a sense of community. For improved understanding, Smiley and Antón exemplified ways to create a sense of community, such as devoting conversation class time about their activities and interests, sharing teacher's life stories, and using humor. Based on the findings, they argued that intentional and responsive use of classroom language was important in learners' development and further suggested that teachers should devote attention to how their roles were expressed through language in the classroom.

In Chapter 14, Amma K. Akrofi, Carole Janisch, Amira Zebidi and Karla Lewis report their study on a second grade teacher's instructional scaffolding to support ELLs in a mainstream class. The purpose of this study was to examine a teacher's social interactional roles that fostered effective literacy learning in an ESL-inclusion second grade classroom. Interactions between the teacher and her students were documented, with special focus on one ELL, Jacques, to demonstrate the effectiveness of the teacher's instruction. The data were collected from 23 literacy lessons for two weeks as well as Jacques' instructional and assessment materials, his journal entries, and all his writings. Through Jacques' participation and writing, they identified two roles that the teacher played: (1) a team builder and, (2) a team captain. One example of the teacher' instructional effectiveness provided was that one of Jacques' desk-mates volunteered to assist Jacques in finishing his poem after observing the teacher's assistance. Supporting the findings of the study by Yoon (2007), this study illustrated that the teacher' positive engagement with the ELL, Jacques, had a significant influence on mainstream students' engagement with ELLs. As ZPD recognized students' individual difference, Jacques' case in this study revealed the effective use of the ZPD in classroom instruction. Akrofi and the colleagues concluded that the teacher's facilitation of learning through peer-collaboration enabled the ELL to make strides and become a more capable peer.

REFERENCES

Bodrova, E., & Leong, D. J. (2006). *Tools of the mind: The Vygotskian approach to early childhood education*. Columbus, OH: Prentice-Hall.

Bruner, J. (1975). From communication to language: A psychological perspective. *Cognition, 3*, 255-287.

Bruner, J. (1986). *Actual minds, possible worlds*. Cambridge, MA: Harvard. University Press.

Chaiklin, S. (2003). The zone of proximal development in Vygotsky's analysis of learning and instruction. In A. Kozulin, B. Gindis, B. Ageyev & S. Miller (Eds.), *Vygotsky's educational theory in cultural context* (pp. 39-64). New York, NY: Cambridge University Press.

Donato, R. (1994). Collective scaffolding in second language learning. In J. P. Lantolf & G. Appel (Eds.). *Vygotskian approaches to second language research*. Norwood, NJ: Ablex.

González, N., Moll, L., & Amanti, C. (2005). *Funds of knowledge: Theorizing practices in households, communities and classrooms*. Mahwah, NJ: Erlbaum.

Gutiérrez, K.D. (2008). Developing a sociocritical literacy in the third space. *Reading Research Quarterly, 43*(2), 148-164.

Kozulin, A. (1990). *Vygotsky's psychology: A bibliography of ideas*. Cambridge, MA: Harvard University Press.

Kozulin, A. (2003). Psychological tools and mediated learning. In A. Kozulin, B. Gindis, B. Ageyev & S. Miller (Eds.), *Vygotsky's educational theory in cultural context* (pp. 15-38). New York, NY: Cambridge University Press.

Lantolf, J. P. (2000). *Sociocultural theory and second language learning*. Oxford:, England: Oxford University Press.

Lee, C. D., & Smagorinsky, P. (Eds.). (2000). *Vygotskian perspectives on literacy research: Constructing meaning through collaborative inquiry*. Cambridge, England: Cambridge University Press.

Moll, L. (1990). *Vygotsky and education: Instructional implications and applications of sociohistorical psychology*. Cambridge, England: Cambridge University Press.

Moll, L. C., Amanti, C., Neff, D., & González, N. (1992). Funds of knowledge for teaching: Using a qualitative approach to connect homes and classrooms. *Theory into Practice, 31*(2), 132-141.

Piaget, J. (1926). *The language and thought of the child* (M. Gabain, Trans.). London: Routledge & Kegan Paul.

Rogoff, B. (1990). *Apprenticeship in thinking: cognitive development in social context*. New York, NY: Oxford University Press.

Tharp, R., & Gallimore, R. (1988). *Rousing minds to life*. Cambridge, England: Cambridge University Press.

van der Veer, R., & Valsiner, J. (1991) *Understanding Vygotsky: A quest for synthesis*. Oxford, England: Blackwell

van Lier, L. (1996). *Interaction in the language curriculum: Awareness, autonomy and authenticity*. New York, NY: Longman.

Vygotsky, L. S. (1962). *Thought and language*. Cambridge, MA: MIT Press.

Vygotsky, L. S. (1971). *The psychology of art*. Cambridge, MA: MIT Press.

Vygotsky, L. S. (1978). *Mind in society: The development of higher mental processes*. Cambridge, MA: Harvard University Press.

Wertsch, J. V. (1991). *Voices of the mind: A sociocultural approach to mediated action*. Cambridge, MA: Harvard University Press.

Wertsch, J. V. (2007). Mediation. In H. Daniels, M. Cole & J. Wertsch (Eds.), *The cambridge companion to Vygotsky* (pp. 178-192). New York, NY: Cambridge Universtity Press.

Yoon, B. (2007). Offering or limiting opportunities: Teachers' roles and approaches to English language learners' participation in literacy activities. *The Reading Teacher, 61*(3), 216-225.

PART I

LINGUISTIC PERSPECTIVES

CHAPTER 1

HOW TEACHER TALK CAN GUIDE STUDENT EXPLORATORY TALK

Communication, Conjecture, and Connections in a Fourth and Fifth Grade ELL Classroom

Maureen P. Boyd

This chapter focuses on a fourth and fifth grade pull-out ELL classroom and through classroom discourse analysis elucidates ways the teacher supported student reasoning and understanding of both content and the target language through three instructional strategies: contingent questioning, positioning students to have interpretive authority, and consistent use of reasoning words. I show how the resulting student exploratory talk marks a classroom culture where both teacher and ELL students are willing to take risks as they reason and learn through talk together.

> *The exploratory uses of language, both in speech and in writing, are important because they lead to understanding rather than mimicry.*
>
> (Barnes, 1969, p. 73)

Teachers' Roles in Second Language Learning:
Classroom Applications of Sociocultural Theory, pp. 3–18
Copyright © 2012 by Information Age Publishing
All rights of reproduction in any form reserved.

This chapter provides an illustrative case study of how one teacher, through her willingness to listen and flexibly wield her pedagogical expertise in service of student talk interests and purposes, supported student reasoning and understanding of both content and the target language in a fourth and fifth grade pull-out English language learning (ELL) classroom. Specifically, I explicate how three instructional strategies: contingent questioning, positioning students to have interpretive authority, and consistent use of reasoning words, guide student communication, conjecture, and connections to what they already knew. The resulting *exploratory talk*: student-led exchanges where students publicly explore ideas offered for joint consideration (Barnes, Britton, & Torbe, 1969; Mercer & Hodgkinson, 2008, marks a classroom culture where both teacher and ELL students are willing to take risks as they reason and learn through talk together.

Building linguistic proficiency, comprehension, engagement, and creation and transfer of knowledge are some of the positive effects associated with student exploratory talk in classrooms. But the desirability of promoting such talk does not minimize the difficulty of promoting it. Simply allowing ELL students to talk in the classroom is insufficient for developing reasoning and understanding or for engendering productive discussions. Purposeful teacher talk can set up and develop patterns of classroom talk that direct students beyond "empty babble" (Pennycook, 1994) and guide students towards educationally effective talk. This chapter shows how purposeful teacher talk can open opportunities for exploratory talk—for it does not happen automatically. The research question that this chapter addresses is: What patterns of teacher talk engender student exploratory talk during a literature based instructional unit in one fourth and fifth grade ELL classroom?

THEORETICAL FRAMEWORK

We internalize talk, and it becomes our link to thought. We externalize talk, and it becomes our link to social reality. We elaborate talk, and it becomes our bridge to literacy. Like the sea, talk is the environment that first incubates and then nurtures our development.

(Rubin, 1990, p. 3)

The role of talk as a mediator and marker of learning is an underpinning tenet of sociocultural theory and constructivist teaching. The social, dynamic, dialogic and co-constructed nature of thought and learning (Bakhtin, 1981; Mercer & Littleton, 2007; Nystrand, Gamoran, Kachur, & Prendergast, 1997; Vygotsky, 1986; Wells, 1999) is captured in both the exploratory nature of talk and the patterns of interaction as we communicate in the moment, grapple to articulate, work to understand in response to a previous utterance and an anticipated response, in relation to what we already know and want to know, and within the norms and structures of the immediate and sociohistorical context.

When teachers position students to think and compose in-the-moment —to internalize, externalize and elaborate talk—students can experience the three functions that student talk performs in learning a language: (1) students become aware of language structures as they apply them; (2) students reflect in and through talk; (3) talk represents the speaker's best guess and provides cues to which teachers and others can respond (Swain, 1995). Through exploratory talk the social and cognitive functions of talk combine as students enter, continue and end conversations, and they practice varied participant roles as they query, respond, initiate and add to contributions as they grapple with substantive content. Exploratory talk is thus often short and choppy as students offer incomplete possibilities and tentative explanations as they talk to understand and make sense of new ideas and experiences in relation to what they already know. Markers of this kind of talk include reasoning words (e.g., might, could, maybe, I think: Mercer, Wegerif, & Dawes, 1999). This talking to learn (Britton, 1969) or experience of talking and talking about experience (Wilkinson, 1970) has been long accepted as supportive of student learning but it is consistently absent in our increasingly scripted mainstream and language classrooms.

Discourse norms of the classroom community are key to inhibiting or encouraging exploratory talk. Patterns of teacher talk position students as having (or not having) interpretive authority, and control the extent to which students can shape the scope of the discourse (Boyd & Galda, 2011; Chinn, Anderson, & Waggoner, 2001). They signify whether thinking in the moment and risking making mistakes are valued and safe practices in the particular classroom and students respond in light of this. Student patterns of talk further influence the likelihood of exploratory talk. For example, the support from other members as they take up one another's ideas and develop them (Mercer, 2002, calls this interthinking), often results in overlapping exploratory talk. However, all too often the excited noise of students making meaning together is shushed.

But promoting student talk in English is an explicit instructional objective in every ELL lesson. The ELL classroom must be a place for real talk where language is played with, rehearsed, and applied—where students grapple to understand, communicate, and make meaning together. Talk cannot be limited to presentational or recitational talk as ELL students need opportunities to experience the necessarily varied participant roles needed to communicate, and talk cannot be confined to social interactions as ELL students need to rehearse the elaborated code of schooling and associated ways of thinking. The ELL classroom can provide a safe, supportive, public context for learning to talk and talking to learn.

LITERATURE REVIEW

It is now appreciated that classroom talk is not merely a conduit for the sharing of information, or a means for controlling the exuberance of youth; it is the most important educational tool for guiding the development of understanding and for jointly constructing knowledge (Mercer & Hodgkinson, 2008, p. xi).

The role of student talk in language learning has been long and widely recognized by teachers and researchers alike (see, e.g., Lantolf, 2002; Mohr & Mohr, 2007; Pica, 1994; Swain, 1995). When students practice the target language they build receptive and productive comprehension, and further develop communicative competence. An underpinning criterion is student time on floor: students need time and opportunity to talk. But consistently across first and second language classrooms teachers talk too much. Across decades research has revealed that teachers talk more than they think they do—and that students speak less than one third of the time (Cazden, 2001; Mohr & Mohr, 2007). But even when they have opportunity for time on floor, not all student talk is equally efficacious. Student talk in and across English language learning (ELL) classrooms range from free-flowing chit-chat to regimented skill and drill, from seeking to provide the interpretation signaled by the teacher to (re) organizing thoughts in discussion based content exploration, and from talk that is devoid of context to talk that reflects relevant and authentic purpose. While different types of talk support and extend different types of student learning, it is the patterning of teacher talk that shapes the types of student talk that can or cannot occur, and thus the type of learning that can occur. In this chapter I am focusing on purposeful teacher talk patterning that engenders student exploratory talk—unfolding reasoning talk that develops conceptual understanding and communicative competence. Through close discourse analysis I show how this ELL teacher employed three particular strategies to support student exploratory talk in her classroom: contingent questioning, positioning students to have interpretive authority, and consistent use of reasoning words.

Contingent Questioning (teacher questioning)

The dominant—and preferred—instructional tool is the teacher question. There is an extensive body of research on types of teacher questioning (for example: display, authentic, clarification request, open, closed) and associated patterns of talk (Dillon, 1982; Mehan, 1979; Nystrand & Gamoran, 1991; Nystrand, Wu, Gamoran, Zeiser, & Long, 2003). Certainly the ubiquitous question is in frequent use by ELL teachers to elicit recall and performance, request clarification, direct thinking, and model appropriate language usage. To be sure, fill-in-the-blank patterns are indicated by questions presuming particular responses and their resulting and necessarily brief student performances provide quick assessments for teachers. In contrast, invitations for student elaborations are indicated with open "why do you think" questions. But simply asking a particular type of question does not guarantee a choppy or elaborated student response. This chapter considers one teacher's use of contingent questioning and in doing so contributes to a growing stream of questioning research that considers two other factors shaping student responses. First, the "third turn" or "follow up" to a student's response to a teacher question as critical to shaping interactions (Boyd & Maloof, 2000; Boyd & Rubin, 2002, 2006; Lee, 2007; Wells, 1993). Second, sociohistoric patterns of classroom talk predispose students to respond in particular ways, independent of the type of question asked (Boyd & Markarian, 2011; Boyd & Rubin, 2006; Smith & Higgins, 2006). Contingent questions are anchored in previous contributions; they explicitly seek to extend what is being currently discussed. For example, when Rosey responds with "Yea, the, the beach," Ms. Charlotte's contingent question, "The beach what happened there?" asks that Rosey elaborate. In this way, contingent questions can be an antidote to what Dillon (1982) called "the presumptive practice" of teacher proffering questions presuming they are furthering student thinking but in fact furthering the teacher agenda. This is not to say that contingent questions are not selective in what student contributions they build upon. Like all instructional tools, their effectiveness lies in the deftness and thoughtfulness of their pedagogical application.

open-ended ?'s

asking student to elaborate

Positioning Students To Have Interpretive Authority

Classroom talk sheds light on instructional stance (see, e.g., recitative, collaborative-reasoning, expressive: Chinn et al., 2001; Soter et al., 2008). When the classroom talk is about literature, the extent to which students are on a treasure hunt to identify the teacher's "right" interpretation or have interpretive authority to articulate their own thoughts and ideas is central to predisposing students to risk exploratory talk. Teacher questioning, and then follow up to a student response to a question, makes transparent the degree to which students are positioned as primary knowers and have interpretive authority (Boyd & Galda, 2011). The frequency and manner in which the teacher uses evaluation (positive or negative evaluative comments terminate the exchange), the extent to which the teacher recognizes, acknowledges, and builds upon student contributions (Bloome et al., 2008), the degree to which teacher questions are contingent—these factors indicate teachers valuing student reasoning and talk.

Use of Reasoning Words

The research of Neil Mercer at the University of Cambridge in England (Mercer & Dawes, 2008; Mercer & Littleton, 2007; Mercer et al., 1999) has identified key reasoning words and associated them with exploratory talk. *Might, could, maybe, I think, because* are examples of words that allow room for reasoning and possibilities, and for considering other viewpoints. He argues for explicitly teaching students this language and for teachers consistently modeling it.

METHODOLOGY

There is no other way to honestly get back at that moment in time and know what was going on without having a transcript.

(Unnamed teacher quoted in Cazden, 2001, p. 6)

Classroom talk reveals the enacted as opposed to intended lesson plan, making transparent instructional stance and indicating what counts as learning in a particular community. It provides markers of student learning. A close look at classroom talk patterns sheds light on the classroom culture shaping what can be learned and how.

In this chapter I draw upon the data bank of a six-week literature based study of whales in a fourth and fifth grade ELL classroom community. I selected this classroom because I had observed it for over four months and witnessed a consistently high amount of student talk participation; I was interested in unpacking the local classroom conditions sustaining and supporting student talk. There were six students (from Mainland China, Mexico, Pakistan, and Taiwan) who received English language "pull-out" services for 45 minutes daily. Each of these students had been studying English for at least a year and could produce age-appropriate thoughts in English. Three of them were not literate in their home language. Gathering these data I witnessed these students eagerly arriving before class officially started and staying until they were told to leave for lunch. Their teacher, Ms Charlotte (a pseudonym as are all the names in this study) was bilingual in English and Spanish, had been teaching ELL for 15 years, and, like many ELL teachers, divided her time between two schools. At the focal school she shared a classroom with the reading specialist. Ms Charlotte taught ELL through literature based instructional units. She planned extensively but was flexible in-the-moment (for more details, see Boyd, 2012). Most lessons began with all six students sitting at a kidney shaped table listening to a teacher picturebook readaloud selected to present information and perspectives about whales and to stimulate discussion about the interactions between whales and people (aligning with guiding questions for unit).

My original analysis of this six week instructional unit was a systematic and comprehensive look at these ELL students' elaborated utterances. Over 90% intercoder reliability was established across myself, graduate students and the teacher for topical episodes and initial coding frames. I then focused on student longer turns of talk that were also coherent and substantively engaged—I called such utterances student critical turns (for more details, see Boyd & Rubin, 2002). But there were many types of student talk in this classroom and for this chapter, I have selected talk data from two lessons to illustrate exploratory talk occurring during a lesson with and without a readaloud focus. These selected exchanges are offered as illustrative excerpts—not formulaic guidelines. They are intended to provide context for in-the-moment instructional decision making and purposeful use of language.

FINDINGS

Each classroom must find its own way of working, taking into account both what each member brings by way of past experience at home, at school, and in the wider community—their values, interests, and aspirations—as well as the outcomes that they are required to achieve

(Wells, 2001, p. 174)

Like most classrooms, the patterns of talk in this language learning classroom community were firmly established by the end of the academic year. In this community, students' contributions regularly shaped the scope of the discourse. In the extended exchange from Friday, April 24 that follows, the focus is on an experience Jordan shared from his social studies class (turns 1-28) and what Lucy has read (turns 29-38). As you pay attention to the role the teacher, Ms Charlotte, plays, notice also the conversational quality of the exchange. Notice how, without prompting, students enter and add to the unfolding conversation. Turn-taking norms are informal and at times there is overlapping talk as students bid for the floor.

1. Jordan: Uh, over by Alaska-well, I hear on the news, Mr. Sims told us in social studies, there were seven whales that were coming to the Pacific Ocean

2. Zach: Oh yea, they got trapped by ice

3. Jordan: And they got trapped by ice over there, by Alaska

4. Zach: [*inaudible*] this story

5. Ms Charlotte: Aha

6. Jordan: They got trapped there were seven whales

7. Zach: Man, they they got to use seven thousand dollars

8. Ms Charlotte: And so, what did they have to do?

9. Jordan: They were trapped, they were trapped there

10. Zach: They use seven thousand dollars to get those whales

11. Ms Charlotte: Why do you think they got trapped?

12. Jordan: Because there was too many ice.

13. Zach: No, no, they didn't go out when the right time should be out

14. Ms Charlotte: Oh, so they didn't go out?

15. Zach: They they stay alone like a few more minutes and eh hour

16. Ms Charlotte: Than when it was time for them to leave and then

17. Jordan: And he said there were like right up

18. Zach: Huge

19. Jordan: Too much ice,

20. Ms Charlotte: Ok

21. Jordan: And they

22. Ms Charlotte: Why do you think there might be too much ice?

23. Ms Charlotte: What about, does that remind you of anything that happened in *Orca Song*? Did anything happen there that would sound like

24. Lucy: Temperature

25. PD: Is very high

26. Jordan: It's been cold over there

27. Zach: It's cold from near pole-North pole

28. Ms Charlotte: Right

29. Lucy: I read in a book and they said em whales em they get stuck in the ice, they like to sit in the water...

30. Ms Charlotte: What about, does that remind you of anything that happened in Orca Song? Did anything happen there that would sound like

31. Rosey: Yeah, they got trapped

32. Jordan: Yea, what d'ya call it?

33. Rosey: The baby whale

34. Jordan: The whale got trapped in the netting

35. Ms Charlotte: The baby got trapped and then what happened, what was the other time? Did he get trapped in any other time?

36. Several students: No

37. Rosey: Yea, the, the beach

38. Ms Charlotte: The beach what happened there?

We see that Ms Charlotte is there as a guide, a support, but not dominating the conversation. She makes less than a third of the utterances (29%, 11 out of the 38 utterances) and when she talks, almost three quarters of the time (8/11), she wields questions, contingent questions that ask her student to push further—either to elaborate on what they have proffered (turns 8, 16, 22, 38), to clarify (turn 14), to extend their reasoning further (turn 11) or to direct their reasoning (turns 30, 35). Ms Charlotte's second most frequent communicative function is place-holding (turns 5, 20, 28). These one-word utterances affirm she is listening rather than serve to evaluate. Ms Charlotte's contingent questions are anchored in her students' contributions. She listens and in-the-moment she "leads from behind" (Wells & Chang Wells, 1992) to support and guide student purposes for discussion about whales. Her questions indicate three things. First, she is listening and interested—there is authentic purpose to them. Second, these questions are anchored in the students' intent for the discussion—they ask for more information or clarification about what they have contributed or they direct student thinking from what they have said to another point. Third, these teacher contingent questions position students as primary knowers with interpretive authority to surmise and answer.

Ms Charlotte's question, "Why do you think there might be too much ice?" models reasoning words that are associated with exploratory talk. The following excerpts from Thursday May 8 make transparent student reasoning and questioning. The first excerpt occurs before the readaloud, the second during the readaloud, of *Kayuktuk, An arctic quest* (Heinz, 1996). Again please note the conversational quality of these classroom interactions. Notice how the students control the scope of the talk through *their* questions (turns 2, 11, 12, 19, 21). Notice also that it is not necessarily the teacher who answers these student questions. In this classroom student can question, and propose answers and "think something else" (turn 34).

1. Charlotte: Ok this, ah, I brought this in (*igloo artifact*) to show you because we are going to be looking at the story that we read yesterday and then we are going to be looking at another story.

2. Jordan: Could we study about them people?

3. Zach: We are studying about whales

4. Charlotte: These are the people that we talked about yesterday, do you remember what they are called?

5. Zach: Yes

6. Charlotte: What?

7. Zach: Kayu (*reading title of book*)

8. Charlotte: Ok, that was his name

9. Jordan: Maybe like they from Alaska

10. Charlotte: They are from Alaska, aha

11. Lucy: How come they speak some kind of other language?

The interaction continues for twelve turns and then Jordan asks a question.

12. Jordan: What do you call this? I forgot.

13. Choral students: Igloo, igloo

14. Jordan: How do they make 'em?

15. Charlotte: It's made of ice

16. Rosey: No, no ice, ice cubes

17. Choral students: Ice, ice

18. Rosey: They cut the exact shape and then put them in the water, I think

[*Lots of overlapping speech*]

19. Jordan: Yea, but how do they make squares?

20. Charlotte: How do they make the squares? Who's going to say that?

21. Jordan: And then how do they make the tent?

22. Charlotte: Who thinks they know how to make the squares?

23. Lucy: Oh, I know

24. Steve: They dig a hole, like a square hole, then put water in it, and then, it change to a....

25. Zach: Ice

26. Steve: Ice

27. Charlotte: Oh, is that how they do it?

28. Choral students: Yeah

29. Steve: Then they put them on

30. Charlotte: Oh ok-so you think they dig a hole, and then they put water in there and the water freezes?

31. Jordan: One more

32. Charlotte: And then they get it out?

33. Rosey: What? No I think....

34. Lucy: No, I think something else

In this exchange—it continues for another 107 turns before Ms Charlotte begins the readaloud picturebook story, *Kayuktuk: An arctic quest*, we see how Ms Charlotte's questioning is in service of student purposes—"Yea, but how do they make squares?" (turn 19) and that she does not claim interpretive authority. With deft restatement of Jordan's contribution she indicates that this is a question worth considering and opens it up, "How do they make the squares? Who's going to say that?" This excerpt illustrates how these students are not afraid to hypothesize. "They cut the exact shape and then put them in the water, *I think*" (turn 18, my emphasis). And Ms Charlotte's feedback, "Oh, is that how they do it?" (turn 27) and "Oh ok-so you think they dig a hole, and then they put water in there and the water freezes?" (turn 30) is less evaluative than Rosey, "What? No, I think..." (turn 33) and Lucy, "No, I think something else." (turn 34). In this classroom students can explore ideas, ask questions, test language and hypothesis knowing the focus is on communicative competence and that their ideas count and will not be shut down.

The consistent willingness of these students to take risks—to ask questions and to provide exploratory responses is captured in the exchange below. It occurs during the same lesson on May 8. Notice how Rosey explains her reasoning (with the accompanying and appropriate student response "whoops" at the mention of the ominous shadow) and then articulates a question that clearly marks her engaged and deep thinking (turns 2-4). Ms Charlotte's response (turn 5) marks her pattern of positioning her students with interpretive authority and then listening attentively to their contributions. Her language allows for possibilities. Having read the story already, she knows Aknik is not blind but her response to PD's suggestion is "Well, I don't think he's blind." When PD postulates "color blind?" she responds, "Well, maybe ... what do you think?" (turns 5-10). Steve's subsequent, "I think" and Zach's "It could" perpetuate the reasoning language of possibility that they hear in Ms Charlotte's language. Such language—and epistemology—allows PD to continue hypothesizing—he is not shut down—and he proposes another possibility (turn 15).

1. Charlotte: *reading story out loud*: "For a feeling instant Aknik's shark eyes fixed on a moving smudge of gray that whisked across the glacial ice and faded away. A shadow he thought, just a shadow. Aknik

reset the snare" (or the trap) "and made the long walk back to the camp of tents."

2.   Rosey: There's a little snow, right? The fox is big, right? Then, he only saw a shadow, right?

3.   Zach: Whoops

4.   Rosey: How come it's a shadow, um, and he didn't see it when there's a lot of grass?

5.   Charlotte: Well, what do you think?

6.   PD: He's blind?

7.   Charlotte: Well, I don't think he's blind

8.   Zach: He's stupid

9.   PD: Color blind?

10.   Charlotte: Well, maybe ... what do you think?

11.   Steve: I think those are probably the shadows

12.   Charlotte: You think those are supposed to be the shadows of the drawings?

13.   Zach: It could

14.   Choral students: *unclear*

15.   PD: I just thought of something, if you trying to kill but it runs away?

Student discussion of what these shadows could foreshadow continues for 47 more turns. The pacing and scope of this discussion, like most in this classroom, are student-directed. Ms Charlotte selects literature to stimulate student interest and thinking and she is sufficiently experienced and patient to allow these ELL students to grapple with language as they talk to generate, shape, develop and validate ideas about books or life or learning together.

DISCUSSION

Exploratory talk provides an important means of working on understanding, but learners are unlikely to embark on it unless they feel relatively at ease, free from the danger of being aggressively contradicted or made fun of.

(Barnes, 2008, p. 6)

In this fourth and fifth grade pull-out ELL classroom children's literature was the springboard for engaging these six English language learners in talk. Literature offers the ideas of others to consider and vicarious experiences to reflect upon; it contextualizes content information and varied language and presentation; it invites engaged purpose for development of ideas and questions. But exploratory talk is not limited to talk about literature. When students grapple with ideas and questions they are interested in, they ask questions they want to answer—and the unfolding exploratory talk is relevant, purposeful and authentic in its communication, conjecture and connections to what is already known. So why is student exploratory talk not common practice in our classrooms? Certainly, the value of such talk for ELL students is clear. This close examination of ELL classroom talk patterns provides some answers.

The sociohistorical patterns of classroom talk predispose students towards particular types of talk. If a teacher asks open, authentic, initiating questions but then never follows up on what students offer in response, students quickly realize that an elaborated thinking response is actually not expected and they figure out what is desired and provide it. If a teacher asks students "what do you think" but then challenges their responses in a face-threatening way then students learn not to risk alternate explanations. On the other hand if the teacher consistently asks questions that further extend student contributions, and share interpretive authority with them, students feel comfortable and confident to risk exploratory talk. In such ELL classrooms the focus is less on grammatical accuracy or mimicry, but rather on thinking and composing in the moment—applying and using language for communication, conjecture and making connections with what is already known.

Classroom talk should be varied in its purpose and focus. A good teacher knows her students; plans an appropriate, engaging, and relevant lesson; and then thoughtfully responds to student cues deciding when to (and when not to) cede the floor and control of scope of discourse to students, and when to ignore or strategically develop and realign student contributions. Good teachers wield a repertoire of instructional strategies and employ them as needed to support student learning. There are times for student listening to teacher explanations, times for directed question and answer, times for literal explications. There are times to instantiate teacher lesson goals and times to honor student intentions for work to be done around texts. But *across* the classroom talk and activities, teachers should be striving to engender student talk where students talk and learn together (collective), listen and share (reciprocal) and build on each other's contributions (cumulative), in a supportive environment where it is safe to take risks and the teacher directs the talk toward some educational purpose (Alexander, 2006). This can be accomplished in many ways and through differing amounts of varied talk.

[handwritten margin note: What balance? many subjects to teach w/ short time]

We see these talk characteristics in these three excerpts from Ms Charlotte's classroom. There is a collective, reciprocal, supportive and cumulative quality to the talk as these students listen, propose, reason, challenge, and evaluate their co-constructed understanding of how whales got stuck, how to build an igloo, what the shadow signified to Aknik. Ms Charlotte supported these student explorations, allowing time, scope and interpretive space for them to communicate and test out ideas. She listened, asked questions, used language of possibilities, anchored her utterances in student contributions—folding in restatements of what they said and nudging them further to clarify, elaborate, extend their reasoning. The classroom talk was not scripted, rather purposively supportive of student explorations—and educationally effective and productive.

CONCLUSION

Awareness of how and why teachers generate particular class patterns help us become more purposeful in our own teaching.

(Boyd & Galda, 2011, p. 3)

An examination of the talk in this ELL classroom has shed light on ways Ms Charlotte employs contingent questioning, positions her students to have interpretive authority, and uses reasoning words to engender student productive exploratory talk. Analysis of her talk takes us beyond anecdotes and calls for more student talk and shows us concrete ways teachers can loosen the reins of classroom talk and risk messy digressions in hopes of fruitful discussions (Bailey, 1996; Duffy & Hoffman, 1999; Fairbanks et al., 2010; Mohr & Mohr, 2007). But for this to be successful, students must feel safe and supported—that their ideas count and will not be shut down -to risk exploration and elaboration.

REFERENCES

Alexander, R. J. (2006). *Towards dialogic teaching: Rethinking classroom talk* (3rd ed.). Cambridge, England: Dialogos.

Bailey, K. (1996). The best laid plans: Teachers' in- class decisions to depart from their lesson plans. In K. Bailey & D. Nunan (Eds.), *Voices from the language classroom* (pp. 15-40). Melbourne, Australia: Cambridge University Press.

Bakhtin, M. M. (1981). *The dialogic imagination: Four essays by M. M. Bakhtin*. Austin, TX: University of Texas Press.

Barnes, D. (2008). Exploratory talk for learning. In N. Mercer & S. Hodgkinson (Eds.), *Exploring talk in school*. Los Angeles: SAGE.

Barnes, D., Britton, J., & Torbe, M. (1969). *Language, the learner and the school*. Portsmouth, NH: Boynton/Cook.

Bloome, D., Power Carter, S., Morton Christian, B., Madrid, S., Otto, S., Shuart-Faris, N., & Smith, M. (2008). *Discourse analysis in classrooms: Approaches to language and literacy research*. New York, NY: Teachers College Press.

Boyd, M. (2012). Planning and realigning a lesson in response to student needs: Intentions and decision making. *Elementary School Journal, 113*(1).

Boyd, M., & Galda, L. (2011). *Real talk in Elementary Schools: Effective oral language practice*. New York, NY: Guilford.

Boyd, M., & Maloof, V. (2000). How teachers build upon Student-Proposal Intertextual Links to facilitate student talk in the ESL classroom. In J. Hall & L. Verplaetse (Eds.), *The Development of second and foreign language learning through classroom interaction* (pp. 163-182). Mahwah, NJ: Lawrence Erlbaum Associates.

Boyd, M., & Markarian, B. (2011). Dialogic teaching: Talk in support of a dialogic stance. *Language and Education, 25*(6) 515-534

Boyd, M., & Rubin, D. (2002). Elaborated student talk in an Elementary ESoL Classroom. *Research in the Teaching of English, 36*(4), 495-530.

Boyd, M., & Rubin, D. (2006). How contingent questioning promotes extended student talk: A function of display questions. *Journal of Literacy Research, 38*(2), 141-169.

Britton, J. (1969). Talking to learn. In D. Barnes, J. Britton, & M. Torbe (Eds.), *Language the learner and the school* (pp. 89-130). Portsmouth, NH: Boynton/Cook.

Cazden, C. B. (2001). *Classroom discourse: The language of teaching and learning* (2nd ed). Portsmouth, NH: Heinemann.

Chinn, C., Anderson, R. C., & Waggoner, M. A. (2001). Patterns of discourse in two kinds of literature discussion. *Reading Research Quarterly, 36*(4), 378-411.

Dillon, J. T. (1982). The effect of questions in education and other enterprises. Journal of *Curriculum Studies, 14*(2), 127-152.

Duffy, G., & Hoffman, J. (1999). In pursuit of an illusion: The flawed search for a perfect method. *The Reading Teacher, 53*(1), 10-16.

Fairbanks, C., Duffy, G., Faircloth, B., Ile, C., Levin, B., Rohr, J., & Stein, C. (2010). Beyond knowledge: Exploring why some teachers are more thoughtfully adaptive than others. *Journal of Teacher Education, 61*(1-2), 161-181.

Lantolf, J. P. (2002). Introducing sociocultural theory. In J. P. Lantolf (Ed.), *Sociocultural theory and second language learning* (pp. 1-26). Oxford, England: Oxford University Press.

Lee, Y. (2007). Third turn position in teacher talk: Contingency and the work of teaching. *Journal of Pragmatics, 39*, 180-206.

Mehan, H. (1979). "What time is it Denise?": Asking knowing information questions in classroom discourse. *Theory into Practice, 1*(6), 89-91.

Mercer, N. (2002). The art of interthinking. *Teaching Thinking, 7*(Spring), 8-11.

Mercer, N., & Dawes, L. (2008). The value of exploratory talk. In N. Mercer & S. Hodgkinson (Eds.), *Exploring talk in schools* (pp. 55-72). Newbury Park, CA: SAGE.

Mercer, N., & Hodgkinson, S. (2008). *Exploring talk in schools*. London: SAGE.

Mercer, N., & Littleton, K. (2007). *Dialogue and the development of children's thinking: A sociocultural approach*. London: Routledge.

Mercer, N., Wegerif, R., & Dawes, L. (1999). Children's talk and the development of reasoning in the classroom. *British Educational Research Journal, 25*(1), 95-111.

Mohr, K. A. J., & Mohr, E. S. (2007). Extending English-Language Learners' classroom interactions using the response protocol. *Reading Teacher, 60*(5), 440-450.

Nystrand, M., & Gamoran, A. (1991). Instructional discourse, student engagement, and literature achievement. *Research in the Teaching of English, 25*, 261-290.

Nystrand, M., Gamoran, A., Kachur, R., & Prendergast, C. (1997). *Opening dialogue: Understanding the dynamics of language and learning in the English classroom*. New York, NY: Teachers College Press.

Nystrand, M., Wu, L. L., Gamoran, A., Zeiser, S., & Long, D. A. (2003). Questions in time: Investigating the structure and dynamics of unfolding classroom discourse. *Discourse Processes, 35*(2), 135-198.

Pennycook, A. (1994). *The cultural politics of English as an international language*. London: Longman.

Pica, T. (1994). Research on negotiation: What does it reveal about second-language learning conditions, processes, and outcomes? *Language Learning, 44*(3), 493-527.

Smith, H., & Higgins, S. (2006). Opening classroom interaction: The importance of feedback. *Cambridge Journal of Education 36*(4), 485-502.

Soter, A., Wilkinson, I. A., Murphy, P. K., Rudge, L., Reninger, K., & Edwards, M. (2008). What the discourse tells us: Talk and indicators of high-level comprehension. *International Journal of Educational Research, 47*, 372-391.

Swain, M. (1995). Three functions of output in Second Language Learning. In G. Cook & B. Seidlhofer (Eds.), *Principle and practice in applied linguistics: Studies in honour of H. G. Widdowson* (pp. 125-144). New York, NY: Oxford University Press.

Vygotsky, L. (1986). *Thought and language*. Cambridge, MA: MIT Press.

Wells, G. (1993). Reevaluating the IRF Sequence: A proposal for the articulation of theories of activity and discourse for the analysis of teaching and learning in the classroom. *Linguistics And Education, 5*, 1-37.

Wells, G. (1999). *Dialogic inquiry: Towards a sociocultural practice and theory of education*. Cambridge, England: Cambridge University Press.

Wells, G. (2001). *Action, talk and text: Learning and teaching through inquiry*. New York and London: Teachers College Press.

Wells, G., & Chang Wells, G. L. (1992). *Constructing knowledge together: Classrooms as centers of inquiry and literacy*. Portsmouth, NH: Heinnemann.

Wilkinson, I. (1970). The concept of oracy. *The English Journal, 59*(1), 71-77.

CHAPTER 2

MEDIATING MEANING IN INTERACTION

Researching the Connection Between Professional Development and Teacher Practice

José David Herazo and Richard Donato

This study compared how two teachers of English as a foreign language mediate their students' meaning-making participation during teacher-led interaction. One of the teachers was trained to mediate students' participation in interaction by the *Colombian National Bilingualism Program* (CNBP) whereas the other was not. Thus, this study examined whether participation in the CNBP training accounted for any notable differences in the mediation-provided by the two teachers. Data for the study consisted of classroom observations, transcriptions of teacher-student interaction, stimulated recall protocols, and teaching materials. Findings show that, contrary to the non-trained teacher, the mediation provided by the CNBP-trained teacher contradicts the CNBP professional development contents, jeopardizing the effectiveness of this training for reaching the CNBP goals. Findings also highlight the importance of understanding how language teaching policy is shaped by local contextual factors and uncover various dimensions of mediation (e.g., time, focus, and tools) that appear underrepresented in the literature.

Teachers' Roles in Second Language Learning:
Classroom Applications of Sociocultural Theory, pp. 19–40
Copyright © 2012 by Information Age Publishing
All rights of reproduction in any form reserved.

The high school class is involved in a discussion in English about students working part time while still in school. Students make multiple contributions to the topic of discussion, debate opinions, and offer alternatives to the teacher's views of the matter. They also answer questions posed by the teacher and provide their own unsolicited ideas on the reasons why some students need to work while in school and how working part time can affect students positively or negatively. During the discussion, the teacher serves as a coparticipant in the conversation by asking probing questions, requesting elaboration of student opinions, and contributing her own points to the development of the discussion. The difference, however, between the discussion in this classroom and a discussion that may take place in the world outside, among family, friends, and colleagues, is that the participants in this discussion are beginning English as a foreign language (EFL) learners who have limited opportunities in their daily lives to have serious conversations in a language which is not yet entirely their own. Another important difference is that one participant in the conversation, the teacher, plays a role that is not often required in conversations among participants who are on relatively equal linguistic and cultural ground. In conversation with EFL students, the teacher is a mediator of the content and the language of the discussion and, as such, provides students with support and assistance for simultaneously developing the meanings and the wordings of the discussion. In this chapter, we examine closely this mediational role of the teacher during classroom discussions. We will show that teacher mediation, a foundational concept in sociocultural theory, is a complex, dynamic, and variable feature that proves to be consequential in the way that students engage in interpersonal communication in the classroom.

Comprehensive educational reforms are often the means to prepare teachers for supporting learners in meaningful and purposeful foreign language interactions, such as the one described above. The *Colombian National Bilingualism Program* (CNBP) (MEN, 2005) is one such reform effort and the context for this study. One of the goals of the CNBP is to prepare teachers of EFL to mediate learners' interpersonal communication skills through meaning-oriented conversations about relevant and interesting topics. Specifically, the CNBP seeks to enable EFL teachers to interact meaningfully with learners, mediating their oral participation through appropriate discourse eliciting strategies, such as questions, and attention to the content of learners' utterances. No research has documented how CNBP-trained teachers mediate their learners' oral participation, one of the major goals of this program. To address this issue, we investigate how two Colombian EFL teachers, one who participated in the training program and one who had not, support the development of their learners' meaning-making participation during instructional interaction.

Based on this cross-case comparison, we examine whether the teachers' verbal support aligns with the explicit goals and training of the CNBP. We use the concept of mediation (Vygotsky, 1978; Wertsch, 2007) from socio-cultural theory (SCT) to examine the realization of the CNBP training efforts in actual classrooms where this research took place.

SOCIOCULTURAL THEORY AND L2 LEARNING

One foundational concept of sociocultural theory is that a more capable other, such as the teacher, plays a major role in mediating novices' learning and development (Vygotsky, 1978). Although in the field of second language acquisition (SLA) this concept has been explored by a variety of research (Hall & Verplaetse, 2000; Lantolf, 2000; Lantolf & Thorne, 2006), several crucial topics appear to be still underrepresented. Notable omissions include the semiotic tools through which mediation occurs (Ohta, 2000a) and the way L2 mediation is shaped by cultural-historical, sociocultural, ontological, and microgenetic influences.

In this chapter, we shed light on these two crucial topics (a) by investigating the *focus*, *time*, and *tools* of teacher mediation of learners' EFL oral participation and (b) by analyzing the relationship between the way this mediation occurs and the goals of the CNBP training program described above. In the first section of the chapter, we discuss the concept of mediation and review some of the research on mediated L2 learning during teacher-student interaction. Next, we describe the methodology for data collection and analysis, and present the findings for each of the two teachers. In the last section, we present the implications of these findings for the CNBP professional development program.

Mediation and L2 Learning

The concept of mediation is based on Vygotsky's view that an individual's mental, social, and material activity is shaped by tools and signs that have been historically and culturally created (Vygotsky, 1978, 1986; Wertsch, 2007). That is to say, an individual's cognitive and affective relationship with the world and others is not direct, but rather mediated through various types of signs, most notably linguistic signs, that have been inherited from others throughout history, learned, and often transformed through recurring cycles of specific cultural and social practices. It is this perspective on mediated mental activity that is referred to as self-, other-, or object regulation (Daniels, 2008) and which most often takes the form of linguistic guidance of participation (e.g., providing verbal cues or using assisting questions of various kinds). Based on this orientation, mediation can be defined as a self-directed or other-directed process resulting in voluntary control over one's social and mental world through the use of cultural artifacts, concepts, and activities (Lantolf & Thorne, 2006). In this chapter, our focus is on mediation provided by the teacher to assist learners as they interact in the EFL classroom. Since learners' use of English in Colombia occurs almost exclusively in the classroom, focusing on teacher mediation is crucial for understanding the dynamics of EFL learning and the way the CNBP prepares teachers for this role in Colombia.

L2 Teacher-Student Interaction as a Mediated Activity

SLA research from a sociocultural perspective has focused on a variety of topics including private speech (Appel & Lantolf, 1994; Ohta, 2000a, 2000b), other-regulation (Anton, 1999; Donato, 2000; McCormick & Donato, 2000), the zone of proximal development and scaffolding (Aljaafreh & Lantolf, 1994; Donato, 1994; Guk & Kellog, 2007), and dynamic assessment (Lantolf & Thorne, 2006; Poehner & Lantolf, 2010). This research shows quite convincingly that SLA can be conceived as social in origin, semiotic in nature, and instantiated in mediated interactions with others. This body of research also shows that a teacher's discourse (what they say, how they say it, how they respond, etc.) is consequential to language learning and development. For example, Aljaafreh and Lantolf (1994) and Ohta (2000b) investigated corrective feedback, attending especially to the verbal moves used by a teacher or tutor to mediate L2 development. The first study looked closely at the cognitive functions of the mediator's utterances, whereas the second approached the issue of mediation from the learners' use of private speech in response to teacher recasts. Aljaafreh and Lantolf's (1994) findings show that mediation needs to be contingent, responsive, and graduated. That is, for mediation to occur and to become the source of learning and development, it must be continuously adjusted to learners' developing understandings. Ohta (2000b) extends this discussion and demonstrates that a learner's private speech can be an important indicator of the effectiveness and saliency of teacher mediation. Her research suggests that private speech during large group instruction may be one indicator of effective mediation that promotes learner assimilation and expansion of new language elements. Research on dynamic assessment in the context of L2 learning is also fundamentally grounded in this basic assumption of Vygotskyan theory (Lantolf & Thorne, 2006).

Other SLA studies have also confirmed the positive effects of teacher mediation on students' L2 learning. These studies have shown that teach-

Importance of teacher discourse

ers' utterances are more than ways to provide input or elicit output, that well managed discursive forms of teacher mediation support cognition and linguistic development in the context of tasks and instructional goals (Gibbons, 2003; Toth, 2011), that this mediation can potentially create whole class and small group ZPDs (Anton, 1999; Guk & Kellog, 2007), and that it may serve as scaffolding and dynamic assistance (McCormick & Donato, 2000).

The specific tools of mediation reported in the SLA literature are diverse, confirming Kozulin's (2003) and Vygotsky's (1978) claims that the forms of adult mediation vary greatly. In addition to questions (McCormick & Donato, 2000), the specific mediational tools that teachers deploy include functional recasts (Mohan & Beckett, 2003), negotiation of meaning requests (Gibbons, 2003), repetition, demonstrations, translation, metalinguistic comments, and the initiation of a solution that learners must complete (Guk & Kellog, 2007).

Although many of the previous studies argue that L2 learning in the classroom can be mediated by teachers' discourse, the research has focused primarily on studying the development of learners' linguistic system rather than on examining how teacher mediation sustains learners' participation in meaningful interactions. For example, previous studies have focused on article use, tense and aspect, use of prepositions, and modal verbs (Aljaafreh & Lantolf, 1994), verb meanings (Ohta, 2000b), and vocabulary (Guk & Kellog, 2007). Two exceptions to this observation seem to be Mohan and Beckett's (2003) and Gibbons' (2003) studies, that described how learners' meaning-making capacity expanded from congruent (non-academic) to non-congruent (academic) discourse realizations (Halliday & Matthiessen, 2004), and how content, meaning, and form in the ESL content-based science classroom were functionally related.

The goals of previous research seem to have been, then, to study how more capable others mediate learners development of the language system, rather than how this mediation helps learners become meaning-makers and participants in interactions. Thus, this study assumes a broader perspective on mediation that focuses on teachers' discourse moves that support student participation and meaning-making during teacher-student interaction.

STUDY DESIGN AND METHODS

This study follows a naturalistic, interpretive line of inquiry (Richards, 2003) to compare the moment-to-moment discourse moves that two Colombian EFL teachers used to mediate learners' meaning-making participation in two different high school classrooms. We use a cross-case design (Duff, 2008) to compare the mediational activity of these two teachers, one who participated in the CNBP training and the other who did not, and to examine the extent to which the mediation of one of them is consistent with the training that she received from the CNBP. Three complementary questions guided our analysis of the two teachers' mediation: (1) what is the *focus* of the two teachers' mediation during their interactions with students? (2) At what *time* during the interaction is teacher mediation provided? and (3) What differences are there in the two teachers' mediational moves? That is, are there differences in the quantity or quality of the mediational *tools* used by the two teachers? Mediation during whole class discussion is analyzed through observations, stimulated recall protocols (SRP), and microanalytical discourse analysis.

Participants and Their Context

Two EFL teachers, Monica and Kelly (pseudonyms), were chosen to participate in this research using a criterion sampling procedure (Duff, 2008). Criteria for selection included language ability level, participation in the CNBP training, and teaching context. Both Monica and Kelly have a C2 English proficiency level according to the QPTtest[1] (Oxford & Cambridge ESOL, 2002), and both hold degrees in English language teaching (ELT). Monica specialized in ELT, but Kelly specialized in English-Spanish translation. Monica and Kelly work in two different high schools on the Colombian North Coast. Monica's school is a designated pilot school for the city's bilingualism project for grades 9th through 11th, which is affiliated with the CNBP. Her school has a multimedia laboratory and provides English textbooks to learners, who are taught two hours of EFL each day during 5 days per week. The textbook Monica uses, *American Adventures: Starter* (Wetz, 2007), was chosen by the local bilingualism administrators, and is the same textbook used by the three pilot schools in the city. In contrast to Monica, Kelly's school is not part of a local bilingualism initiative and learners are taught only 3 hours of EFL per week (1 hour on 1 day and 2 hours on another day). Kelly and her students use sections from the textbook, *Go for it* 3B (Nunan, 2005), that Kelly selected.

Monica completed 120 hours of professional development offered by the CNBP in order to promote teaching practices appropriate for communicative language teaching. To this end, Monica was taught to mediate learners' meaningful participation in EFL during theme-based, personalized interactions. The following transcript, taken from the course materials (MEN, 2009), shows the type of teacher-student interaction that the CNBP promoted.

Teacher: *What did you do over the weekend?*
Student: *I ... play basketball*
Teacher: *Oh you played basketball. Where did you play?*
Student: *I played at the school.*
Teacher: *Did you win the game?*

As this example shows, the CNBP training encouraged Monica to attend to the meaning of learners' utterances, to use initiating and follow-up questions for sustaining learners' participation, and to correct learners' mistakes through recasts or reformulations (e.g., *"You played basketball"* in the above interaction). Kelly did not take part in the ELT training offered by the CNBP, but attended a course to improve her proficiency in English. In addition to her position in the school, Kelly teaches English to pre-service EFL teachers at a local university.

Data Sources

We observed 6 hours of teaching during 5 lessons for Kelly and 3 hours of class work during 3 lessons for Monica in the middle of the school year. We kept field-notes during lessons, collected artifacts, and videotaped and audio recorded all lessons. After each lesson, we identified and transcribed episodes in which teacher-student oral interaction occurred. We used these episodes for the stimulated recall protocols (SRPs) (Gass & Mackey, 2000) that took place in the teachers' L1 within 2 days after each lesson. We identified and transcribed a corpus of 46 episodes, 21 episodes for Monica and 25 episodes for Kelly. To maximize corpus variability (Bauer & Aarts, 2000), we transcribed all the episodes in which teacher and learners engaged in oral communication. Data about the CNBP training consisted of the syllabus of this course.

Data Analysis

Talk is one of the major historical and cultural mediational tools we possess to create relationships of various kinds, be they social, professional, or instructional. For this reason, conversations between teacher and learners and learners with each other constitute a window (Ohta, 2000a) through which mediation can be seen and analyzed. Thus, we view teacher and learner interaction as the text where the microdynamics of L2 learning can be read. Reading this text, however, requires a recursive and careful analytical process. To this end, the software NVivo 8 (QSR International) was used to analyze the data. Analytical coding was based on the SLA and sociocultural literature or derived from the data to address the three perspectives of mediation described above (focus, time, and tools). Although these perspectives are often realized simultaneously in teachers' discourse, the coding process for each category occurred separately. Inter-rater reliability checks yielded a Kappa agreement of 0.82, 0.83, and 0.90 for the categories of focus, time and tools respectively. Concerning the focus of mediation, we used three categories: focus on *meaning*, focus on *affect*, and focus on *language*. Focus on *meaning* refers to mediation that supports learners' production of meaningful content, focus on *affect* refers to teacher moves that mediate learners' willingness to participate (MacIntyre, Dörnyei, Clément, & Noels, 1998), and focus on *language* deals with mediation of learners' linguistic accuracy, typically morphosyntax.

The sociocultural SLA literature refers to the temporal feature of mediation as contingency, meaning that mediation occurs only *when* it is needed and is removed when learners show they can perform independently (Aljaafreh & Lantolf, 1994). We used three categories to code for *time* of mediation. *Proactive mediation* orients learners' attention to their forthcoming participation, pushes them to say more, or sets up expectancies (van Lier, 1996) for the content or form of what they will say. *Ongoing mediation* corresponds to "procedural assistance" (Toth, 2008), and occurs while learners are trying to formulate an utterance. We call this type of mediation "ongoing" to emphasize its temporal orientation. Finally, *reactive mediation* refers to the teacher's supportive moves that orient learners' attention to previous utterances, usually to the inaccurate form of these utterances rather than to their meanings.

To analyze the *tools* of mediation, we used eleven different categories, such as, "recasts," "follow-up questions," "forced-choice questions," "provision of example options," "elaborations" and "continuatives" (see Table 2.1, p. 33). Since many of these categories have been reported in the existing sociocultural and SLA literature, they will not be explained here.

As the coding process was taking place, we interviewed the two teachers using transcripts as stimulus to validate the coding system and enhance its reliability. The SRP provided self-reported reasons for the two teachers' discourse moves. The SRP data and the CNBP documents were analyzed through the procedure of constant comparison (Strauss, 1987). This comparative procedure allowed for the identification, confirmation, or disconfirmation of recurrent patterns of mediation in the data.

FINDINGS

We present the findings in terms of the focus, time, and tools of mediation. To report the analysis of these dimensions, we will use only one interaction episode for each teacher. Rather than seeking quantitative representativeness with these episodes, our goal is to show the variability and patterns of mediation for each teacher.

Monica as Mediator

As Episode A shows below, Monica's mediation efforts (underlined) centered primarily on accuracy issues and occurred reactively in most cases. Episode A occurred in the first lesson of a new unit in which learners were discussing famous people. Before episode A, Monica had questioned her students about the occupation of famous people whose pictures appeared in the textbook. She then tried to mediate learners' use of a relational identifying clause[2] (Halliday & Matthiessen, 2004) to produce their own examples of famous people and their occupations.

Episode A[3]

1. M   okay, now guys/ <u>can you say like, Alex Rodriguez is a sports sta::r</u>, right, now let's do it umm, with a singer please yeah a singer, <u>can you say like SHAKIRA is a singer</u>, right another one, S4 ((*points to S4*))

2. S4 Paris Hilton is a singer too

3. M   well she's not a singer SINger

4. S1   └Leona Lewis

5. S2   └Leona Lewis

6. M   who/

7. S2 Leona Lewis

8. M   okay Leona Lewis

9. S3 Daddy Yankee

10. S4   └Gavilan

11. M   <u>but say it like the whole sentence</u>, again

12. S3 Daddy Yankee

13. M   <u>Daddy Yankee what/</u>

14. S5 Diomedez Diaz

15. M   <u>What does he do?</u>

16. S   laughter

17. M   <u>Daddy Yankee is/</u>

18. S6 a singer

19. M   └a singer okay, S3/ ((*points to S3*))

20. S? Eminen

21. M   <u>Eminen is a singer</u> ((*points to S6*))

22. S6 my mom is a [business] person

23. M   <u>a BUSINESS person</u> really/

24. S6 ((nods))

25. M   coo::l okay, so <u>S6's mom is a business person</u>, very good, S7

26. S7 Diomedez Diaz

27. M   <u>Diomedez Diaz is a singer</u>, that's right

28. SS laughter

29. M   yeah, he's a very good, well he used to be a very good singer

As this episode indicates, Monica's mediation focused on assisting learners' production of the relational identifying clause "*(name of person) IS + determiner (occupation)*" accurately, or what teachers might anecdotally refer to as responding to questions in a complete sentence. To this end, she used several reactive mediational moves. In turn 1, she gave learners two models of the form of the desired utterance ("*Alex Rodriguez is a sports star*" and "*Shakira is a singer*"). This initial proactive mediation assisted S4 but clearly failed to help other learners who simply listed names of famous people with no identification of the profession (turns 4, 5, 7, 9, and 10).

After turn 10, Monica used reactive mediation to direct learners' attention to the morphosyntactic accuracy of their utterances. For example, Monica used a metalinguistic request in turn 11("*say it like the whole sentence*") to explicitly ask S3 to correct the answer that he provided in turn 9. Next, she used an implicit evaluative move (turn 13), signaled by the interrogative "what" in end position ("*Daddy Yankee what/*"), to indicate that something was missing in S3's utterance in turn 9. Following this prompt for a full sentence, she used a follow-up question in which she explicitly requested an identification of Daddy Yankee's occupation (turn 15). The fact that Monica already knew the answer (*Daddy Yankee is a singer*) suggests that the intention of this mediational move was to prompt learners to notice the syntactic form of their production rather than to express interest in the content of their contribution. This mediational move was again unsuccessful, resulting in another evaluation in the form of an incomplete declarative with raising intonation (turn 17). This move provided simultaneously an evaluative response and the correct syntactic frame that learners need to use (Toth, 2008). Monica's concern for morphosyntactic accuracy (here a full identifying clause) can also be seen in turn 23, where she recasted S6's answer (turn 22) to provide the correct pronunciation of the word "*business*," and repeated S6's complete utterance, concluding with an evaluation of its syntactic accuracy with "*very good*" (turn 23). Interestingly, S4's (turn 2) and S6's (turn 22) responses were the only instances when students produced the teacher's expected response. Monica replied to S6 with a verification request ("*really?*") with tonic prominence on the lexical item (*business*) rather than with a follow-up request for more information (e.g., *in what type of business is she working?*). Her follow-up move is evidence of Monica's focus on accuracy rather than on supporting the learner's elaboration of the content and meaning of the exchange.

Monica's focus on form through reactive mediational moves was the most common pattern of mediation throughout the data set. Analysis of the corpus showed that she oriented her mediation to *language* 54% of the time, while *meaning* received only 34% of her attention, and *affect* received the remaining 12%. Her orientation to form focused on morphosyntactic accuracy (76%) and pronunciation (14%), was reactive 78.5% of the time, and occurred mainly through recasts, incomplete declaratives with raising intonation, follow-up questions, and metalinguistic requests of the 'whole sentence' type. Her focus on accuracy through reactive mediation was corroborated in the SRP.[4] Monica reported that she expected learners "to produce whole sentences and not only say the names of the singers." She also explained that for learners to be able to participate meaningfully during oral interaction, "they first need language models they can follow to create their sentences." As shown in the analysis, she regularly corrected the form of learner contributions by redirecting their attention to these model utterances.

Monica's moderate focus on meaning (34%) occurred almost always proactively through follow-up questions, elaborations of her own questions, and yes/no questions with the wrong answer (e.g. asking "*is he a composer?*" when discussing the picture of a soccer player). Her minimal orientation towards affect occurred through ongoing moves like continuatives (e.g. *uh huh*) (Halliday & Matthiessen, 2004). The majority of the cases of mediation of meaning and affect occurred within an initiation-response-evaluation pattern of discourse (Cazden, 2001), and rarely engaged students in extending their production during their response turn.

In summary, the data present a profile of Monica's mediation that can be described as primarily form focused, reactive, and motivated by her belief that learners need to control form as a prerequisite to expressing opinions, feelings, and new information. What is surprising is that Monica participated in the teacher development program the CNBP offered, in which the preferred orientation to interaction was *not* of the type found consistently in her corpus.

she believed form was necessary for expression

did teacher dev. program discuss this?

Kelly as Mediator

In contrast to Monica, Kelly's mediation was primarily proactive and oriented toward the goal of learners' meaning-making participation. Episode B below, taken from the fifth lesson in the unit, illustrates these findings. Before this episode, the class had been discussing the problem of adolescent drug addiction, using the example of a learner who left school due to this problem. During this discussion, learners shifted the topic from drug addiction to reasons why learners drop out of school, a topic shift that Kelly did not realize until turns 14 and 15.

Episode B

1. K   so, tell me WHY, <u>is only about problems/ is only about companies/ or is about MY DECISION</u>
2. S1   money
3. K   is about money/
4. S2   is my decision
5. K   <u>money is another factor/</u>
6. S3   no
7. K   money is another factor/
8. SS   yes, yes
9. K   <u>why? why?</u>
10. S4   *yo creo que si* ((I think so))
11. K   <u>why? why? is it important?</u>
12. S4   *la necesitan en el colegio para trabajar* ((they need it in school, to work))
13. K   <u>if you work you get drugs/</u>
14. S5   no teacher, *quieren estudiar y no tienen la posibilidad de negociar* ((they want to study and don't have the chance to do business))
15. K   <u>uh hu/ they don't have the/</u>
16. S?   possibility
17. K   possibility <u>they don't have the possibility</u>
18. S3   └teacher
19. S3   in the work don't affect
20. K   <u>uh hu/</u>
21. S3   *osea porque::: * ((I mean because::))
22. K   └<u>why:::?</u>
23. SS   ((giggles))

24. S3 └is … two *jornal* ((*jornal*: one section of the day, morning or afternoon))

25. K   └yeah/

26. S3 in … in a one *jornal* work/ in the ot- in the other *jornal*::: study

27. K   └uh uh/

28. K oh:: so:: they can study/, so according to S3 <u>money is not a factor because…in the morning they can study/ and in the afternoon/ in the afternoon/</u>

29. S3 work

30. K <u>they can/ work\ … in the afternoon/ they can work\</u> okay

  Three different but complementary patterns of mediation occurred in episode B. First, Kelly used proactive mediation to promote learners' meaning-focused participation. That is, she provided conversational support in advance of the learners' responses followed by meaning-focused questions that sustained learner participation. For example, in turn 1, she gave learners contrasting options from which to choose, which resulted in an answer from S1 (turn 2) consisting only of the clause residue ("*money*"),[5] and another response from S2 in turn 4. Kelly reacted to S1's response with a follow-up question requesting confirmation (turn 3, 5, and 7), focusing on the meaning of S1's statement rather than on the fact that it consisted of a single-word reply. Once the entire class confirmed S1's answer (turn 8), she asked a follow-up question demanding justification (turn 9: "*why? why?*"). Because S4 answered in Spanish, she asked the same question again (turn 11) and then made it more specific by using a yes/no interrogative instead of a "wh-" construction (turn 11: "*is it important?*"). Kelly's mediation allowed S4 to continue his answer, still in Spanish (turn 12), and Kelly responded with another verification request (turn 13) that helped her realize the topic shift. As Kelly reported during the SRP, one of her goals was to make learners "feel they could participate in conversations in the L2, even if their participation had language errors or occurred in Spanish sometimes." Her goal for meaningful participation explains why she reacted to the content of S4 answers in turn 10 and 12 with a justification request (turn 11) and a confirmation request (turn 13), even though the learner's utterances were in Spanish. In this way, she implicitly accepted these contributions as valid for the ongoing conversation and mediated conversational participation for meaning over form.

  The second mediation pattern occurred from turn 14 to 17 and again from turn 28 to 30. Interestingly in both cases, Kelly focused on form through reactive mediation only after learners had conveyed their meaningful contribution to the topic of conversation. To S5's response in L1 (turn 14), Kelly provided an incomplete translation (turn 15: "*they don't have the/*"), which she ended with raising intonation signaling an invitation to the class to assist in the completion of the utterance. This invitation was taken up by one learner who provided the missing word in turn 16 ("*possibility*"), allowing Kelly to incorporate the word into a full clause containing the subject, finite element, and verb (turn 17: "*they* [subject] *don't* [finite element] *have* [verb] *the possibility*"). As the SRP revealed, Kelly's intention was to send the subtle message that participation in L2 was required and to model, without explicit correction, the form-meaning mapping needed. This same form-focused, reactive pattern repeated from turns 28 to 30, where Kelly's mediation resembles a functional recast (Mohan & Beckett, 2003) that seeks to edit learners discourse, illustrating acceptable forms for expressing particular L2 meanings.

The third recurring pattern of mediation is Kelly's attention to learner affect. Mediation of affect occurred from turns 15 to 27 and was mainly realized by the continuative "*uh hu/*" (turns 15, 22, 25, and 27), with raising intonation, as a way to show interest and encourage elaboration. This form of mediation appeared to have prompted S3 to engage in sustained participation over several turns, while attempting the complex formulation: "*in the work don't affect* [because] *is two 'jornal', in one 'jornal'* [students can] *work in the other 'jornal'* [they can] *study.*" Our interpretation of Kelly's use of continuatives was confirmed during the SRP, where Kelly said that she used "*uh hu/*" to mean "go on, I'm listening" and encourage learners to say more.

Episode B clearly shows the patterns that occurred in Kelly's mediation throughout the corpus. Our analysis revealed that her mediation focused primarily on meaning (57%) and occurred proactively through follow-up questions that advanced the topic, elaborations of her own questions, and the provision of response options. Her focus on language represented approximately one-third of her mediation (29%), and was achieved reactively through recasts and incomplete declaratives. Her focus on form addressed morphosyntax and lexis in similar proportions, and targeted functional chunks, such as whole phrases or clauses to construct specific meanings. Kelly's mediation of affect was her least common form of mediation (14%), and in almost all cases occurred through continuatives to support ongoing participation.

In summary, the data show a profile of Kelly's mediation that is primarily focused on meaning, proactive, and motivated by her belief that learners need first to construe meaning and present their ideas before attending to language forms. Although Kelly was not a participant in the CNBP professional development program, she displayed mediational patterns that match what this program advocates in terms of teacher-student interaction in the EFL classroom.

Cross-Case Comparison

Table 2.1 summarizes the distribution of mediation moves by Kelly and Monica. It shows the frequency of each type of mediation within each dimension and the variety of discourse tools each teacher used throughout the corpus.

Table 2.1 confirms that Monica's mediation was oriented toward form and occurred mostly reactively, whereas Kelly's mediation was primarily oriented towards meaning and participation, and occurred proactively in most cases. What is more, Monica first oriented learners' participation towards producing specific language forms and used recasts or incomplete declaratives to help them focus on accuracy. At least half of her follow-up questions were yes/no agreement requests ("*do you agree?*") addressed to the whole class. Conversely, Kelly first focused on meaning and participation, usually allowing learners to use both Spanish and English. Once learners provided their ideas, she used continuatives to sustain their participation in English over several turns. As Cummins (2007) has argued, when learners' L1 is invoked as a

Table 2.1.   Cross-Case Comparison of Mediational Moves

	Monica	*Kelly*
Total Moves	75	228
Focus of mediation:		
Meaning	34%	57%
Form	54%	29%
Affect	12%	14%
Time of mediation		
Proactive	38%	60%
Reactive	59%	30%
Ongoing	2.7%	10%
Tools of mediation	• Recasts (26.7%) • Questions (17.3%) • Incomplete declarative ending with rising intonation (10.7%) • Elaboration moves (9.3%) • Forced choice questions (8%) • Repetition (8%) • Metalinguistic requests (5.3%) • Modeling (4%) • Translation (4%) • Example options (4%) • Continuatives (2.7%)	• Questions (33%) • Elaboration moves (12.7%) • Recasts (11%) • Continuatives (11%) • Translation (8.8%) • Incomplete declarative ending with rising intonation (8.3%) • Example options (7%) • Repetition (4.4%) • Metalinguistic requests (1.8%) • Forced choice questions (0.4%) • Modeling (0.4%)

cognitive and linguistic resource, it can function as a stepping stone to scaffold more accomplished performance in the L2. Clearly, Kelly has an intuitive sense of this claim. Contrary to Monica, only when learners had produced their thoughts on the topic did Kelly direct their attention to L2 accuracy. As we will argue below, these two mediation profiles have different implications for learners' L2 development and for the goals of the CNBP reform.

DISCUSSION

It is somewhat surprising that there is little correspondence between Monica's mediation and her training by the CNBP. Although the CNBP course explicitly trained EFL teachers to engage learners in meaning-making participation and to address language forms implicitly once meaning was established (MEN, 2009), Monica's mediation concentrated on form over meaning and on eliciting accurate language before meaningful learner contributions to discussions. Ironically, Kelly's mediation aligns more closely than Monica's with the professional development goals of the CNBP. Kelly's continued use of questions that advance topic development orients learners' attention to meaning and sustains participation. Her correction of learners' mistakes is, for the most part, implicit. She attends to the meaning of learners' utterances continually, recognizing learners as valid interaction participants despite their frequent use of L1. This type of interactional activity not only matches the CNBP goals, but seems to provide learners with frequent affordances to engage in meaning-making, a necessary condition for L2 development (van Lier, 2004) advocated by the CNBP.

Although the data are insufficient to arrive at conclusive explanations, we suggest two reasons for this low correspondence between Monica's mediation and the CNBP training goals. One may be found in Monica's belief that learners need to practice and master language models before they are able to engage in authentic communication, and that real communication consists of complete and accurate sentences. This belief, common among EFL teachers in Colombia (Herazo, Jerez, & Lorduy, 2009), matches her focus on accuracy rather than meaningful L2 participation by learners. Interestingly, she stated that reflecting on her own discourse during the SRP had helped her realize she focused more on accuracy than on meaningful communication.

Another explanation might lie in the textbook that Monica uses and in her attitudes towards it. Although the CNBP favors a meaning-focused orientation to interaction (MEN, 2006), Monica's textbook follows a grammar-based syllabus with little emphasis on oral interpersonal com-

 # textbooks — remember mine had little oral comm. practice — what it school districts expect it?

munication. The textbook unit Monica taught during this study includes only two speaking activities whose goals were to practice grammatical forms. Because this textbook is the one mandated by the local bilingualism program, Monica's attitude towards it was one of compliance. As Monica stated during the SRP, "I had to use it [the textbook] because it was the one chosen for the pilot schools." By way of contrast, Kelly often prepared handouts for her class using textbook material that she selected. During the SRP, Kelly spoke of adapting the textbook to suit her teaching goals and her students' needs. Additionally, her textbook provided frequent activities for oral interpersonal communication throughout the chapters, which clearly matched Kelly's expressed goal to promote students' meaningful use of English.

The previous situation suggests a clear contradiction between the CNBP professional development goals and what actually occurs in an EFL classroom such as Monica's. In this particular case, the conditions created by the local bilingualism project appear to shape Monica's discursive decision-making, jeopardizing the effectiveness of the CNBP training for reaching the national reform goals of communicatively competent interpersonal communication. This interpretation confirms Fullan's (1999) warning that the "deeper reason that transferability is so complex is that successful reforms in one place are partly a function of good ideas, and largely a function of the *conditions* under which the ideas flourished" (p. 64, emphasis added). In other words, local constraints and affordances seem to be influential in determining the course and outcome of the CNBP rather than the contents of its professional development programs. Although this research supports this assertion in the specific case of one teacher, albeit with a small data set, more research is needed to explore this situation across different contexts of instruction and different beliefs that teachers hold about the process of language learning.

From a theoretical perspective, the two different patterns of mediation we found confirm the position that mediation is not a unitary, undifferentiated activity (Kozulin, 2003). Rather, teachers use a variety of tools for different pedagogical intentions in the moment-to-moment construction of meaning. Even though both teachers preferred certain types of discourse tools for certain purposes, they also used the same mediational tools for different purposes, or at different times in the interaction. This suggests that during professional development programs, teachers need to learn to analyze mediational tools from various perspectives. By analyzing their own discourse moves, teachers might become conscious of how and for what purposes they mediate, and in so doing develop agency in their practice.

CONCLUSIONS AND RECOMMENDATIONS

The study presented here provides strong evidence for the need to monitor closely at the classroom level the efforts of comprehensive educational reform. This imperative is especially important when dealing with reforms that are intended to influence the moment-to-moment practice of EFL teachers when supporting the development of interpersonal communication in the EFL classroom. Unlike curricular reform dealing mainly with content to be taught, the CNBP requires a change of teachers' beliefs and verbal behavior, and the skill to respond in unrehearsed and unplanned ways to the interactional dynamics of conversation as they unfold in real time. This study has shown that expanding the concept of the function of mediation is a viable way to assess how teachers orient themselves within classroom interaction.

This study has also shown that the concept of mediation, when used as the lens to analyze teacher support for students' oral participation and to assess the goals of instructional reform, needs further refinement and explanation to be a useful tool for teachers to improve their practice. Re-conceptualizing mediation as being composed of three complementary and interdependent dimensions (time, focus, and tools) seems to be a clear and accessible way to improve how conversational management is explained to teachers during professional development. However, more research is still needed to explore in detail the nature of such interdependence, in particular concerning the contingent dimension of mediation, described in this chapter as proactive, reactive, and ongoing. This research has also found that the study of mediation needs to be anchored in teacher beliefs about the nature of their interactions with learners and motivated by the desire to understand how contextual factors influence a teacher's mediation. As this study has shown, the sociocultural context, including teacher beliefs, may promote or obstruct the realization of the goals of national reform efforts (Fullan, 1999).

Finally, our research has direct implications for national reform efforts in Colombia that may be applicable elsewhere. Professional development sessions need to raise teachers' awareness of local conditions and previously held beliefs that may impede or contradict the recommendations of reform movements. As Smagorinsky, Cook, and Johnson (2003) have suggested, teachers can reenvision their teaching by analyzing and discussing a central and unifying concept that will challenge teachers' beliefs and instructional practices. We maintain that mediation is one such concept that can serve as a centerpiece for reforming classroom interpersonal communication, a way to identify and analyze classroom verbal interactions, and a tool for assisting teachers to overcome local constraints that are often subtle and imperceptible.

ACKNOWLEDGMENTS

This research was supported by a student field-research grant from the Center for Latin American Studies and the University Center for International Studies at the University of Pittsburgh, and a summer research grant from the Fulbright Commission. We express our gratitude and appreciation to the two teachers who agreed to be part of this study and to Professor Ellice Forman for her comments on earlier drafts of this chapter.

NOTES

1. This test is used by the CNBP to measure teacher English proficiency. The test rates proficiency along six levels, from elementary to advanced proficiency, using the Common European Framework of Reference scales (A1 to C2).
2. Throughout the chapter, we will use systemic functional linguistics (SFL) to describe the lexicogrammatical realization of the two teachers' discourse moves. SFL provides useful categories for describing how teachers achieve functional goals through specific lexicogrammatical choices.
3. Transcription conventions were adapted from van Lier (1988). $^{\llcorner}$ indicates concurrent talk, a slash (/) indicates raising intonation, question marks (?) indicates a question structure, ellipsis (…) indicate one-second pause, a hyphen (-) indicates an abrupt cut-off, colons (:::) indicate lengthening of preceding sound, italics correspond to talk in L1, mispronounced words appear in square brackets, comments or translation appear in double parentheses, unintelligible talk is marked as XXX, and unclear or probable items appear in single parentheses.
4. As mentioned in the methods section, SRPs were conducted in Spanish, the two teachers' L1. Teachers' comments were translated into English for this chapter.
5. Using only the clause residue (language that follows the subject and finite verbal element) is common with novice language learners of English. Here the structure for stating the proposition is incomplete since it lacks the subject and the finite element (tense marking on the verb *to be*). Kelly does not focus on this formal property of the utterance, however. That is, she does not mediate for the provision of a subject and finite element but rather seeks confirmation of S1's meaning located in the clause residue.

REFERENCES

Aljaafreh, A., & Lantolf, J. P. (1994). Negative feedback as regulation and second language learning in the zone of proximal development. *Modern Language Journal, 78*(4), 465-483.

Anton, M. (1999). The discourse of a learner-centered classroom: Sociocultural perspectives on teacher-learner interaction in the second-language classroom. *The Modern Language Journal, 83*(3), 303-318.

Appel, G., & Lantolf, J. P. (1994). Speaking as mediation: A study of L1 and L2 text recall tasks. *The Modern Language Journal, 78*(4), 437-452.

Bauer, M., & Aarts, B. (2000). Corpus construction: A principle for qualitative data collection. In M. Bauer & G. Gaskell (Eds.), *Qualitative researching with text, image and sound* (pp. 19-37). Thousand Oaks, CA: SAGE.

Cazden, C. B. (2001). *Classroom discourse: The language of teaching and learning* (2nd ed.). Portsmouth, NH: Heinemann.

Cummins, J. (2007). Rethinking monolingual instructional strategies in multilingual classrooms. *The Canadian Journal of Applied Linguistics, 10*(2), 221-240.

Daniels, H. (2008). *Vygotsky and research*. New York, NY: Routledge.

Donato, R. (1994). Collective scaffolding in second language learning. In J. P. Lantolf & G. Appel (Eds.), *Vygotskian approaches to second language research* (pp. 33-56). Norwood, NJ: Abblex.

Donato, R. (2000). Sociocultural contributions to understanding the foreing and second language classroom. In J. Lantolf (Ed.), *Sociocultural theory and second language learning* (pp. 27-50). New York, NY: Oxford University Press.

Duff, P. (2008). *Case study research in applied linguistics*. New York, NY: Lawrence Erlbaum Associates.

Fullan, M. (1999). *Change forces: The sequel*. London: Falmer.

Gass, S. M., & Mackey, A. (2000). *Stimulated recall methodology in second language research*. Mahwah, NJ: Lawrence Erlbaum Associates.

Gibbons, P. (2003). Mediating language learning: Teacher interactions with ESL students in a content-based classroom. *TESOL Quarterly, 37*(2), 247-273.

Guk, I., & Kellog, D. (2007). The ZPD and whole class teaching: Teacher-led and student-led interactional mediation of tasks. *Language Teaching Research, 11*(3), 281-299. doi: 10.1177/1362168807077561

Hall, J. K., & Verplaetse, L. S. (2000). *Second and foreign language learning through classroom interaction*. Mahwah, NJ: Lawrence Erlbaum Associates.

Halliday, M. A. K., & Matthiessen, C. M. I. M. (2004). *An introduction to functional grammar* (3rd ed.). London: Hodder Education.

Herazo, J. D., Jerez, S., & Lorduy, D. (2009). Learning through communication in the EFL class: Going beyond the PPP approach. *Ikala, 14*(23), 117 - 136.

Kozulin, A. (2003). Psychological tools and mediated learning. In A. Kozulin, B. Gindis, B. Ageyev & S. Miller (Eds.), *Vygotsky's educational theory in cultural context* (pp. 15-38). New York, NY: Cambridge University Press.

Lantolf, J. P. (2000). *Sociocultural theory and second language learning*. New York, NY: Oxford University Press.

Lantolf, J. P., & Thorne, S. (2006). *Sociocultural theory and the genesis of second language development*. Oxford, England: Oxford University Press.

MacIntyre, P. D., Dörnyei, Z., Clément, R., & Noels, K. A. (1998). Conceptualizing willingness to communicate in a L2: A situational model of L2 confidence and affiliation. *The Modern Language Journal, 82*(4), 545-562.

McCormick, D. E., & Donato, R. (2000). Teacher questions as scaffolded assistance in an ESL classroom. In J. K. Hall & L. S. Verplaetse (Eds.), *Second and foreign laguage learning through classroom interaction* (pp. 183-202). London: Lawrence Erlbaum Associates.

MEN. (2005). Bases para una nación bilingüe y competitiva [Basis for a bilingual and competitive nation]. *Altablero, 37.* Retrieved from http://www.mineducacion.gov.co/1621/propertyvalue-32266.html

MEN. (2006). *Estándares básicos de competencias en lenguas extranjeras: Inglés* [Basic foreign language competive standards: English]. Bogota, Colombia: Ministerio de Educación Nacional.

MEN. (2009). *Teacher development program: B1 course guide*. Bogota, Colombia: Ministerio de Educacion Nacional.

Mohan, B., & Beckett, G. (2003). A functional approach to research on content-based language learning: Recasts in causal explanations. *Modern Language Journal, 87*(3), 421-432.

Nunan, D. (2005). *Go for it 3B*. Boston, MA: Thompson Heinle.

Ohta, A. (2000a). Rethinking interaction in SLA: Developmentally appropriate assistance in the zone of proximal development and the acquisition of L2 grammar. In J. P. Lantolf (Ed.), *Sociocultural theory and second language learning* (pp. 51-78). New York, NY: Oxford University Press.

Ohta, A. (2000b). Rethinking recasts: A learner-centered examination of corrective feedback in the Japanese language classroom. In J. K. Hall & L. S. Verplaetse (Eds.), *Second and foreign language learning through classroom interaction* (pp. 47-71). London: Lawrence Erlbaum Associates.

Oxford, & Cambridge ESOL. (2002). Quick Placement Test, QPT [Computer software]. Oxford, England: Cambridge University Press.

Poehner, M. E., & Lantolf, J. P. (2010). Vygotsky's teaching-assessment dialectic and L2 education: The case for dynamic assessment. *Mind, Culture, and Activity, 17*(4), 312-330.

QSR International. Nvivo [Computer software] (Version 8).

Richards, K. (2003). *Qualitative inquiry in TESOL*. New York, NY: Palgrave Macmillan.

Smagorinsky, P., Cook, L., & Johnson, T. (2003). The twisting path of concept development in learning to teach. *Teachers College Record 105*(8), 1399-1436.

Strauss, A. L. (1987). *Qualitative analysis for social scientists*. New York, NY: Cambridge University Press.

Toth, P. D. (2008). Teacher- and learner-led discourse in task-based grammar instruction: Providing procedural assistance for L2 morphosyntactic development. [Article]. *Language Learning, 58*(2), 237-283. doi: 10.1111/j.1467-9922.2008.00441.x

Toth, P. D. (2011). Social and cognitive factors in making teacher-led classroom discourse relevant for second language development. *The Modern Language Journal, 95*(1), 1-25. doi: 10.1111/j.1540-4781.2010.01144.x

van Lier, L. (1988). *The classroom and the language learner: Ethnography and second-language classroom research*. New York, NY: Longman.

van Lier, L. (1996). *Interaction in the language curriculum: Awareness, autonomy, and authenticity*. London: Longman.

van Lier, L. (2004). *The ecology and semiotics of language learning: A sociocultural perspective*. Norwell, MA: Kluwer Academic Press.

Vygotsky, L. (1978). *Mind in Society: The development of higher psychological processes*. Cambridge, MA: Harvard University Press.

Vygotsky, L. (1986). *Thought and language*. Cambridge, MA: The MIT Press.

Wertsch, J. V. (2007). Mediation. In H. Daniels, M. Cole & J. Wertsch (Eds.), *The cambridge companion to Vygotsky* (pp. 178-192). New York, NY: Cambridge University Press.

Wetz, B. (2007). *American adventures starter: Student book*. London: Oxford University Press.

CHAPTER 3

MEDIATING LEARNING AND NEGOTIATING CURRICULAR IDEOLOGIES IN A FOURTH GRADE BILINGUAL CLASSROOM

Lara J. Handsfield

In this chapter, I illustrate how a fourth grade bilingual teacher engaged and blended multiple and sometimes competing curricular approaches and discourse patterns during a science unit on plant life to support her students' English language and academic content development. Illustrative examples are drawn from a 2-year qualitative study exploring multilingualism, multiliteracies, and K-8 teacher development. Using critical sociocultural theory and microethnographic discourse analysis, I highlight how the teacher mediated students' language and learning through meaningful contextualization and careful linguistic scaffolding while she simultaneously tactically negotiated multiple ideologies of teaching and learning. She accomplished this by moving between different teacher roles within and across learning events. Findings provide helpful lessons for other teachers who find themselves pulled in multiple directions with respect to curricular expectations in linguistically and culturally diverse classrooms.

In the hall one day at lunchtime, Isabel (all names are pseudonyms), a fourth grade bilingual teacher, invited me into her classroom to observe

Teachers' Roles in Second Language Learning:
Classroom Applications of Sociocultural Theory, pp. 41–61
Copyright © 2012 by Information Age Publishing
All rights of reproduction in any form reserved.

during science. I asked her what she would be doing, and she replied that her students would be doing "a true/false test." This surprised me. At the time, Isabel was a participant in a research study I was conducting. I had spent many hours observing in her classroom during literacy time, and saw her students writing graphic novels, discussing literature, and blogging on classroom computers. These practices seemed unaligned with true/false tests, which I associated with ideologies such as standardization, teacher as primary authority and gate-keeper of knowledge, individualized achievement, and knowledge as either "known or not known," rather than socially-constructed. Indeed, scholars have made clear how narrow, decontextualized, and individualized assessment measures may disadvantage emergent bilingual students (Brisk & Harrington, 2000; García, 2005). However, I later learned that the true/false test was embedded within a larger instructional sequence that complicated ideological categorization, and was implemented in ways that aligned more closely with sociocultural theories of teaching and learning.

In this chapter I illustrate how Isabel took on multiple roles to engage and blend multiple curricular approaches and discourse patterns in a science unit on plant life (including the true/false test) to support her students' English language and academic content development. In the process, she not only mediated students' language and learning through meaningful contextualization and careful linguistic scaffolding, but also negotiated multiple ideologies of teaching and learning. Understanding how different ideologies of teaching and learning are negotiated in practice is important because of the multiple and often conflicting expectations teachers face in their work. While teachers of emerging bilingual students are expected to build on students' diverse funds of knowledge (González, Moll, & Amanti, 2005), they are also held accountable to standardized and high stakes assessments and curricula that construct difference as deficit. Working from tenets of critical sociocultural theory (Lewis, Enciso, & Moje, 2007), I show how Isabel engages in linguistic and curricular scaffolding *along side* her tactical negotiation (de Certeau, 1984) of competing curricular expectations and their concomitant ideologies.

RELEVANT LITERATURE REVIEW

For decades, research has suggested that nontraditional classroom interaction patterns support learning opportunities for emergent bilinguals and students from marginalized communities (e.g., Au & Jordan, 1981; Cazden, 2001; Enright, 1986; Heath, 1983; Thomas & Collier, 1997). Teachers can successfully adapt their instruction to support English learners' content learning by emphasizing meaning and communication in learning activities, combining large and small group with individualized learning opportunities, and shifting their discourse. Discursive scaffolding may entail using sensory aides, and contextualizing and recontextualizing student utterances (Cazden, 2001). Furthermore, while the traditional Initiation-Response-Evaluation (IRE) discourse pattern (where teachers ask known-answer questions, students respond, and teachers evaluate the response) may hinder opportunities for language development when used excessively, when combined with collaborative and responsive discourses and activities, it may scaffold language production and learning (Cazden, 2001; McIntyre, Kyle, & Moore, 2006).

The discourse patterns used and legitimized in classroom contexts may also impact content area learning, particularly when specific academic registers, or ways of speaking specific to different fields, are called for. As English learners engage in science learning, they will not only be expected to learn content-specific English vocabulary, but also to acquire scientific registers, on top of basic communication skills (Genesee, Lindholm-Leary, Saunders, & Christian, 2006; Saville-Troike, 1994). A challenge for teachers, then, is to engage in curricular approaches and classroom engagements that scaffold both in content area instruction.

Such curricular engagements, however, are not value-free. Different classroom discourse patterns index different ideologies of learning and teaching (Bloome, Power-Carter, Morton Christian, Otto, & Shuart-Farris, 2005). IRE, for example, suggests an ideology of teacher-as-authority, knowledge as provided and evaluated by the teacher, and the student as a more passive knower-in-training. Responsive-Collaborative Discourses (Gutiérrez, Rymes, & Larson, 1995), on the other hand, situate the teacher as a mediator of knowledge and students as participants in learning communities. Some research has examined how teachers negotiate multiple curricular ideologies in their instruction to support the learning of historically marginalized students (Dixson & Bloome, 2007; Handsfield, Crumpler, & Dean, 2010). However, in a political context characterized by increased standardization of curricula and student-teacher interactions, teachers may be dissuaded from engaging in collaborative and responsive discourse. Furthermore, when teachers do attempt these discourse patterns, their students may resist or have difficulty participating, having been socialized into more traditional teacher-centered discourse patterns (Maloch, 2004). Thus, the discourse patterns teachers and students use reflect both learning opportunities and the ideological commitments and institutional structures of authority that govern curricular engagements.

While researchers have examined teachers' blending of discourse styles in terms of scaffolding student learning, and how teachers negotiate complex ideological and curricular tensions in their work, few have examined teachers' discursive scaffolding as it occurs within and along side such ideological negotiations. This may be because most research on classroom discourse has been informed by sociolinguistics and traditional iterations of sociocultural theory, which have been criticized for not adequately addressing issues of power and ideology (Collins & Blot, 2003). This criticism is particularly important with respect to teaching historically marginalized students, such as emergent bilinguals. In response to such criticism, I ground my work in critical sociocultural theory (Lewis, Enciso, & Moje, 2007).

THEORETICAL GROUNDING

Critical sociocultural theory was developed by language and literacy researchers to extend traditional sociocultural theory to account for how learning and teaching both influence and are influenced by power relations (Lewis, Enciso, & Moje, 2007). It embraces Vygotsky's (1978) concepts of semiotic mediation and appropriation, recognizing that as learners engage in socially mediated activity alongside more knowledgeable others, they appropriate new knowledge and ways of speaking relevant to the field in which they are being apprenticed. However, critical sociocultural theory also views teaching and learning as historically situated (Barton, 1994) and grounded in complex networks of power (Lewis, Enciso, & Moje, 2007). That is, teaching and learning are not only social, but also ideological: the semiotic mediation through which learners appropriate knowledge and language also involves the simultaneous appropriation of ideologies of language and language learning. Teachers and students are viewed as both consumers and agents of curriculum with the power to appropriate curricular texts and discourse in creative ways. While instructional practices, including patterns of classroom discourse and curricular design, are largely shaped by and within dominant power structures, teachers and students may also play with, tactically negotiate, and even shift dominant power structures and social roles in small ways (Collins & Blot, 2003; de Certeau, 1984).

Applied to teaching emergent bilinguals, a critical sociocultural approach embraces social interaction and scaffolding, including moderating language, opportunities for student-student interaction, relating content instruction to students' funds of knowledge (González, Moll, & Amanti, 2005), and engaging collaborative and experiential learning (Dixon-Krauss, 1995). Such an approach supports students in negotiating multiple expectations for social and academic language use and the power relationships that they imply. Isabel'sperformance of multiple roles through her use of different discourse patterns may seem ideologically inconsistent. However, these tactical negotiations help her scaffold academic English and content for her students as well as their successful participation in both nontraditional and traditional classroom practices.

RESEARCH CONTEXT AND METHODS

The data I present are drawn from a research study exploring multilingualism, multiliteracies, and K-8 teacher development.[1] The study included two teacher study groups: one on literacy for linguistically diverse learners (fall 2006) and one on multimodal literacy instruction (fall 2007). The following spring, a subset of teachers set pedagogical goals based on the study groups, and were observed during instruction (spring 2008).

Participants and Setting

Isabel, a White, middle class third year bilingual teacher who was a native English speaker and also fluent in Spanish, participated in all three phases of the study. I observed her science instruction to understand how she incorporated literacy in that content area; however, for this analysis I focus on Isabel's language use and curricular negotiations.

Isabel taught at Southend Elementary, which housed a transitional bilingual education program, designed to move children as quickly as possible from Spanish- to English-medium instruction. The bilingual program only went through grade four, and in fifth grade students were placed in all English classrooms and provided with pull-out ESL support for 30 minutes a day. Isabel's instructional context was unique in that her bilingual fourth grade class consisted entirely of eight boys. The gender distribution occurred by chance, and the low numbers resulted from a large number of the previous year's third graders being reclassified into English only classrooms. Isabel's eight students were all native Spanish speakers from Mexico and Central America at varying stages of oral English proficiency. The vast bulk of Isabel's instruction was in English, although she often conversed in Spanish with individual students as needed.

Data Sources and Analysis

The science unit I describe focused on plant life and occurred in early May 2008. I videotaped students' engagement in activity-based learning, during which time they measured and monitored their own plants and noted their observations in science notebooks. This activity was preceded by the true/false test, which was student-led and done orally. (The larger unit, the activity-based learning event, and the true/false event are described in further detail in the findings section.). Descriptions are also informed by formal and informal interviews with Isabel.

Consistent with critical sociocultural theory, analyses identified both dominant instructional approaches and ideologies, and how Isabel negotiated competing expectations for language learning and teaching. This was achieved using Constant Comparative Analysis (CCA) (Glaser & Strauss, 1967) and microethnographic discourse analysis (Bloome et al., 2005). Interviews and observation data were first analyzed using CCA to identify general patterns and themes. These included codes such as "IRE," "experience-based learning," "responsive-collaborative discourse," and "academic language." I then identified broader categories of themes related to ideologies of teaching and learning (e.g., teacher as authority, standardization, knowledge as co-constructed) into which the initial codes were grouped. I analyzed the true/false event in a more focused manner, using microethnograpic discourse analysis, which attends to language in use, examining how utterances and body language enact different ideologies and position participants in relation to those ideologies. As such, it responds to critical sociocultural theory's concern with how people negotiate authority structures in everyday practice.

Transcript conventions are included in the appendix. I used speaker turns, semantic features of their speech, and other cues (such as movement and intonation) to separate utterances into "message units," which Green and Wallat (1981) characterize as the smallest units of meaning in conversation (potentially smaller than sentences, or even clauses). I then divided the transcript into larger interaction units, or "conversationally tied message units," (p. 200) using contextualization cues and shifts in the interaction, such as a change in discourse structures (e.g., IRE to more collaborative conversation) or changes in topic. Breaks in interaction units often correspond to shifts in ideologies honored in the event.

Instead of standard punctuation, I used conventions that reflect specific intonation, pitch, and other elements of speech. For example, some questions are not spoken with a rising pitch at the end (e.g., "Why is your plant drooping?"). A question mark represents a grammatical form rather than how an utterance is actually spoken. Thus, a question (or other utterance) with a rising tone at the end would be represented with an upward arrow: "Can you tell me why your plant is drooping↑" In addition, I underlined words spoken with extra emphasis, and capitalized words or phrases that were loud or shouted. While these conventions may be cumbersome to some readers, they allow for more nuanced analyses. Relevant notes that are not reflected in transcript conventions, such as participants' gaze and body movements, are described in the far right-hand column of the transcript, and are aligned with specific utterances.

FINDINGS: MEDIATING LANGUAGE, LEARNING, AND CURRICULAR IDEOLOGIES

I begin this section by describing Isabel's general instructional approach as related to her professional context, followed by the hands-on activity in her plant life unit that immediately followed the true/false activity. My goal in these two first subsections is to provide the reader with a context in which to consider the true/false activity. I then describe the true/false activity, offering key examples to illustrate how Isabel's scaffolding was intertwined with her performance of different roles and her tactical negotiation of competing curricular ideologies.

Isabel's Instructional Approach

Isabel's instructional approach leaned toward active learning with ample opportunities for social interaction and collaboration. She emphasized student responsibility for both longer-term projects (e.g., completing reports on time) and daily tasks (e.g., setting up the classroom LCD projector). Isabel valued learning processes in addition to final products, and situated knowledge as unstable, rather than as given, or to be passively received by students. For example, when introducing a writing unit on graphic novels, she challenged students' preconceived notions about characters or settings implied by certain colors:

> A student asserts that pink and purple are not scary. Isabel says, "what if there's a big monster with fangs and he's pink and blue?" One student says it would be scary, but others aren't so sure. Isabel adds, "Or a girl with a lollypop jumping rope, but she's red and black?" A student says, "scary!" Many students seem to not be sure; they appear to be pondering this. A student then says, "if the letters are dripping, then that's scary," as if they're dripping blood. There's then a student conversation about black and white and how that's scary. Isabel says, "so if I put on a black sweater, I would be scary?" The debate, however, is left unresolved. (Observation fieldnotes, 2/08)

In this example, meanings are made unstable through questioning, conversation, and debate. While Isabel's questioning could be loosely categorized as a traditional IRE, the broader context of debate and expectations of students as knowers and knowledge as socially constructed changes how her questions are taken up: students' responses are authentic and worthy of debate.

Isabel also often grounded instructional examples in students' cultural knowledge or experiences, such as the legend of La Llorona and students' popular culture interests. For example, she based the graphic novels unit on her students' interests in comics, Nick Jr., and art, and she encouraged her students as they wrote fan-fiction based on Rebelde, a Spanish-language soap opera. Isabel also built on their native language knowledge by teaching cognate strategy for word identification (Jiménez, García, & Pearson, 1996) and by encouraging their Spanish use as they engaged with texts and academic content.

Isabel used a "Kidwatching" approach across her curriculum (Owocki & Goodman, 2002), generating opportunities for students to work without her direct intervention or participation, and observing their practices and interactions to inform her teaching. Isabel stated that she sometimes pretended to be writing something of her own, but would actually write down her students' conversations to try to understand their thinking. She would also use photo and video to document her students at work, and then share those images with her students:

> Today … I showed them a PowerPoint … "Oh, look at all of the great things that you guys are doing." I like how their heads are together, I like how even though only one person is writing, everybody looks like they're contributing. (Study group conversation, 11/06)

At the same time, it was not uncommon to see Isabel leading more traditional activities (e.g., spelling tests or students completing individual math problems at their desks)—practices that suggest a view of teacher as knower, and knowledge as stable and demonstrated to the teacher by students to assess individual competence. Such practices more closely mirrored the more teacher-fronted approaches of most of her colleagues. She explained, "when they go to 5th grade that is what they are going to do, so I let them get used to that" (Interview, 9/07). Pressure to conform to standardized approaches also came from Southend's status with regard to Adequate Yearly Progress (AYP), as required by the No Child Left Behind Act (2002). In 2006 Southend did not make AYP due to low test scores among its English learners. Isabel was critical of high stakes tests, and frustrated that she sometimes had to put beneficial learning activities (such as science journals) on hold because they had to "bubble in a thousand things" (Interview, 1/08).

Tensions are evident between two broad sets of ideologies of learning and teaching that Isabel negotiated: (1) Knowledge as collaboratively constructed in social contexts, building on students' cultural and linguistic competencies, knowledge as unstable (up for debate), and teacher as mediator and facilitator of knowledge; and (2) knowledge as universal, autonomous (separated from social contexts), and stable, teacher as knower, and individual achievement. Similar negotiations were evident in her science instruction, including her unit on plant life.

Plant Life Unit and Activity-Based Learning

Plant life was not part of the science curriculum for fourth grade. However, Isabel had engaged her previous years' students in this unit, which she felt benefitted them in terms of learning science content. She stated that many of her students' families had gardens or experiences working with plants. She strived to connect learning with her students' home lives, and so she continued to do this unit on top of the expected science curriculum. In fact, on the same day I observed during the plant life unit, she also led a lesson on solids, liquids, and gasses that involved reading their science text and dramatic simulations of solid, liquid, and gas molecules.

During the plant life unit, students planted vegetables, which they kept in a movable "greenhouse"—a multishelf cart with a plastic cover that could be kept in the classroom or wheeled directly outdoors from Isabel's classroom into a small paved area. Isabel and her students researched homemade plant foods online and experimented with different plant food combinations, including dog food, soda, and coffee. Each student kept two plants: one that received only water, and one that received an alternate food. They recorded plant growth and other observations in journals twice a week for two months and also took a fieldtrip to a local nursery.

During the unit, Isabel used alternative assessments that reflected ideologies of learning as socially constructed and grounded in students' cultural and linguistic knowledge:

> I let them meet in a group and do some sort of artistic form of showing me how they understand photosynthesis either through making a model or- They all wanted to do a rap because they think they are Daddy Yankee [a Puerto Rican Regetón artist] (laughter). I mean they even have the little movements down and everything, and this kid wrote this two-page rap in Spanish that rhymes, that's very detailed; every single detail, even stuff I had mentioned once and did not expect them to know, he put in there.... Yeah, if I was just a regular teacher and didn't understand what he had written I would think he had no clue what I was talking about and that he never paid attention. (Interview, 9/06)

Immediately following the true/false activity (which I discuss in the next section), students spent about 20 minutes checking their plants' moisture, providing their plants with water or experimental foods, measuring the plants' height, and closely observing them for signs of health or distress (e.g., browning leaves, wilting, vigorous growth, "tiny hairs" on the leaves). In the process, they moved about the classroom and outdoor space. Teacher and student interactions during this time included a combination of discourse patterns (e.g., teacher-led IRE exchanges and directives), but consisted mostly of authentic teacher-student ("so what you're saying is..." "that's interesting. I wonder why...") and student-student ("dude, that's too much water") interactions. These exchanges engaged key content vocabulary, and Isabel and her students made a vocabulary chart that they used as a resource in their science journals.

Isabel's role in this activity was less authority-driven and more responsive and facilitative, reflecting ideologies of learning as contextualized and socially constructed. While such ideologies may contrast with true/false tests as an assessment practice, on close analysis, the true/false activity illustrates Isabel's tactical negotiation of multiple ideologies.

True/False Activity: Negotiating Roles, Ideologies, and Learning

Isabel let her students choose how they demonstrated their knowledge of plants, and Avery and Tomás partnered up to create a true/false test. The test was conducted orally, almost entirely in English, with students sitting in their desks and Avery and Tomás at the front of the class. Isabel took up multiple and at times contradictory roles: Teacher as authority, teacher as critic (of both traditional authority structures, and students' knowledge displays), teacher as facilitator, and teacher as participant. While each of these roles carries different ideological commitments, Isabel performed them in complex, even simultaneous, ways. This makes presenting her performance of these roles difficult. To mitigate this, I present four key moments during the event, highlighting how, within each moment, she took up these roles.

Moment 1: Establishing Rules of Participation

At the beginning of the event, Tomás frames the activity by stating, "We're gonna play a game. It's true and false." However, other boys question the expectations for the activity by asking "is this a game?" and "can we stand up?":

Line	Speaker → Hearer	Utterances	Add. Contextualization
015	Tomás→ Class	Okay, let's play it	Announcing to the
016		Tru:e | a:nd | false | |	class, moves to front of
017		C'mon, Avery	classroom to sit down
018	David → Isabel	Is this a game↑	
019	Isabel → Class	They're testing your knowledge	Avery walks around the
020		True or false	desks up to the front to
021	S → Isabel	False	join Tomás
022	Jesús → Isabel	Can we stand up↓	Pointing empty soda
023	Alej. → Isabel	Can we stand u:p↑	bottle toward Isabel
024	Isabel ?Jesús		bottle toward Isabel
025	Tomás → Avery	Okay, I read number one Avery	Waits for Avery to look
026		Avery|	at him.
027		I read number one	Pronounces "cells" as
028	Tomás → Class	Most plants are made of millionsofcells	"sails"
029	S → Tomás	Cells?	
030	Tomás → S	Yeah	
031	Ss	TRUE	
032	Tomás → Ss	*Correct*	

Teacher as authority. With her negation of Jesús's and Alejandro's request to stand, and her response to the question regarding whether the activity was a game ("they're testing your knowledge"), Isabel positions herself as an authority, setting the stage for traditional interaction structures, such as IRE. Isabel also expected her students to assume authoritative teacher (and tester) roles. Tomás's exaggerated evaluation of his peers (line 32) emphasizes this and the expectation of tester as dominant authority and knowledge as stable—either right or wrong.

Teacher as critic. Importantly, Isabel also leaves authority structures open to critique. Her expectation that students take on teacher-like roles can be viewed as a challenge to traditional teacher authority. Moreover, she does not explicitly deny that the activity is a game with presumably less hierarchical interactions (lines 18-20). Thus, while she uses her authority to reinforce ideologies aligned with standardized assessment approaches (e.g., individual achievement, testing), a degree of ideological ambiguity is established, tacitly inviting the contestation of traditional structures of learning and teaching.

Moment 2: Content Integrity

Teacher as authority. Three minutes later, we again see Isabel taking up an authoritative role, intervening to reassert herself as initiator and evaluator of responses (lines 46-47) (side conversations have been replaced with ellipses: ...):

Line	Speaker → Hearer	Utterances	Add. Contextualization
042	Avery → Class	Leaves stems and roots are plants	
043	David	TRUE	
044	José and other S	TRUE	
045	Avery → Class	All leaves look [the sa-	
046		[Well |wait a	
047	Isabel → Ss	second	
		Is that true ↑	
		...	
057	Isabel → Avery	Can you read that question again ↑	Lots of overlapping
		...	speech
070	Avery → Isabel	Leaves, stems, and roots are	Isabel leans forward to
		plants	hear
071	S	True	
072	David	False	
073	Alejandro	FALSE	
074	Isabel	Fa::lse	
075	Tomás → Class	Cah-RECT	

076	Isabel → Class	Fa:lse	
077	Avery → ?	Why is it false	
078	Alej. → Avery	Because they're not a:ll plants	
079	Avery → ?	XXX	
080	Alejandro → ?	Like XXX	
081	Isabel → Alej.	Can you say that a little louder Alejandro↑	
082	Alej. → Avery	Leaves are a part of the plant	
083	Isabel → Avery	A pa:rt of the plant	
084		A root is *part of* a plant	
085		It isn't a plant	Pronounces "a" with long vowel
086	Tomás	<u>Allleaveslook</u> the <u>same</u>	
087	Ss	False	Isabel nods affirmatively

She continues in this role through line 87, nodding in response to students' answers.

Teacher as critic. Isabel often asserted her authority when she felt students' understanding of core concepts was faltering. Even as she reinstates an authoritative IRE discourse, her questioning simultaneously serves to critique the authority of the test (and testers, in this case Avery and Tomás). In short, Isabel uses a teacher-as-authority discourse (IRE) to subvert a different authority structure (tests and testers). This tactical use of one authority structure to discredit another opens the door for Avery's question, "why is it false?" (line 77), prompting Isabel to assume a facilitator role.

Teacher as facilitator. After Alejandro responds, Isabel facilitates the discussion by asking Avery to repeat his answer (line 81), and then builds on his response by distinguishing a *part* of a plant from *a* plant (lines 83-85). We see a more refined view of knowledge than typical true/false tests allow, in which high expectations are supported through social interaction and scaffolding. The invitation to question authority structures is taken up by students in moment 3.

Moment 3: "Let's Talk About That"

About half way into the event, Tomás reads a test item: "Cactus do not have leaves." As the true/false test continues, the discourse is characterized by a back and forth IRE pattern, reinforcing an ideology of knowledge as black/white, or right/wrong, rather than as socially mediated and constructed. This is punctuated by Tomás's evaluation of a peer's answer, in which he says "Nope!" and makes a loud buzzer sound. He explains, "It's false because cactuses don't have leaves. They have those <u>spikes.</u>" However, Avery counters Tomás's response much in the same way Isabel questioned their evaluation in moment 2. When students' claims are limited to unsupported assertions or vague rationales (e.g., "They don't <u>have</u> no leaves. Only plants has leaves"; "They're different in a <u>lot</u> of ways"), Isabel once again intervenes:

Line	Speaker → Hearer	Utterances	Add. Contextualization
107	Isabel → Class	I don't <u>know</u>	
108		That's a <u>question</u>	
109		So, wait, let's talk about that	
110		Avery says, I thought the spikes	
111		<u>were</u> leaves	
112		Is that considered a leaf ↑	Looks at José, on her
113	Ss	U::m	left
114	Alex	Mm hmm, mm hmm	Avery walks around the
115	Jesús	Some are	José shrugs
116	Avery → Isabel	THEY'RE ALL DIFFERE:NT	Looking at Isabel,
117	Isabel → Avery	Explain	water in his mouth
118		What do you mean by they're all different	Nodding and looking at Avery
119	Avery → Isabel	Um	because some are <u>brown</u>ish and <u>yellow</u>ish-	
120	Tomás. → Isabel	-Like, different colors ↑	Isabel nods
121	Isabel ?Jesús	Like XXX	
122	Avery → Isabel	And some are- are- are	a different <u>shape</u>↓	

Teacher as facilitator. Because Avery challenged Tomás's answer, Isabel did not need to. She intervenes not to provide an answer or critique, but to scaffold further debate ("I don't know/That's a question/So, wait, let's talk about that"). By stating that she doesn't know (line 107), validating the question (line 108), and inviting talk (line 109), Isabel positions herself as facilitator rather than as authority, or sole evaluator of knowledge. This is different from taking a participant role because she intervenes to prompt student discussion rather than to take part in it.

Teacher as critic. While facilitating student discussion, Isabel resituates the "test" as a mode of assessment that is open to critique. She also takes up a critic role with respect to her students' assertions, demanding sound argumentation regarding academic content. She requires her students to articulate details ("Explain. What do you mean by they're all different", line 118), specific characteristics of leaves (e.g., color and shape), maintaining high expectations for language use.

Moment 4: Personal Narrative

Moment 4 occurred just after moment 3 and is marked by a different kind of discourse: Isabel abruptly redirects the activity into a personal narrative about a plant she has at home:

Line	Speaker → Hearer	Utterances	Add. Contextualization
124	Isabel → Class	Oh, I should bring a-	
125		I have a plant at home called a	
126		Lavender Mona↑	
127	S → Isabel	Huh	Spoken with interest
128	Isabel → Class	Because what's my favorite	Extending final syllable
		colo::r	of "color"; Isabel
129	Alej. → Isabel	[Lavender	glances at students with
		[Pu:rple	face slightly down, but
131		And you know what	eyes gazing ahead
132		The unders- The top of the leaf is	
		green	

(Moment 4 continues on next page)

Line	Speaker → Hearer	Utterances	Add. Contextualization
133	Ss	And the bottom is purple	
134	Avery → Isabel	Cool	
135	Isabel → Class	And so I'll bring it in	
		And once it starts producing	
136		flowers	
137		It produces purple and white	
		trumpets	
138		The flowers look like trumpets	
139		I'll bring it in so you can see it	

Teacher as participant. In shifting the discourse structure, Isabel positions herself as a participant in the event. At first glance, this might be viewed as a side conversation, loosely related to the activity at hand. However, Isabel's narrative builds directly on Avery's and Tomás's previous statements regarding the coloring of leaves. After a brief IRE sequence (lines 128-130) to recruit students' participation, she details the characteristics of her plant's leaves and flowers with respect to color (lines 132-133, line 137). While narrative is typically not associated with formal authority structures and academic content knowledge, she describes the plant using vocabulary (e.g., "producing", lines 136, 137) characteristic of a scientific register. This is precisely the kind of detail and talk that she wants her students to engage in. By positioning herself as a participant, she provides key modeling to support her students in attaining the high expectations that she requires in her teacher as critic role. Her narrative and conversational tone also legitimize personal/experiential knowledge within content learning.

Moment 5: Logical Reasoning

Toward the end of the event, students have still not resolved whether cactus spikes are leaves. Isabel initiates an IRE sequence, with simple known-answer questions ("What about your Christmas tree? Is it a plant?" "Where are its leaves?"), to prompt their reasoning about how such plants grow. Alejandro answers, "the spiky things," and Isabel continues:

Line	Speaker → Hearer	Utterances	Add. Contextualization
163	Isabel → Class	[And the spiky things	
164		or the needles	
165		Are those leaves ↑	
166	David → Isabel	XXXX	Isabel gestures with
167	Alej. → Isabel	No	hands open, palms up;
168	Avery → Isabel	I hav a electric tree	does not respond to
169	Isabel → Class	Well, then how does-	David's comment
		Tomás just told us that in the	
		little-	
171	Avery → Isabel	-I got a electric tree	
172	Isabel → Class	| Well, okay, if you ha- If you get	Isabel turns to Avery
173		a real tree	
174		You know what a real Christmas	
		tree would look like, right ↑	Gestures with her hands
175	Alejandro	It's green	in a triangle, tree shape
			in the air
176	Isabel → Class	If you see one growing outside	
177		Or somebody has one	
178		Tomás just told us	Avery nods
179		Um, that the leaves of a	affirmatively
180		planttakein the sun	
181		And there's a process called	
		photosynthesis	
182		that makes energy for the plant|	
183		togrow |	
184		How does a Christmas tree grow↓	

(Moment 5 continues on next page.)

Line	Speaker → Hearer	Utterances	Add. Contextualization
185	Alex	By a seed↑	Looking at David, Alex and Esteban's table
186	David → Isabel	By its- by its leaves	Pointing finger in air,
187	Alej. → Isabel		leaning forward
188	Isabel → Class	How does it-	
189	Isabel → Alex	Well it grows from a see:d	
190		Of some so:rt	
191	Alej. → Isabel	By- it gets some from its leaves↑	
192	Isabel → Alej.	*But you just said	Feigned frustration
193		it didn't have leaves*	spoken quickly, with rising tone

Teacher as authority. Isabel assumes a teacher as authority role in the IRE sequence, positioning herself as director of the conversation and evaluator of knowledge. However, this is tempered by inviting her students to connect to a plant that is familiar to them (Christmas trees), using their cultural/experiential knowledge to facilitate learning.

Teacher as facilitator. In this example, we again see Isabel engaged in discursive scaffolding, rephrasing Alejandro's "spiky things" to the conventional "needles" (lines 160-164) and providing simplified descriptions of key concepts (e.g., photosynthesis, lines 181-183), and accounting for students' personal experiences (e.g., Avery's electric tree). Ideologically, Isabel's divergence from traditional true/false interactions by scaffolding the students' content-oriented debate values knowledge as socially-mediated and constructed rather than individual, predetermined, and stable, and her facilitator role is critical in making this happen.

Teacher as critic. Isabel also requires her students to provide warrants for their claims based on sound logic and content knowledge. This is evident when Isabel challenges Alejandro's contrary assertions that Christmas tree needles are not leaves (line 167) and that it gets energy via photosynthesis (lines 187, 191). She later poses counter-arguments (e.g., "But it's not just water," "But where does the sun go?") are not unlike those in the short example at the beginning of the findings section, in which she and her students focused on color representations.

DISCUSSION AND IMPLICATIONS

While at first glance the discourse in the true/false event may appear unremarkable; on close inspection, we see Isabel performing multiple roles to tactically negotiate competing expectations and ideologies of teaching and learning while maintaining high expectations for academic language and content learning. We get a sense of both deference to traditional authority structures, such as tests and testers, *and* a clear understanding of tests and content knowledge as open to question and debate. That is, Isabel is simultaneously compliant with and resistant to standardized curricular expectations. At a surface level (which is often where teacher evaluation remains), Isabel not only had the true/false test (and the ideologies that it stands for as an abstract idea) on her instructional plan, but she also carried it out. However, this standardized discourse and assessment practice was situated in a broader context that limited the effects of its corresponding ideologies. In its implementation, the abstract "traditional" true/false test became rewritten as an opportunity for rich language scaffolding, contextualized and socially constructed learning, and high standards for academic language and content knowledge.

The integrated scaffolding and ideological negotiation that Isabel engaged in provides helpful lessons for other teachers who, like Isabel, find themselves pulled in multiple directions with respect to their curriculum and teaching. In short, the devil is in the details. Teachers of emergent bilinguals who are asked to implement more restrictive forms of instruction and assessment might consider the following questions as they plan learning engagements:

- How can I integrate restrictive curricular requirements into more active and socially-mediated activities and contexts?
- In what ways might I carry out such engagements in alternative ways (e.g., conduct a test orally with room for discussion; position students as test-makers)?

The conversations we had with Isabel during our research helped her become aware of her own tactical negotiations, and other teachers may find it informative and useful to engage in close examinations of their own teaching and discourse. Recordings of their own teaching may prompt teachers to consider how less socially-oriented instructional and assessment activities might be reframed within curricular units or lesson and carried out in alternative ways.

Thomas and Collier (1997) found that language minority students "who participate in classes that are very interactive, with discovery learning facilitated by teachers so that students work cooperatively together in a socioculturally supportive environment, do better than those attending classes taught more traditionally" (p. 50). While this is encouraging for teachers seeking to use approaches grounded in sociocultural theories of teaching and learning, Isabel was also cognizant of local pressures and practices that did not validate such approaches. Although I did not collect any systematic achievement data for Isabel's students, her simultaneous scaffolding and careful negotiation of multiple and conflicting curricular ideologies and expectations will likely support her students in their language and content learning, *and* as they themselves are expected to participate in both nontraditional and traditional curricular activities.

ACKNOWLEDGMENT

1.   The research study reported here was funded by a grant from the Spencer Foundation.

REFERENCES

Au, K. H., & Jordan, C. (1981). Teaching reading to Hawaiian children: Finding a culturally appropriate solution. In H. T. Trueba, G. P. Guthrie & K. H. Au (Eds.), *Culture and the bilingual classroom: Studies in classroom ethnography* (pp. 139-152). Rowley, MA: Newbury House.

Barton, D. (1994). *Literacy: An introduction to the ecology of written language*. Malden, MA: Blackwell.

Bloome, D., Power-Carter, S., Morton Christian, B., Otto, S., & Shuart-Farris, N. (2005). *Discourse analysis and the study of classroom language and literacy events: A microethnographic perspective*. Mahwah, NJ:Erlbaum.

Brisk, M. E., & Harrington, M. M. (2000). *Literacy and bilingualism: A handbook for all teachers*. Mahwah, NJ: Erlbaum.

Cazden, C. B. (2001).*Classroom discourse: The language of teaching and learning*. Portsmouth, NH: Heinemann.

Collins, J., & Blot, R. (2003). *Literacy and literacies: Texts, power, and identity*. New York, NY: Cambridge University Press.

de Certeau, M. (1984). *The practice of everyday life*. Berkeley: University of California Press.

Dixon-Krauss, L. (1995).*Vygotsky in the classroom: Mediated literacy instruction and assessment*. Boston, MA: Allyn & Bacon.

Dixson, A., & Bloome, D. (2007). Jazz, critical race theories, and the discourse analysis of literacy events in classrooms. In M. V. Blackburn & C. T. Clark (Eds.), *Literacy research for political action and change* (pp. 29-52). New York, NY: Peter Lang.

Enright, D. S. (1986). "Use everything you have to teach English": Providing useful input to young language learners. In P. Rigg & D. S. Enright (Eds.), *Children and ESL: Integrating perspectives* (pp. 113-162). Washington, DC: TESOL.

García, E. E. (2005). *Teaching and learning in two languages: Bilingualism and schooling in the United States.* New York: Teachers College Press.

Genesee, F., Lindholm-Leary, K., Saunders, W. M., & Christian, D. (2006). *Educating English language learners: A synthesis of research evidence* (Eds.). New York, NY: Cambridge University Press.

Glaser, B. G., & Strauss, A. L. (1967). *The discovery of grounded theory.* Chicago: Aldine.

González, N., Moll, L. C., & Amanti, C. (Eds.). (2005). *Funds of knowledge: Theorizing practice in households, communities, and classrooms.* Mahwah, NJ: Erlbaum.

Green, J. &Wallat, C. (1981). Mapping instructional conversations. In J. Green & C. Wallat (Eds.), *Ethnography and language in educational settings* (pp. 161-195). Norwood, NJ: Ablex.

Gutiérrez, K., Rymes, B. & Larson, J. (1995). Script, counterscript, and under life in the classroom: James Brown versus Brown v. Board of Education. *Harvard Educational Review, 65*(3), 445-471.

Handsfield, L. J., Crumpler, T. & Dean, T. R. (2010). Tactical negotiations and creative adaptations: The discursive production of literacy curriculum and teacher identities across space-times. *Reading Research Quarterly, 45*(4), 405-431.

Heath, S. B. (1983). *Ways with words: Language, life, and work in communities and classrooms.* New York: Cambridge University Press.

Jiménez, R. T., Garcia, G. E., & Pearson, P. D. (1996). The reading strategies of bilingual Latina/o students who are successful English readers: Opportunities and obstacles. *Reading Research Quarterly, 31*(1), 90-112.

Lewis, C., Enciso, P. & Moje, E. B. (2007). *Reframing sociocultural research on literacy: Identity, agency, and power* (Eds.). Mahwah, NJ: Erlbaum.

Maloch, B. (2004). One teacher's journey: Transitioning into literature discussion groups, *Language Arts, 81*(4), 312-322.

McIntyre, E., Kyle, D.W., & Moore, G.H. (2006). A primary-grade teacher's guidance toward small-group dialogue.*Reading Research Quarterly, 41*(1), 36–66.

Owocki, G., & Goodman, Y. (2002). *Kidwatching: Documenting children's literacy development.* Portsmouth, NH: Heinemann.

Saville-Troike, M. (1994). What really matters in second language learning for academic achievement? *TESOL Quarterly, 18*(2), 199-219.

Thomas, W. P., & Collier, V. (1997).*School effectiveness for language minority stdents.* Washington, DC.: National Clearinghouse for Bilingual Education.

No Child Left Behind (NCLB) Act of 2001, Pub. L. No. 107-110, § 115, Stat. 1425 (2002).

Vygotsky, L. S. (1978). *Mind in society: The development of higher psychological processes.* Cambridge, MA: Harvard University Press.

CHAPTER 4

TEACHER AND STUDENTS' USE OF GESTURE AS A MEANING-MAKING AFFORDANCE FOR SECOND LANGUAGE LEARNING

Alessandro Rosborough

The purpose of this study was to explore how a teacher's use of gesture assisted in the learning of English as a second language in a second grade classroom. Using sociocultural theory, this study demonstrates how gesture was an important affordance in assisting second language learners' meaning making of their spelling words. Particular to the activity, the teacher created multiple opportunities for the students to use gesture as an embodied form for learning the word. The embodied form played a central role in extending dialogue about the subject. Most importantly, the use of gesture provided joint-attention and shared meaning-making between the teacher and her students. Findings include how gesture was a vital part of the language learning experience. Implications include the recommendation that teachers heighten their conscious awareness of gesture and formally recognize its role in the second language learning process.

This chapter demonstrates how teachers should consider gesture as a central component to meaning-making to facilitate second language learning. Of the many affordances (i.e., signs or signals, or symbolic acts),

Teachers' Roles in Second Language Learning:
Classroom Applications of Sociocultural Theory, pp. 63–80
Copyright © 2012 by Information Age Publishing
All rights of reproduction in any form reserved.

63

found in a school, language is the central message system (Halliday, 1993) for creating and carrying meaning between teachers and students, and gesture is a fully integrated part of language (Gullberg, 1998; Kendon, 2004; McNeill, 1985). The common school practices and tasks concerning reading, writing, speaking, and listening in any subject is made possible through language. Language as the central modality for carrying content in a classroom setting or ecology is not limited to speech or arbitrary linguistic signs, but also contains fully integrated nonverbal communication signs.

Bronfenbrenner (1979) explained that within the ecology of a classroom, multiple social ecosystems (i.e., family, friends, community, and so forth) are present. The interrelationship between humans and the environment or ecology (Gibson, 1979) presents teachers with unique, if not chaotic, affordances and opportunities that extend or constrain teaching and learning. Spontaneous use of hand gestures between teachers and students is an ubiquitous modality of communication found naturally in the social interactions of the classroom environment. In this study, gesture is viewed for its contribution to understanding second language learning as affordances in the ecosocial spaces of the classroom (van Lier, 2004). According to the aforementioned researchers, ecosocial spaces have to do with the relationship between an organism, the artifacts or tools that provide affordances for learning, and the environment. In second language learning, an ecosocial approach is an interactional context that offers or provides affordances that the learner or child may perceive and act on (van Lier, 1996). In relation to second language learning, this perspective has to do with viewing and understanding the learning during its activity *in*-vivo, or in its live use in the context in which it takes place.

Understanding teaching and learning through an ecosocial linguistic perspective demonstrates/supports a sociocultural theoretical (SCT) perspective in that the study of language is made microgenetically *in-vivo*, or in other words during its activity. SCT provides a means of understanding language in use and takes into account the complexities of learning and development that comes with the movement of time (Thibault, 2004). In addition, SCT positions gesture as an integrated part of language and as a mediational tool for meaning-making between participants (Vygotsky, 1978, 1986). Particular to this research, I attempt to demonstrate how using a SCT perspective can help teachers understand how gestures create extended spaces of learning between instructors and their students. In this study, gesture is presented as an affordance or meditational tool that assisted in teaching English language learners (ELLs).

LITERATURE REVIEW

Gesture Promotes Interaction in Second Language Learning Activities

Gestures serve many functions in second language learning. It is part of nonverbal communication as a whole and is also a fully integrated part of learning a first (McNeill, 1992; Tomasello, 2008) and second language (Gullberg, 1998; Gullberg & McCafferty, 2008; McCafferty, 2008, McCafferty & Stam, 2008). Gullberg (2006) lists many reasons for studying gesture such as providing insights into communicative and cognitive aspects of language learning, being used as a compensatory part of communication, and as a tool for handling language challenges or difficulties. In addition, gesture can be viewed for its psychological and interactional functions in thinking and speaking a second language (McCafferty, 2008; Stam, 2008).

Viewing second language learning as a socially situated activity places gesture as an important artifact of the environment and an important resource for teachers and students to recognize in their classroom discourse (Kida, 2008; Sime, 2006). In a SCT perspective, gesture is a full part of what it means to participate with all tools in the ecology of the classroom and cultural reality (Kramsch, 1998/2009). Gesture as a meditational tool for meaning-making is a fundamental part of a person's ability to establish dialogic and reflective language learning practices. Gesture as an affordance provides a physical and psychological way to manifest self-investment in their language learning and is a fundamental means for entering a new culture and language. This process may best occur when humans are allowed volition and agency in their learning to mediate their interactions with each other and their surroundings (Vygotsky, 1986).

Concerning younger children, Vygotsky's (1986) explanation of the direction of development of thinking going from the social to the individual is applicable to second-language learners (SLLs). Using this perspective, any overt systematic and structured second-language learning curriculum is only one source to the child's bilingual development. Vygotsky (1978) addressed a role of gesture concerning some aspects of children's symbolic play as a "complex system of 'speech' through gestures that communicate and indicate the meaning of playthings" (p. 108). This idea may be particularly significant for second language learners. They often go through a phase of practicing the second language through translating the information to their first language—a complicated and cognitively challenging process (Lantolf & Thorne, 2006). However, learning a second language may be better understood as processes where there is space to continually play with the new language during interac-

tion with interlocutors (da Silva-Iddings & McCafferty, 2007), and intrap-
ersonally through gesture that promotes inner and private speech
(McCafferty, 1998).

Children do not enter a new language setting with the same linguistic
and cultural background knowledge as their L1 peers. Agar's (1994) 'languaculture' concept explains this background knowledge as an inseparable intertwining of language and culture, which encapsulates the contexts,
speech acts, and conceptual metaphors that drive meaning-making in
language. Indeed, L2 learning includes much more than explicit linguistic knowledge concerning such concepts as syntactic conventions and lexical pieces in the second language. Instead, the primary source for
children's bilingualism in the L2 culture is found in the practicing community itself. In this case, *imitation* and *mimesis* plays a leading role in children's learning of an L2 (Rosborough, 2011). McCafferty (2008) explains
mimesis as having to do with imitation, joint attention, identity, and
group placement—all important aspects of learning a new language and
fitting in the classroom. He specifically addressed gesture as mimesis for
having two functions: "The first is its role as a materializer for both the
purposes of thinking and communicating (i.e., creating meaning), and
the second relates to being and doing in a L2 languaculture (i.e., identity)" (p. 163). According to Donald (2001), "Physical self-familiarity is
one of our cognitive touchstones, perhaps the basis of all higher forms of
self-awareness. Our bodies set the stage not only for conscious experience,
but also for memory" (p. 135). Gesture use as a form of mimesis, provides
second language learners the opportunity to not only engage in a comprehensible interaction (i.e., comprehensible input), but also to gain self-
regulation and consciousness of speech, image, and thought in the L2. In
regards to learning in general, Donald explains, "Conscious ideas and
images are always owned. This owning is highly physical and body-based"
(p. 134). In this case, owning has to do with the physical manifestation of
ideas and images as a form of understanding and meaning-making.

According to Lantolf and Thorne (2006), thinking and doing is the
activity of bringing signs into the organization of consciousness. This consciousness process is highly embodied as children work within the con-
fines of the classroom and school to understand how to line up, when to
move, how to respond, and other physical movements that include and
extend beyond the writing, reading, and mathematical problem solving
often envisioned as typical learning tasks. The child is surrounded in the
L2 culture with meaning-making in context. Hence, it is in the students'
social environment, with the accompanying naturally situated affordances
that provides the learner with a holistic and syncretic understanding of
language. The combination of language learned in a situated and embodied manner includes both linguistic and image components. This embod-

ied ecosocial combination provides a strong foundation for learning a second language. As Vygotsky (1986) explained, meaning-making inhabits the speaker and is made present on both the social and psychological plane. This combination is addressed specifically to second language acquisition as a whole by McCafferty (2008), "Any truly comprehensive theory of SLA will need to move beyond the mind-body dualism that currently pervades the field and take into account our material experience in the world as an aspect of living and learning" (p. 164). Gesture needs to be viewed for its invaluable function in meaning making in a second language and as a more centralized aspect for understanding the dynamics of second language teaching and learning.

Awareness of Pedagogical Restrictions

Most educators would accept the idea that the success of second language learners in identifying, refining, and developing their voice and understanding to the environment around them is best accomplished in a social atmosphere that fosters communication in a reflective and purposeful way. However, many "school friendly" English for speakers of other languages (ESOL) models centralize their theories of teaching and learning on historic comprehensible input theories with what might be termed a "dash-of-salt" addition of contemporary perspectives on how to make appropriate accommodation and modification strategies. Hence, certificates, curriculums, and texts for ESOL teaching are usually based on "strategy training" techniques and not on understanding authentic language issues in educational settings, especially in how to meet needs in the active moment. In some ways, many best strategy-building models replace the idea that teachers should be educated in depth concerning second language theories or methodologies. A disconnect occurs in such systems where models promote the idea of flexibility but at the same time provide a system for teachers to follow that may actually hinder the space created by affordances, such as gesture, to create a more meaningful practice. Instead, many components of language that cannot be easily compartmentalized are often termed para-linguistic, a type of second positioning for such aspects such as prosody, stress, and gesture. As a result of such compartmentalization or dualisms promoted by many cognitive theories (e.g., performance vs. competence), much more attention is given to formalized language components such as syntax or lexicon, form or function, or the four popular language modalities (i.e., speaking, listening, reading, and writing). Many ESOL models (Echevarria & Graves, 2011) encourage teachers to "assign real-life activities" to learn a new language; but often these preconstructed teaching frameworks relegate real-life prosodic and imagistic functions of

[Handwritten marginalia: "Everyone knows authentic learning contexts are best — why strategy training?"]

language to simplistic categories or neglect them completely. Hence, telling teachers to perform "tailored-support" and "adjustments to speech" (Echevarria, Vogt, & Short, 2000) places gesture and other meaning-making affordances as just a static tool and only as one of many input-output based techniques for working with ELLs (Wooldridge, 2001).

The simplification and reductionist approach to learning language by many ESOL programs stand in contrast to Vygotsky's (1978, 1997) and Bahktin's (1981) work concerning meaning-making and dialogic paths of discourse. According to Dunn and Lantolf (1998) and van Lier (1996, 2004), the effect of the learning and changing process for the second language learner is dynamic and not a linear form of additive scaffolding as recommended by Krashen (1981, 1982) and currently used by many popular language learning models or programs.

In contrast to more linear language learning models, the purpose of this study was to explore how gestures were used as mediational tools for teaching English Language Learners at the elementary school level. Although previous studies have explored the use of gesture and second language learning in the classroom (Faraco & Kida, 2008; Lazaraton, 2004; Sime, 2006, 2008; Zhao, 2007), research is needed through a SCT perspective to understand how gesture is used as a mediational tool for teaching and learning a second language at the elementary level. Differing from mainstream educational views of gesture's form and function in the classroom, this study placed the analysis of gesture as a fully integrated part of language and communication for the understanding and interpretation of meaning-making in an L2 setting.

METHODOLOGY

Subjects, Setting, and Procedure

The data for this study is based on the observation and video recording of interactions and dialogues in a classroom specifically developed for ELLs. Participants included one teacher and 19 second graders. The teacher in the classroom was a female English speaker with beginning Spanish language experience acquired mainly through her 19 years of employment as an elementary educator of which 17 years was as an ESL instructor. Many of the students were recent immigrants to the United States and all students were identified and labeled as limited English proficient (LEP) by government standards. The first languages of the students in the classroom were Spanish, Bengali, Arabic, and Tagolog, with Spanish being the predominant type. Collection of data occurred for 28 working days using three triangulated cameras in the classroom. The participants were unaware of any particular research aspect of this study other than the general observation of communication in the classroom. As such, they conducted themselves according to the agenda and tasks assigned through the teacher and curriculum. The larger study is composed of a variety of tasks found in most elementary classrooms. This study displays an excerpt of gesture use as identified through the data sources of observation notes, analysis of video, and post-videotaping interviews with the teacher. The teacher was unaware of the focus on gesture until after the videorecording days of the classroom experience. Only after the 28 classroom days, were videoclips analyzed, selected for function categories, and presented for the teacher to review and elicit feedback concerning possible meanings.

Coding and Transcription

This transcript is coded for gesture stroke in bold, with turn-taking between participants being assigned a new number. The coding process is a modified pattern based on McNeill (1992) (see Appendix A). Although there were a variety of gestures, with some overlapping or serving other functioning capacities simultaneously, specific coding is focused on the gesture phrase by placing it within brackets with the actual stroke in bold. A description of the other gesture motions are described in detail in italics but not specifically classified for their semiotic values. Gesture functions for 17 days were categorized in a theme-based matrix from which this study's examples were selected. Quicktime and Elan software was used to hear and see the gestures in up to one-tenth of a fraction of real-time speed. Instead of referring to names, students were assigned numbers and are coded as S1, S2, and so forth. The teacher is represented as T or Mrs. Dee.

FINDINGS

Examples of gesture playing a central role in communication and extending the space of practice to make meaning through language in areas not readily accessible through the oral/aural or written modalities included functions such as joint-attention, interpersonal communication, and as a material carrier of the content and meaning. Although there were multiple examples of the functions of gesture in holistic, small group, and one-on-one activities, only one small group setting was used for this particular study.

During a small group spelling time, the teacher, Mrs. Dee, embedded phonological awareness, vocabulary development, and meaning-making into the task of spelling 10 words on a list. In the following examples, the use of the teacher's gesture provided additional space in the practice to make of the spelling words. In the first excerpt, Mrs. Dee and three students work together during small group spelling time to practice phonemes and blends of "cr" and "dr." A space for gesture was allowed and promoted by the teacher, which developed interpersonal communication, personal narratives, and clarity to definitions (see Examples 1 & 2). Mrs. Dee provided an embodied experience to assist the students in learning the word with one particular gesture becoming the central mode for carrying meaning.

Example 1
Day 2:   1M.2 & 3 4-13 (01:50:00– Camera Viewing Teacher) and 3M.1
         4-13 (1:21:14- Camera Viewing Students)

14   T: S11?
15   S11: It's an animal that lives in the sea-d and it's [red, //]
              Left hand fingers are slightly apart and move up and down imi-
              tating a crab's walk, performed at her side, at shoulder level near
              her chin, quickly and subtly
16   T: They often are red, aren't they, [uh, huhmmm]
              Points at S16 with left index
              finger

(Skip to line 23)

23   S11: When I lived in Cuba with my grandma and my family,
              when we went to the beach, when we were, when we were
              going home, a crab, a crab bit my, my grandma [in the
              foot,] a baby crab.
              Repeats her previous crab walking movement (line 14) with fin-
              gers going up and down, very quickly and subtly

Example 2
17   S16: [And they go under][water,]
              Moves right hand from reaching above his head, to a five spread
              out finger motion extending from below his chest area towards the
              teacher parallel to the table; left hand is placed above the right
              arm during the motion coinciding with the words "under water"
              and sometimes they [snip your nose]

Has both elbows on the table and hands up and out in front of his face and pinches fingers and thumb together with both hands on his nostrils

[and in the movies//]

Releases his nostrils and opens both palms up vertical to desk top at head level

[they snip,]

18   T: begins to mimic S16 by using both hands as pinchers/ claws with all fingers pinching down on the thumb at chin level in front of her face between her and S16

19   S16: *Mirrors Mrs. Dee and pinches his fingers together like a claw at the same time as her; they share the same pinching beat a couple of times*

20   T: I would so not want a crab to snip my nose

21   S16: No, in the movies

Points at teacher (to correct her)

22   T: Oh, only in the movies, okay, good. Yes (Cam.1.M. 2&3 (0:02:40))

In these two examples, both students shared explanations and personal narratives concerning the word they were given both in a verbal and gestural mode. Two students respond with two gesture productions for the word "crab". S11's gesture demonstrated the movement of the crab; whereas, S16 created a pinching motion between the fingers. During review of video clips in interview 1, Mrs. Dee explained that S11 was the most advanced English speaker in that group. Although S11 contributes a gesture, it is performed at the side of the body in fractions of a second. It did reveal additional information not carried by verbal communication such as the movement of the crab. In this case, Mrs. Dee provides an affordance for learning by allowing the students the opportunity to interact and hold dialogue about particular spelling words. Although the teacher did not use the gesture by S11, it became a mediational tool that provided a potential reference point or tangible artifact to be used as needed for future meaning-making. Indeed, S11 refers to this same movement later in the conversation (line 23). However, there is no evidence of the teacher responding mimetically to S11's gesture.

In contrast to the teacher's and S11's speech-based interaction, S16's use of gesture becomes the focal point of meaning-making for the word. In lines 16-18, S16 defined crab in a hypothetical, yet personal manner. His personal connection is developed and represented by the iconic and metonymic gesture representation of pinching crab claws. Line 16 contains his use of the pronouns "they" and "your" in connection to seeing them in the movies. Yet Mrs. Dee's first reaction is not in a verbal response but through the mimicking of the pinchers - even before S16 has finished his statement. The data demonstrates a joint production and sharing of the pincher motion as both participants pinch fingers in synchrony at 1/10 of a second. The remaining narrative concerning the misunderstanding between S16's movie experience and real life is residual to the joint-attention made between participants. Mrs. Dee and S16 develop interpersonal communication concerning the word crab by implementing a gesture modality. The teacher's attentiveness to how the student responded, beyond the oral/aural modality was important to the creation of meaning-making through a newly created tool. By acknowledging and demonstrating this new tool to each other and the group, all three participants participated in using this new artifact later in the dialogue (see line 30 next page).

Of note between S11's and S16's gestures, the pincher motion represented a distinct feature of a crab, which performs a representational function not developed by S11's undulating fingers for a "moving crab". The pinching motion between the fingers and thumb is taken up by the teacher and is highly iconic of a crab's claw. S11s "moving crab" gesture may be seen as less iconic in that it may represent any moving creature with multiple legs. The teacher's acknowledgment and advocacy of the pinching motion demonstrates her particular preference in this moment for this gesture to represent the word and its meaning. In addition, as this iconic and metonymic gesture becomes the mediational tool of choice, the teacher continued to reference this newly developed artifact in an attempt to assess S15's background knowledge of crab.

Example 3

29   T: I don't think, I don't think crabs are poisoned, no.
                    [But a crab definitely has claws.]
                    Repeats crab claw pinching motion in front of S15. She pinches both hands open and close 3 times
                    [Do you know a crab?]
                T: *Turns towards S15, points to S15 and then repeats the claw pinching motions with fingers and thumb coming together on both hands at shoulder level*
30   S11 & S16: *Both repeat the claw pinching gesture*
31   S15: Yeah
                    Unlike S11 & S16, there is no motion at this time with his reply
32   T: [Do you know the word for crab in Spanish?]
                    Continues to pinch with her hands

[handwritten margin note: ✴ creating new, shared meaning through gestures]

| 33 | | S15: | Hmmm, ///I don't know |

34   T: I'm looking, I have a dictionary in Spanish// S8, do you, is there a Spanish dictionary next to you, [by that white notebook?]

Looks around at her shelf and the shelf by S8 then points with left hand index finger at shoulder level towards the bookshelf near S8

35   S8: Right here?

36   T: Next to that? Is there a Spanish Dictionary? It's yellow and blue, no, okay,// thank-you.

S16: Uh, uh, what was I going to tell you?

37   T: I don't know. [All right, so this word is crab.]

Points to the word with her right index finger

38   S15: I see, [I see crab]/// I see one and I eat it.

Places fingers and thumb together before closing hand in a holding/pinching motion in the same metonymic pattern as S16, S11 and T.

In reproducing the pincher motion, Mrs. Dee then directs an embodied form for sharing and joining the process of meaning-making of the word towards the most recent immigrant and less English experienced student in the group, S15. It is important to note that Mrs. Dee produced the pincher gesture in line 29 and both S11 and S16 respond in like manner. However, this gesture is not taken up by S15 even though he verbally states that he understands. The attentiveness and perception by the teacher used the newly created and unplanned tool during the process of teaching. According to Mrs. Dee's interview response, she knew that he had the least English background. In addition, review of the video clip demonstrated that he was the only student who did not respond through the use of the newly created gesture tool. Mrs. Dee demonstrated awareness of this situation and the potential for meaning-making the gesture tool represented and asked the question again. With S15 showing no gestural movement to affirm a shared understanding of the word, Mrs. Dee turns to other tools to assess his ability to comprehend crab. After failing to find an alternative means of communication such as searching for a Spanish-English dictionary, Mrs. Dee returns to the same embodied tool of making a pinching motion between the fingers to represent "crab" again. At this point, S15 takes up the non-verbal request for shared understanding by the teacher and responds with a smaller pincher gesture, using one finger and thumb accompanied with a self-disclosure about eating them (line 38). Mrs. Dee's responses and ability to adjust by using newly created tools provided a new process and space for extending the student's knowledge beyond a simple recall spelling activity. This provided the students with new performance based responses, which demonstrated how they gained additional meaning of the word in English, including an embodied knowledge of the subject.

DISCUSSION

The purpose of this research was to investigate gesture's role in meaning-making between a teacher and her students in a second-grade ELL classroom. One finding demonstrated gesture as a part of the ecosocial space where affordances helped the ELLs create meaning in a spelling and phonemic awareness task. Gesture use by both the teacher and students provided joint-attention that led to extended meaning-making for all the participants. Gesture played a central role as a material-carrier of new content that was shared between the participants in the very moment it was needed.

In this second grade classroom the teacher created space in the assignments through the acknowledgement and use of gesture, which provided evidence of extending an activity from a more linguistic form based practice to one that added joint-attention and narrative identity sharing that was not necessarily available through a verbal channel dominated practice. As explained by van Lier (1996), many practices that use a traditional recitation process such as initiate-respond-evaluate (IRE) between teachers and students may result in limiting the space, creation, and expansion of the tools available for learning. In examples 1-3, a recitation practice focusing on the literal spelling of letters combined with a phonemic awareness task through only oral/aural methodology could have met the lesson's objectives. Instead, Mrs. Dee provided space for gesture where students could demonstrate their abilities to not only comprehend but also develop the content knowledge. In other words, all the participants were able to amplify and build on the new gestural tool that the teacher and the ecosocial setting afforded. As a result of the teacher allowing and promoting embodied interaction for learning a word, a new unplanned but completely appropriate experience for joint-attention, meaning-making, and shared intentionality occurred.

Specific to this data, the small group spelling time demonstrated how a teacher was aware of gesture as an affordance for learning, including her ability to use it as a tangible foundational reference point to assess comprehension. Although some gestures were not as readily acknowledged (Example 1, line 15) the affordance for space was available and one gesture became a new artifact to be used for learning the content. In particular, the spontaneous but highly iconic gesture created by S16 turned into an emblematic and symbolic tool for understanding the word; whereas, S11's more ambiguous moving gesture lacked the metonymic characteristics somewhat unique to crabs. These examples support Kida's (2008) suggestion that using gestures that are highly iconic may be more beneficial for SLLs. In addition, although S11 may not have needed this particular mediational tool to gain understanding, the shared production of the gesture allowed Mrs. Dee a formative assessment to understand the needs of all the students.

Findings from the data also reveal that similar to Gullberg (1998), Mrs. Dee used the gesture for assessment purposes to assist and overcome a struggling student's (S15) ability to share in the meaning of the conversation. In addition, the use of gesture by both the teacher and students provided a foundational reference point providing both participants with an ability to refer back to a past aspect of the narrative – a speech act often deemed difficult for new SLLs. This dialogue example, based on a spontaneously constructed gesture demonstrates language complexity well beyond just a technique or cue to scaffold or gain comprehensible input.

Implications for Practitioners

Although gesture played a variety of functions for communication in this study, a central point emerged from its role: the teacher provided time and space for gesture to be a fully integrated part of meaning-making of the content in the students' second language. As explained by Chandler (2007), meaning-making is not found in relationship to other signs in a language system but in "the social context of its use" (p.9). Ultimately, it is the users of the language in an embodied experience that determines the meanings created and shared according to their ecosocial affordances (Thibault, 2004).

An SCT approach places the students' learning path as central to learning and development in their L2 since it is *their* meaning-making experience. Teachers that provide and encourage space for gesture, allow themselves another modality to join the student in their learning path without placing limitations or reductions on how to use the language. Traditional pedagogical practices for the English language in the United States are built on the premise that the curriculum helps the child move from the simple understanding of using words to a more academic understanding of the word itself. It is understood that helping students attend to the components of English orthology will help them to learn and improve their reading and writing. However, many second language speakers come without the background knowledge of the sample of words used in early grades as their English-speaking peer. In examples 1-3, the English learners do not have the same advantage of the English speakers in that phonemes may be added to obtain a word already identified and known through the students' background knowledge. Instead, the L2 learner may find themselves connecting phonemes to create a word that they do not recognize and turn to a search for the meaning of the word and why they are performing that particular practice – a challenge that does not as readily occur for L1 learners. Gesture and space for meaning-making assisted the students in creating meaning which required the teacher to adjust the practice in the moment, thus going beyond the idea of just preconceived correct comprehensible input/output production.

Gesture, as one of many affordances, embodies the students' *languacultural* (i.e., language and cultural background knowledge) realities and provides a teacher physical insight and a shared path into students' learning and development in a second language through joint-attention and interpersonal communication. As Wells (1999) explained, "by contributing to the joint meaning making with and for others, one also makes meaning for oneself and, in the process, extends one's own understanding" (p. 108). Teachers that consciously increase their awareness and ability to use spontaneous gestures in the classroom, create an opportunity and affordances to understand how new words in a new language are taken up by the learners and how to meet their needs. Participation in joint gesture exchange will help teachers and students not only comprehend meaning but also gain insights as to how learning a new language goes beyond words and comprehensible input since it is an embodied and experiential situation (Hoffman, 1989). Teachers should keep in mind that young students typically want to understand and make meaning of their world and this often entails more than simple accommodations or modifications to first language learning practices.

Gesture as a mediational tool for meaning-making is a fundamental part of a person's ability to establish dialogic and reflective language learning practices. As an affordance found in the ecosocial practices of the classroom, gesture provides a physical and psychological way for the teacher to manifest joint investment with the students in their new language learning experience. Gesture is a fundamental means for entering a new culture and language; this study shows that this process occurs when teachers allow for space in their lesson plans or activities for the exchange of gestures to mediate their interactions with each other and their content.

Practical application of this study should include the idea that teachers make a more conscious effort to raise their attention to gesture. When teachers realize that their SLLs do not respond in an embodied fashion, they would do well to provide space and time for students to use their hands to create potential affordances for learning. As teachers help students to embody the language, especially the less experienced second language users, both participants should benefit from this additional modality with the potential to gain joint attention and meaning-making.

The teacher that brings a higher consciousness to the functions of gesture in the classroom will be better able to understand and view the processes of second language development. Teachers would do well to provide space and time in activities that invite gesture production. In essence, this means that they should be better able to meet development needs from the diverse second language learners that come with many different communicative experiences. With this heightened consciousness for gesture, it is hoped that both teachers and students see new changes and transformations in their teaching and learning of a second language.

APPENDIX A: TRANSCRIPTION DATA DESCRIPTION

A transcription code modified and based on McNeill (1992) Speech and Gesture.

1. Speech is transcribed fully from the videotape in ordinary orthography

2. Gesture is typed in italics below the speech. Gesture codes include the following:

> [ ]   gesture phrase (stroke in boldface)
>
> /   silent pause (multiple slashes for longer pauses)
>
> (////)   Stroke not associated with speech
>
> ^   Rise in voice intonation
>
> ( )   Additional information to providing context to the situation by the researcher
>
> T1   The main teacher of this study, also referred to as Mrs. Dee
>
> T2   The assisting adult that comes in the afternoon, also referred to as Mrs. Mee

S1 through S-19—Student names were assigned a code of S1 (Student one), S2 (Student two), and so forth for every child participant in the classroom

Numbers were assigned to every speech turn performed by the participant. Although transcriptions were done for entire scenes, some examples only demonstrate partial dialogues. Hence, shifts or jumps in numbers provide the reader knowledge of a break in the dialogue or context. "Skips" are noted in the transcriptions. It should also be noted that extended speech is segmented by conventional commas and periods to best match the pauses and meaning of the participant's speech. However, it should be noted that periods and commas are not a part of speech and they are placed according to this researcher's understanding of the dialogue.

3. Gestures were analyzed according to the following points:

    1. Identification of the movements that are gestures (particularly the hands but also the arm, head, and body movements).
    2. Identification of the stroke phase, and in some cases the preparation or retraction phases. In the stroke, a concentration was placed on the trajectory, shape, and posture.
    3. Location the boundaries of the gesture phases in the relevant part of the phonological transcription.

4. Codings for gesture types include the following:

    1. Representational (i.e., represents attributes, actions, or relationships of objects or characters); two kinds: 1. Iconic 2. Metaphoric
    2. Deictic (i.e., finger points or other indications of either concrete or imaginary objects or people)
    3. Beats (i.e., formless hands that convey no information but move in rhythmic relationship to speech). This category can be confirmed by means of the beat filter below.
    4. Emblems/Italianate: (i.e., deliberate and standardized movements that have a direct verbal equivalent known to others in the same speech community. Typically these movements continually demonstrate the same meaning when performed).

REFERENCES

Agar, M. (1994). *Language shock: Understanding the culture of conversation*. New York, NY: William Morrow.

Bakhtin, M. (1981). *The dialogic imagination*. In M. Holquist (Ed.), (C. Emerson & M. Holquist, Trans.). Austin, TX: University of Texas Press.

Bronfenbrenner, U. (1979). *The ecology of human development: Experiments by nature and design*. Cambridge, MA: Harvard University Press.

Chandler, D. (2007). *Semiotics: The basics*. New York, NY: Routledge.

Da Silva-Iddings, C., & McCafferty, S. (2007). Carnival in a mainstream kindergarten classroom: A Bakhtinian Analysis of Second Language Learners' off-task behaviors. *The Modern Language Journal, 91*(1), 31-44.

Donald, M. (2001). *A mind so rare*. New York, NY: W.W. Norton.

Dunn, W., & Lantolf, J. (1998). Vygotsky's zone of proximal development and Krashen's i+1: Incommensurable constructs, incommensurable theories. *Language Learning, 48*(3), 411-422.

Echevarria, J., & Graves, A. (2011). *Sheltered content instruction: Teaching English learners with diverse abilities*. Boston, MA: Allyn & Bacon.

Echevarria, J., Short, D., & Vogt, M. (2000). *Making content comprehensible for English language learners: The SIOP Model*. Boston, MA: Allyn & Bacon.

Faraco, M., & Kida, T. (2008). Gesture and the negotiation of meaning in a Second Language classroom. In S. McCafferty, & G. Stam (Eds.), *Gesture: Second language acquisition and classroom research* (pp. 280-297). London: Routledge.

Gibson, J. J. (1979). *The ecological approach to visual perception*. Boston, MA: Cornell University.

Gullberg, M. (1998). *Gesture as a communication strategy in second language discourse: A study of learners of French and Swedish*. Lund, Sweden: Lund University Press.

Gullberg, M. (2006). Some reasons for studying gesture and second language acquisition (hommage à Adam Kendon). [Electronic version]. *IRAL: International Review of Applied Linguistics in Language Teaching,44*(2), 103-124.

Gullberg, M., & McCafferty, S. (2008). Introduction to gesture and SLA: Toward an integrated approach. *Studies in Second Language Acquisition, 30*, 133-146.

Halliday, M. (1993). Towards a language-based theory of learning. *Linguistics and Education, 5*, 93-116.

Hoffman, E. (1989). *Lost in translation. A life in a new language*. New York, NY: Dutton.

Kendon, A. (2004). *Gesture: Visible action as utterance*. Cambridge, England: Cambridge University Press

Kida, T. (2008). Does gesture aid discourse comprehension in the L2? In S. McCafferty & G. Stam, (Eds.), *Gesture: Second language acquisition and classroom research* (pp. 131-156). London: Routledge.

Kramsch, C. (2009). *Language and culture*. Oxford, England: Oxford University Press. (Original work published 1998)

Krashen, S. (1981). *Second language acquisition and second language learning*. Oxford, England: Pergamon.

Krashen, S. (1982). *Principles and practice in second language acquisition*. Oxford, England: Pergamon.

Lantolf, J., & Thorne, S. (2006). *Sociocultural theory and the genesis of second language development*. Oxford, England: Oxford University Press.

Lazaraton, A. (2004). Gesture and speech in the vocabulary explanations of one ESL teacher: A microanalytic inquiry. *Language Learning, 54*(1), 79-117.

McCafferty, S. (2006). Gesture and the materialization of second language prosody. Special Issue, Gullberg, M. (Guest Editor), *IRAL, 44*(4), 195-207.

McCafferty, S., & Stam, G. (2008). *Gesture: Second language acquisition and classroom research*. London: Routledge.

McCafferty, S. (2008). Mimesis and second language acquisition. *Studies in Second Language Acquisition, 30*, 147-167.

McCafferty, S. G. (1998). Nonverbal expression and L2 private speech. *Applied Linguistics, 19*, 73-96.

McNeill, D. (1992). *Hand and mind*. Chicago, IL: Chicago University Press.

McNeill, D. (2005). *Gesture and thought*. Chicago, Il: University of Chicago Press.

Rosborough, A. (2011). *Gesture as an act of meaning-making: An eco-social perspective of a sheltered-English second grade classroom* (Unpublished doctoral dissertation). University of Nevada, Las Vegas.

Sime, D. (2006). What do learners make of teachers' gestures in the language classroom? *International Review of Applied Linguistics in Language Teaching, 44*(2), 211-230.

Sime, D. (2008). "Because of her gesture, it's very easy to understand"—Learners' perceptions of teachers' gestures in the foreign language class. In S. McCafferty & G. Stam, (Eds.), *Gesture: Second language acquisition and classroom research* (pp. 259-279). London: Routledge.

Stam, G. (2008). What gestures reveal about second language acquisition. In McCafferty, S. &G. Stam, (Eds.), *Gesture: Second language acquisition and classroom research* (pp. 231-255). London: Routledge.

Thibault, P. (2004). *Brain, mind, and the signifying body.* London: Continuum.

Tomasselo, M. (2008). *Origins of human communication.* Cambridge, MA: MIT Press.

van Lier, L. (1996). *Interaction in the language curriculum: Awareness, autonomy, &authenticity.* New York, NY: Longman.

van Lier, L. (2004). *The ecology and semiotics of language learning: A sociocultural perspective.* Boston, MA: Kluwer.

Vygotsky, L. (1978). *Mind in society: The development of higher psychological processes.* Cambridge, MA: Harvard University Press.

Vygotsky, L. (1986). *Thought and language.* Cambridge, MA: MIT press.

Vygotsky, L. S. (1997). *The collected works of L. S. Vygotsky: Vol. 4. History of the development of higher mental functions.* In R. W. Reiber, & A. S. Carton, (Eds.). New York, NY: Plenum Press.

Wells, G. (1999). *Dialogic inquiry: Towards a sociocultural practice and theory of education.* Cambridge, England: Cambridge University Press.

Wooldridge, B. (2001). Foreigner talk: An important element in cross-cultural management, education and training. *International Review of Administrative Sciences, 67*, 621-634.

Zhao, J. (2007). *Metaphors and gestures for abstract concepts in English academic writing* (Unpublished doctoral dissertation) University of Arizona, Tucson.

CHAPTER 5

TEACHER DISCOURSE AND CODE CHOICE IN A SWEDISH EFL CLASSROOM

Kristy Beers Fägersten

In this chapter, examples from classroom interaction are presented to illustrate how language functions in and is influenced by the sociocultural setting of the EFL classroom. The chapter features two distinct focal points: First, the predominant use of English by the teacher and the minimal use of English by the students are proposed as instrumental activities where English can be considered a mediating semiotic tool. I suggest that English-language interaction in the EFL classroom represents Vygotsky's concept of a social semiotic tool that is specifically related to an institutional context (Wertsch 1998). Conversely, the second focus of the chapter is on the inverse use of Swedish, which mainly features as the students' language of social speech and the teacher's language of regulatory, disciplinary discourse. The teacher's code choice and the established practice of code-switching thus serve to redirect the students' focus, either to engaging in the learning of English, or to behaving according to the institutional context.

Scandinavians have been recognized as having a high level of English proficiency, and it has been suggested that English has attained the status of a second language in the Scandinavian countries, "rather than a foreign language, as the number of domains where English is becoming

Teachers' Roles in Second Language Learning:
Classroom Applications of Sociocultural Theory, pp. 81–98
Copyright © 2012 by Information Age Publishing
All rights of reproduction in any form reserved.

indispensible in Scandinavia is increasing constantly" (Phillipson, 1992, p. 25). In Sweden, English is used not only as a lingua franca in international contexts, but also intranationally, as Swedes can be observed incorporating English words and phrases in their Swedish-language communication with each other (Sharp, 2007). This practice of code-switching reflects the powerful influence English has historically exerted on the Swedish language and, by extension, on Swedish culture. Because English has no official second language status in Sweden, it remains, technically, a foreign language. However, the historically deliberate promotion and appropriation of English in Sweden has resulted in an unofficially bilingual national speech community. This status is reflected and further perpetuated by the prominence given English in Sweden's school system according to the national school curriculum, where it is stipulated that English instruction should reflect communicative methodology to develop receptive, interactive and productive skills. Communicative competence is positioned as the ultimate goal, encompassing sociolinguistic, strategic, and grammatical competence, according to Hymes' model (1972), and daily passive or active encounters with English are assumed.

English foreign language (EFL) instruction at Swedish elementary schools is jump-started by the fact that, even before the first years of instruction, pupils have been regularly exposed to English. Unlike initial exposure to truly foreign languages, instruction in English is characterized by generally preexisting familiarity and basic skills. By the seventh grade, when pupils in Sweden are 13 years old, English lessons are often conducted entirely in the target language. It is at this point, then, that classroom discourse, particularly the discourse of the teacher, becomes interesting from the perspective of language choice. The more English is established as the language of instruction in addition to being the subject of instruction, the more marked the use of Swedish becomes. The contrastive use of English and Swedish in classroom discourse can thus reveal the sociolcultural practices and functions associated with each language.

PURPOSE OF THE STUDY

This chapter aims to analyze and interpret classroom discourse according to Vygotsky's (1986) theory of language as a mediating tool. Drawing from empirical data, I will present examples of classroom discourse which illustrate how language functions in and is influenced by the sociocultural setting of the Swedish, EFL classroom at the seventh grade level. The chapter features two distinct focal points: first, the predominant use of English by the teacher and the minimal use of English by the students are considered in terms of the sociocultural associations of marked and unmarked code choices (Myers-Scotton, 1983, 2001). I suggest that English-language interaction in the EFL classroom, as an example of external, communicative speech, represents the unmarked code choice, established by the discursive practices of the teacher. Conversely, the second focus of the chapter is on the use of Swedish, particularly by the teacher, which, in the specific instructional environment of a Swedish EFL classroom, is suggested to be a marked case of language use. English is established as the main language of teacher-to-student interaction, serving instructional and regulatory functions according to Bernstein's (1996) model. The teacher's code-switches to Swedish are proposed as serving solely regulatory discourse-related purposes, and in this chapter, it is proposed that the teacher's use of Swedish fulfills a specifically disciplinary function, as direct responses to pupils' spontaneous, off-task verbalizations. This chapter thus aims to examine how students' utterances can predispose the teacher to regulate classroom interaction by choosing a particular communicative code. Language choice is proposed to have a sociocultural function in its use as a mediating tool to promote pupil learning and behavior appropriate to the culture of the EFL classroom.

THEORETICAL FRAMEWORK

This chapter adopts a theoretical framework based on Vygotsky's (1978, 1934/1986) theories of the role of culture and social communication in a child's individual development, and, significantly, the role of language as a mediating tool in this process. Vygotsky proposed that it is social interaction that serves as the platform for a child's acquisition of cultural practices and social conventions, and it is language which functions as the crucial tool for mediation. Vygotsky's (1986) observations of linguistic behavior in young children led him to theorize that, initially, language is outside of the child, existing solely within the external, social context. The acquisition and use of language reflects the psychological and cognitive progression of children from social beings acquiring culturally shared knowledge to individuals who have appropriated that knowledge as their own. Individual mental activity is thus a product of social learning, which in turn can be understood as the process of mastering tasks via social interaction with others. Social learning among children is normally via interaction with adults or other interlocutors who can be considered "more knowledgeable others." Language is a communicative tool, but also a mediating tool of thought, ultimately allowing individuals in a social context to "co-construct knowledge together" (Mercer, 1995, p. 4).

Specifically, the theoretical framework of this chapter positions language as a mediating tool, to consider how code choice is socioculturally mediated and directly related to the extent of functional differentiation of social speech in the communicative language context of a Swedish, EFL classroom. In the next sections, I prepare the presentation of analyses of classroom discourse by briefly outlining key studies concerning teacher discourse and classroom code-switching, and the methodologies of sociocultural discourse analysis and ethnographic communication.

LITERATURE REVIEW

Relevant to the discussion of language as a mediating tool is pedagogic theory concerning classroom discourse and the application of discourse analytic methodology. On the one hand, language is used in the educational context as a mediating tool of social interaction; on the other hand, in the EFL classroom, language is also the subject of instruction. In other words, it is at once the means and object of mediation. In this chapter, I analyze teacher discourse as the realization of this dual nature of English, focusing on the sociocultural significance of the teacher's contrastive use of English and Swedish.

Classroom Discourse

Classroom discourse has been shown to pattern rather rigidly with regards to activities that are dominated by teacher talk. The most standard type of teacher-student discourse is one that follows an Initiation-Response-Follow-up (IRF) sequence (Sinclair & Coulthard, 1975; Wells, 1993) or an Initiation-Response-Evaluation (IRE) sequence (Cazden, 1988; Mehan, 1979). Teachers commonly engage in IRF/IRE sequences primarily for large group activities: when a question is posed, one pupil or group of pupils answers or is selected to answer, and the teacher comments on the response. Hicks (1995) suggests that the IRF/IRE sequence represents the unmarked case of classroom discourse, as it "constitutes somewhat of a norm" (p. 66). Wells (1993) seems to agree with Hicks' assessment, but qualifies that the IRF/IRE sequence as a form of triadic discourse may generally apply to structure, but vary according to function.

Pupils vary in their individual need to be initiated into the specific classroom culture of the IRF/IRE sequence, or even into general classroom discourse or culture. Theories of socialization (Bernstein, 1971; Halliday, 1978) consider the effects that different sociolinguistic and sociocultural backgrounds can have on pupils' successful assimilation of classroom culture. Pupils furthermore need to learn classroom speech activities (Gumperz, 1982), "in which participants share assumptions about who does the talking and what forms of talk are appropriate. Speech activities ... can be identified by characteristic forms of discourse that are fairly predictable from the setting" (Hicks, 1995, p. 71). Thus in addition to learning subject matter, pupils need to learn how to learn, by performing the role of pupil. According to Stubbs (1976), "social roles such as 'teacher' or 'pupil' do not exist in the abstract. They have to be acted out, performed and continuously constructed in the course of social interaction" (p. 99). In extreme cases,

> the task of the teacher as an orchestrator of discourse then becomes much more complex. She or he not only must apprentice children into authentic disciplinary practices but must also orchestrate multiple voices reflective of the differing discourses that children acquire in home and community settings. (Hicks, 1995, p. 76)

Teachers assume, accordingly, a minimum of two roles. On the one hand, they are responsible for subject-matter instruction, and, on the other hand, they establish and maintain the social context of the classroom. Teacher discourse will certainly reflect this dual role, as suggested by Bernstein's (1996) principle of pedagogic discourse, which consists of two embedded discourses,

> the discourse which creates specialized skills and their relationship to each other as *instructional discourse*, and the moral discourse which creates order, relations and identity [as] *regulatory discourse* ... the instructional discourse is embedded in the regulatory discourse, and the regulatory discourse is the dominant discourse. (p. 46)

It is through pedagogic discourse that teachers are able to perform their dual roles, and participate in creating, negotiating, or co-constructing the institutional and sociocultural environment of the classroom. In this chapter, examples of classroom talk illustrate the structural and functional aspects of teacher discourse, considering how "language simultaneously reflects and constructs the situation in which it is used" (Gee & Green, 1998, p. 134). A further aspect to consider with regards to the Swedish EFL classroom, however, is code choice.

Classroom Code-Switching

Code-switching has been defined as "the use of more than one language in the course of a single communicative episode" (Heller, 1988, p. 1); "the alternating use of more than one language" (Auer, 1984, p. 1); and "the use of two or more languages in the same conversation" (Myers-Scotton, 1993, p. vii). These definitions suffice to represent the basic act of switching codes, but, according to Nilep (2006), they are inadequate for a sociocultural linguistic analysis of code-switching discourse. A "useful definition" should instead recognize code-switching as "an alternation in the form of communication that signals a context in which the linguistic contribution can be understood" (p. 17). Interactional functions of code-switching are thereby accounted for, such as making salient aspects of situation, interlocutor identity, or discursive background (p. 15).

Particularly significant to the scholarship of code-switching is Myers-Scotton's "markedness" model. The underlying assumption of the model is that interlocutors have a common understanding of the social meanings associated with their available codes. The markedness model is robust in terms of its potential to account for motivations for and processes of code-switching. It is also particularly applicable to analyses of second and foreign language classroom discourse, where the marked and unmarked codes may clearly correspond to interaction type, sociocultural values, or discursive goals.

Auer (1995) claims that code-switching research does not support the predictions of the markedness model with regards to speech activities corresponding to particular codes. The concept of markedness is, however, not infelicitous with Auer's (1999) own dichotomy of code-switching as having discourse-related and participant-related functions in interactional contexts, indexing either aspects of the situation or features of the speaker, respectively. In Auer's dichotomy, markedness can be considered to be accounted for, albeit somewhat neutralized, as the meaningful contrast of "otherness." For example, Auer particularly characterizes discourse-related code-switches as occurring in social contexts in which it is "possible to identify the language of interaction which is valid at a given moment." Departure from the valid code of the moment "signals 'otherness' of the upcoming contextual frame, and thereby achieves a change of 'footing'" (p. 312). From a sociocultural perspective, code-switching can be approached as the use of language as a mediating tool to establish and co-construct context-embedded social functions of language choice. It can therefore be likened to Gutiérrez's (2008) "specific semiotic resources such as use of the L1 ... to gain control over the task in hand, and to facilitate knowledge co-construction and L2 development" (p. 145), (cf. Swain & Lapkin, 2000).

METHOD

Data for the present study were collected during observations of a seventh grade (13-year-old pupils) English class at a public middle school in a suburb of Stockholm, Sweden. Over a period of 5 weeks, one 60-minute lesson of the English course was observed (as a participant observer, Heigham & Crocker, 2009) on five different occasions. Additional permission to video- or audio-record the observed lessons was not granted; the data presented here represent the researcher's own written recordings of classroom interaction. Due to the inability to manually and simultaneously transcribe classroom interaction at length, recordings were limited to short intervals of student-teacher discourse, or longer intervals of student-only or teacher-only speech. At the end of each lesson, a consultation with the teacher contributed to determining the accuracy of the written recordings, insofar as the teacher was able to recall the interaction. The three sequences of discourse presented in this chapter were collected during the fourth and fifth observations. It is proposed that, by this time, the pupils and teacher were more accustomed to the researcher's presence, and manual recording skills were sufficiently honed to accurately and completely represent the short sequences of interaction. The recorded extracts featured in this chapter include a student-teacher interaction taking place over approximately 6 minutes, and a sequence of teacher-only discourse, spanning an approximately 15-minute long discussion activity.

The analyses included in this study are informed by methods of sociocultural discourse analysis and ethnography of communication. Mercer's (2004) methodology of sociocultural discourse analysis has been applied, representing a departure from linguistic discourse analysis by focusing on the functions of language as collaborative negotiation instead of on language itself. Similar to the methods of linguistic ethnography and conversation analysis, sociocultural discourse analysis includes commentated examples from the transcribed discourse. The ethnographic approach to language use seems to complement sociocultural discourse analysis particularly well, judging from Spindler and Spindler's (1987) explication of ethnography, in which they suggest that linguistic, nonlinguistic, and para-linguistic expressions constitute culturally constructed dialogue, which is the subject of ethnographic study.

In the present study, I apply a combination of sociocultural discourse analytic and ethnographic methodology, acknowledging Nystrand's (2006) observation that classroom discourse lends itself well to a combination of methods. Luke (1995) credits Gumperz and Hymes (1972) and Hymes (1995) for stressing the social aspects of language use in ethnography, stating that their research agenda recognizes that language development is a product of socialization, itself characterized by norms, rules, and conventions for behavior, each of which contribute to establishing classrooms as institutional discourse communities. Gee and Green (1998) identify two key tasks of ethnographers: exploring part-whole relationships and contrastive relevance (p. 126). Citing Erickson (1979), they argue that the ethnographer's goal is to achieve a holistic understanding of the social context, and suggest that this can be done by considering even single lessons. Erickson thereby alludes to Hymes' (1972) description of contrastive relevance, in which he suggests that an ethnographer can demonstrate the relevance of contrast in choices regardless of the size of data. Gee and Green (1998) support this position, claiming that contrast in language use can be investigated regardless of the size of the unit of analysis (for example, an utterance, a series of turns, or a complete text).

Sociocultural discourse analysis and ethnographic methodology are applied to the selected extracts of classroom discourse, suggesting their value as parts of the historical, cultural, and social context of the classroom, and as illustrations of the contrastive linguistic choices that may contribute to establishing the classroom as a discourse community characterized by conventions of appropriateness. This study is not proposed as an ethnographic investigation in the pure sense of term, due to the limited scope of time and observation data. Nevertheless, ethnographic methodology is applied in the form of a close analysis of the discourse extracts with regards to the social context of the classroom. Methods of sociocultural discourse analysis are also applied in order to determine how the teacher and students together take part in a dialogic process, establishing language use as directly related to distinct discursive functions.

RESULTS

Two examples of classroom discourse are presented in this chapter. The first example presents a brief pupil-teacher interaction illustrating the unmarked use of English and the marked use of Swedish in the Swedish EFL classroom. At the point of observation, the pupils were to have finished reading *Georgie*, a young-adult novel by Malachy Doyle (2001). Leading up to the point of the recording presented in Example 1, the teacher has engaged the pupils in general, but structured, teacher-led discussion. At one point, the teacher poses a question to no one pupil in particular, and indeed no pupil answers, prompting the teacher to select a specific pupil, calling on "Jonas." The transcriptions reflect the recording situation in that focus was directed at achieving "a faithful representation of what is actually said, to the extent that speakers' utterances are not misrepresented and as much information relevant to the analysis is included as is practically possible" (Mercer, 2004, p. 147). In all examples, standard punctuation is used to represent the utterances as grounded in a grammatical organization. A period also denotes a falling intonation, a question mark denotes a rising intonation, and a comma denotes a steady intonation. Exclamation marks denote plosive utterances, and bold type denotes louder volume. English translations of Swedish-language utterances are provided subsequently, denoted by italics, and paralinguistic information is included in parentheses. Names of the pupils have been changed.

Example 1: In English?

1. Teacher: Jonas! Don't you want to say something? Something about the book?
2. Jonas: I don't know what to say because I only read up to page 116.
3. Teacher: What about when he eats breakfast with the group. That happened in the beginning of the section.
4. Jonas: No, I don't think I remember that.
   (silence; the teacher looks around the room)
5. Alice: Finns det en film till det här?
   Is there a movie for this?
6. Teacher: In English?
7. Alice: Mm-hmm.
8. Teacher: No, say it in English.
9. Alice: Ah men! (sighs)
   Oh jeez!
10. Finns det en film till det här?
    Is there a movie for this?
11. Teacher: But say it in English.
12. Alice: Ah men Gud! (addressing her neighbor, Roger). Va' fan ska jag saga?
    Oh God! What the heck should I say?
13. Roger: Is there a movie based on the book?
14. Teacher: Ah! Thank you Roger!
15. Alice: (laughs) Det är min sekretärare!
    That's my secretary!
16. Teacher: We can find out if there's a movie. Are you interested in seeing it?

Example 1 illustrates the status of English in this Swedish, EFL classroom as being the language of instruction. The pupils are expected to interact in this language, and contributions in Swedish are normally not sanctioned by the teacher, by virtue of not being overtly recognized as meaningful. Instead, pupils are prompted to use English, by way of meta-language such as is found in lines 7 and 9. The pupil Alice is clearly resistant to using English as evidenced by her persistent use of Swedish, but her opposing disposition is particularly salient in line 8, where she does not recognize the teacher's metalinguistic prompt, *in English?*, and instead interprets it as a meaningful response to her original question, as if the teacher were inquiring whether Alice wants to see an English-language movie. When Alice understands the goal of the teacher, namely to get Alice to use English, she expresses exasperation, *Ah men Gud/Oh God*, but makes no effort to accommodate the request for rephrasing. In fact, Alice's appeal to her neighbor, Roger, for help suggests an inability to express her question in English. The teacher makes no overt move to prohibit Roger from helping, who indeed provides an acceptable English translation of Alice's question. The teacher immediately acknowledges the contribution and continues the discussion, now directed at gauging interest in seeing a movie version of the book. In this way, the teacher ratifies the content of Alice's original contribution while at the same time establishing zero tolerance for her use of the L1.

The teacher's discourse in Example 1 can be analyzed in terms of Bernstein's (1996) construct of pedagogic discourse. According to Bernstein, discourse that creates and maintains social order serves to regulate the classroom environment; discourse that promotes the acquisition of specialized competencies serves to instruct. In pedagogic discourse, instructive discourse is always embedded in regulatory discourse.

> Pedagogic discourse refers not only to the scientific contents and competences to be transmitted, but also to their transmission and evaluation—that is, it refers to the *what* that is transmitted, *how* it is transmitted, and also which student realizations are considered legitimate. (Morais, 2002, pp. 559-560)

In Example 1, Alice's use of L1 Swedish as a realization of her competence is not recognized as legitimate, and the teacher instructs her to attempt a new realization by prompting *In English?* and *No, say it in English*. It is not until Roger expresses the question in English that the teacher takes up Alice's contribution, incorporating it into the subsequent interaction. In Morais' terms, the *what* is firmly embedded in the *how*. The teacher's own use of English is part and parcel of the pedagogic discourse: it serves both regulatory and instructional purposes. Significantly, the teacher's dominant, regulatory discourse overtly establishes English as the default language of interaction in this EFL classroom, the unmarked (Myers-Scotton, 1983) code of classroom discourse. Example 1 illustrates how pupils' use of the marked code, Swedish L1, is not received as legitimate but overtly regulated.

In Example 2, the teacher's use of Swedish L1 capitalizes on its status as the marked code to perform specific regulatory discursive functions. Prior to the recording of this sequence, the students had just completed a walking tour of the classroom, featuring ten information stations related to various Anglophone cultures. The pupils walked in groups of three from station to station, reading an English-language text accompanied by a picture, and answering one multiple choice question. When each of the ten questions was answered, the pupil groups returned to their seats. Examples 2a-2c present the teacher discourse during the evaluation phase of the activity. During this phase, the teacher allowed the pupils to contribute at will, resulting in many overlapping and unintelligible responses. For this reason, only the teacher's utterances were recorded; general indications of pupils' contributions are provided when relevant. In the interest of space, only extracts of the discourse are presented below; the complete teacher discourse is available in the Appendix.

Example 2a: You can say this in English.

1. The first question. How many states are there?
    (various pupils call out answers in Swedish)
2. You can say this in English.
    (various pupils call out answers in Swedish and English)
3. No, (pause) 52? I don't think so.
    (pupils disagree)

Example 2b: *Ah men tyst!*

17. Okay number three then?
18. Simon?
     (Simon answers "Washington")
19. And what does DC stand for?
     (suggestions from the pupils)
20. No, I think it's District of Columbia.
21. *Ah men **tyst**! Jag hör inte vad Rasmus **säger**.*
     Oh be **quiet**! I can't hear what Rasmus is **say**ing.

Example 2c: *Pratar du hela tiden?*

39. Next one?
40. Jane.
     (private communication among one group of male students, including David)

41.   *Pratar du **hela** tiden David?*
      Do you talk **all** the time David?
      (David responds affirmatively)

42.   Ah, **hela tiden**? *Du måste försöka vara tyst för jag hör inte vad de andra säger.*
      Oh, **all the time**? You have to try to be quiet because I can't hear what the others are **saying**.

The activity begins in Example 2a with the teacher addressing the first of the walking tour questions, and encountering a number of responses in the L1, she immediately regulates the discussion with a prompt, *You can say this in English,* to use the L2 (English), the established code of interaction. The activity then proceeds according to the IRF/IRE sequence, as the teacher systematically works through each of the ten questions.

Like the discourse presented in Example 1, the teacher's activity-based, pedagogic discourse features regulatory and instructive discourse. Each of the IRF/IRE sequences (see, e.g., lines 17-20, 31-35, or 53-55 in the Appendix), represent instructive discourse with regards to the teacher's initiation, selection of pupil to answer, and evaluation of the answer. The instructive discourse is, however, embedded in much regulatory discourse, which in this representative example is often realized as recurring direct addresses of pupils engaged in nonelicited, off-task behavior or interaction. One fourth of the teacher's discourse (twelve utterances: lines 8, 9, 11, 12, 14, 15, 26, 27, 29, 30, 36, 38) is comprised of instances of such direct address that is not for the purpose of eliciting a contribution or response, but rather to discipline the pupil in question. The direct address signals to the pupil to focus his attention to the task and/or cease or rectify his current, off-task behavior.

On two occasions (line 21 and lines 41-42), the regulatory discourse takes on a decidedly disciplinary function, realized via a code-switch. The teacher's abrupt switch to Swedish L1 establishes a significant contrast to the ongoing English-language interaction, and thrusts all of the pupils into a new frame. In triggering the reframing, the code-switch resituates the pupils as participants in a sociocultural context, and reminds them of the norms of social behavior in the classroom environment. Significantly, the code-switch capitalizes on the force of this contrast between codes.

The teacher's deliberate cultivation—by example and by metalinguistic discourse—of English as the unmarked code of interaction in the Swedish EFL classroom establishes a sociocultural aspect of code choice in that shared knowledge of appropriate language use is co-constructed. The teacher's contrastive use of Swedish as the marked code introduces an otherness that allows her to change her footing, performing her role as one who establishes and maintains social order. The code-switch thus serves discourse-related functions, indexing the inappropriateness of the nonelicited verbalizations to the current IRF/IRE frame. The teacher's code-switch is thus in direct response to behavior she finds distracting; it is a culmination of repeated attempts to regulate the speech activity by directly attending to those pupils whose constant and competing verbalizations threaten the structural integrity of the instructional activity and the salience of the instructional discourse.

DISCUSSION

In the sociocultural perspective of the classroom environment, the language use of the pupils and the teacher both reflect and construct the social environment, such that it is co-constructed and vulnerable to the possibility that the instructional goals of the teacher may not always be in line with the social instincts of the pupils. The examples presented in this chapter suggest that in this Swedish, EFL classroom context, the co-construction of the sociocultural environment in terms of establishing and cultivating changes *in* and new patterns of thought and behavior *via* social interaction is an ongoing process. The examples furthermore indicate that some pupils may not be as initiated into the sociocultural environment of the classroom as others. Examples 1 and 2a-2c suggest that the contrast between the unmarked and marked codes can foreground such interpersonal variation, making the sociocultural practices of the classroom salient.

The code-switching examples presented in this chapter illustrate an as yet unexplored function with regards to the sociocultural perspective of classroom discourse. They do not represent a topic-switch, nor do they have an affective, socializing or repetitive function (Mattsson & Burhenhult, 1999; Sert, 2005). They instead contribute directly to establishing the sociocultural norms of classroom behavior and classroom discourse, constructing the "internal structure" of the class as a group, complete with standards for behavior (Dörnei & Murphy, 2004). The teacher's code-switches to Swedish serve to initiate and acculturate the students; they do not have any bearing on the subject instruction. Instead, they serve to break the frame of instruction, thrusting the students into a native-language frame which is more closely associated with the sociocultural context of institutional discourse. By code-switching to Swedish, the teacher asserts the authoritative status awarded her by the institutional context, so as to more effectively regulate the discourse.

*not content based, behavior managment based code-switching

IMPLICATIONS

The focus of the study on a Swedish, seventh grade EFL classroom is against the background of the privileged status English holds in Swedish

what if you can't fluently speak languages of your students?

society. Wide-spread exposure to English in both formal and informal domains, and national efforts to promote the learning of English allow for it to be established as the default code of instruction, the *unmarked code* in Myers-Scotton's (1983, 2001) terminology. English is co-constructed as the unmarked code discursively: the teacher uses English as a mediating tool representing both the means and object of instruction, responding metalinguistically to pupils' use of the marked code, Swedish. The advantages to co-constructively establish an unmarked code extend beyond promotion of the target language, to recognition of the true bilingual context in which the contrastive use of the marked code can be exploited to make a "meta-pragmatic comment on the ongoing interaction" (Auer, 1999, p. 310). The teacher's persistent use of English as instructive discourse in response to the students' use of Swedish establishes a clear linguistic contrast which encourages or even requires the students to acknowledge the teacher's discursive goals by adjusting their own behavior. Similarly, the teacher's sporadic, but nevertheless seemingly predictable, use of Swedish as the language for regulatory discourse creates a linguistic contrast that breaks the frame of the English lesson. The students are reminded of the classroom context and its corresponding rules, norms, and conventions of behavior. The teacher's code choice, including the established practice of code-switching, thus serves to redirect the students' focus, either to actively engaging in the learning and use of English, or to behaving according to the conventions of the institutional context.

APPENDIX I: FULL TRANSCRIPT OF EXAMPLES 2A-2C

Example 2: Ah men tyst! *(Oh be quiet!)*

1. The first question. How many states are there.
   (various pupils call out answers in Swedish)
2. You can say this in English.
3. No, (pause) 52? I don't think so.
   (pupils disagree)
4. Well, we have someone from America here with us. Let's ask her.
   (answer provided)
5. Yes, that's what I thought.
6. Okay next one.
   (several female pupils raise their hands)
7. No. Take it out of your ear.
8. Rasmus. **Rasmus**!
9. Jonaton.

10. (gestures to a female pupil, who answers) Yes.
11. Max!
12. David.
13. (attending to the female pupil's answer) The queen?
     (discussion of who lives at 10 Downing Street)
14. Sebastian, wait please.
15. Simon.
16. The correct answer was Prime Minister. Number two.
17. Okay number three then?
18. Simon?
     (Simon answers "Washington")
19. And what does DC stand for?
     (suggestions from the pupils)
20. No, I think it's District of Columbia.
21. Ah men **tyst**! Jag hör inte vad Rasmus **säger**.
     Oh be quiet! I can't hear what Rasmus is saying.
22. And then there was a question about Halloween.
23. And we-
24. So I guess you- (unintelligible)
     (pupils call out answers)
25. (hearing correct answer) Yes.
26. Max!
27. Anders. **Anders**!
28. Then there was a picture of-
29. David.
30. Jonas **please**.
     (female pupil raises her hand)
31. What is it? (referring to the question; looks around classroom)
32. (attending to pupil who has raised her hand) **Ida!**
     (Ida answers)
33. World Trade Center. The World Trade Center.
34. Good.
35. So that's X.
36. David? David.
     (male pupil asks for a repetition of the answer)
37. World Trade Center.
38. Simon? Simon!
39. Next one?

40. Jane.
     (private communication among one group of male students,
     including David)

41. *Pratar du **hela** tiden David?*
     Do you talk all the time David?
     (David responds affirmatively)

42. Ah, **hela tiden**? Du måste försöka vara tyst för jag hör inte vad de
     andra **säger**.
     Oh, all the time? You have to try to be quiet because I can't hear
     what the others are saying.

43. Ylva, yes.

44. David? Do you know David?

45. The statue on the island?
     (many pupils raise their hands)

46. Anders?
     (Anders answers Statue of Liberty)

47. What is liberty in Swedish?

48. Sebastian?
     (Sebastian answers)

49. What about number nine?

50. Has anyone been to London?
     (some pupils raise their hands)

51. Okay, did you see the square?

52. X, yes. Trafalgar Square.

53. Question ten. That was about the policemen and the strange hats.
     (a female pupil, Jane, raises hand and waves it in the teacher's
     face)

54. Jane!

55. Good. A bobby.

REFERENCES

Auer, P. (1984). *Bilingual conversation*. Amsterdam: John Benjamins.

Auer, P. (1995). The pragmatics of code-switching: A sequential approach. In L.
Milroy & P. Muysken (Eds.), *One speaker, two languages: Cross-disciplinary per-
spectives on code-switching* (pp. 115-135). Cambridge, England: Cambridge
University Press.

Auer, P. (1999). From codeswitching via language mixing to fused lects: Toward a
dynamic typology of bilingual speech. *International Journal of Bilingualism*,
3(4), 309-332.

Bernstein, B. (1971). *Class, codes and control I: Theoretical studies towards a sociology of language*. London: Routledge & Kegan Paul.

Bernstein, B. (1996). *Pedagogy, symbolic control and ideology: Theory, research, critique*. Bristol, PA: Taylor & Francis.

Cazden, C. (1988). *Classroom discourse: The language of teaching and learning*. Portsmouth, NH: Heinemann.

Dörnei, Z., & Murphy, T. (2004). *Group dynamics in the language classroom*. Cambridge, England: Cambridge University Press.

Doyle, M. (2001). *Georgie*. New York, NY: Bloomsbury.

Erickson, F. (1979). *On standards of descriptive validity in studies of classroom activity*. (Occasional Paper #16). East Lansing, MI: Institute for Research on Teaching.

Gee, J. P., & Green, J. (1998). Discourse analysis, learning and social practice: A methodological study. *Review of Research in Education, 23*, 119-69.

Gumperz, J. J. (1982). *Discourse strategies*. Cambridge, England: Cambridge University Press.

Gumperz, J. J., & Hymes, D. (1972). *Directions in sociolinguistics: The ethnography of communication*. New York, NY: Holt, Rinehart & Winston.

Gutiérrez, A. G. (2008). Microgenesis, method and object: A study of collaborative activity in a Spanish as a foreign language classroom. *Applied Linguistics, 29*(1), 120-148.

Halliday, M.A.K. (1978). *Language as social semiotic: The social interpretation of language and meaning*. London: Arnold.

Heller, M. (1988). *Codeswitching: Anthropological and sociolinguistic perspectives*. Berlin. Germany: Mouton de Gruyter.

Heigham, J., & Croker, R. (2009). *Qualitative research in applied linguistics*. Basingstoke: Palgrave.

Hicks, D. (1995). Discourse, learning, and teaching. In M. W. Apple (Ed.), *Review of research in education, 21*, 49-95. Washington, DC: American Educational Research Association.

Hymes, D. (1972). On communicative competence. In J. B. Pride & J. Holmes (Eds.), *Sociolinguistics* (pp. 269-293). London: Penguin.

Hymes, D. (1995). *Education, linguistics, narrative inequality.* London: Taylor & Francis.

Luke, A. (1995). Text and discourse in education: An introduction to critical discourse analysis. In M. W. Apple (Ed.), *Review of research in education, 21*, 3-48. Washington, DC: American Educational Research Association.

Mattsson, A., & Burenhult, N. (1999). Code-switching in second language teaching of French. *Working papers, 47*, 59-72.

Mehan, H. (1979). *Learning lessons: Social organization in the classroom*. Cambridge, MA: Harvard University Press.

Mercer, N. (1995). *The guided construction of knowledge*. Clevedon, England: Multilingual Matters.

Mercer, N. (2004). Sociocultural discourse analysis: Analyzing classroom talk as a social mode of thinking. *Journal of Applied Linguistics, 1*, 137-168.

Morais, A. (2002). Basil Bernstein at the micro level of the classroom. *British Journal of Sociology of Education, 23*(4), 559-569.

Myers-Scotton, C. (1983). The negotiation of identities in conversation: A theory of markedness and code choice. *International Journal of the Sociology of Language, 44,* 115-136.

Myers-Scotton, C. (1993). *Social motivations for codeswitching: Evidence from Africa.* Oxford, England: Clarendon Press.

Myers-Scotton, C. (2001). The matrix language frame model: Developments and responses. In R. Jacobson (Ed.), *Trends in linguistics. Codeswitching worldwide II.* Berlin, Germany: Walter de Gruyter.

Nilep, C. (2006). "Code switching" in sociocultural linguistics. *Colorado Research in Linguistics, 19,* 1-22.

Nystrand, M. (2006). Research on the role of classroom discourse as it affects reading comprehension. *Research in the Teaching of English, 40,* 392-412.

Phillipson , R. (1992). *Linguistic Imperialism.* Oxford, England: Oxford University Press.

Sert, O. (2005). The functions of code-switching in ELT classrooms. *The Internet TESL Journal.* Retrieved http://iteslj.org.Articles/Sert-CodeSwitching.html.

Sharp, H. (2007). Swedish-English language mixing. *World Englishes,26,* 224-240.

Sinclair, J., & Coulthard, M. (1975). *Towards an analysis of discourse: The English used by teachers and pupils.* London: Oxford University Press.

Spindler, G., & Spindler, L. (1987). *Interpretive ethnography of education: At home and abroad* (Eds.). Hillsdale, NJ: Erlbaum.

Stubbs, M. (1976). *Language, schools and classrooms.* London: Methuen.

Swain, M., & Lapkin, S. (2000). Task-based second language learning: The uses of the first language. *Language Teaching Research, 43,* 251-274.

Vygotsky, L. S. (1978). *Mind in society: The development of higher psychological processes.* Cambridge, MA: Harvard University Press.

Vygotsky, L. S. (1986). *Thought and language* (A. Kozulin, trans.). Cambridge, MA: MIT Press. (Original work published 1934)

Wells, G. (1993). The complimentary contributions of Halliday and Vygotsky to a "language-based theory of learning." *Linguistics and Education, 6,* 41-90.

CHAPTER 6

HOW DO TEACHERS PARTICIPATE, MEDIATE, AND INTERVENE IN THE CO-CONSTRUCTION OF LANGUAGE KNOWLEDGE DURING LEARNER INTERACTIONS?

Melinda Martin-Beltrán

Applying a sociocultural theoretical lens, this chapter examines the teacher's role in socially mediated language learning processes that occur during student interactions. Drawing from data collected during a year-long ethnographic study in a dual language elementary school, findings in this chapter focus on how teachers' discourse and instructional decisions influence students' opportunities for language learning. Discursive analysis of learner and teacher interactions and patterns identified in teaching practices over time offer insight to teachers who seek to create a context for language learning among students. Examples from classroom practices illustrate how teachers model languaging and how teachers decide when and how to intervene productively in peer interactions. Findings from this study can inform teacher education as we apply a sociocultural theoretical lens to encourage teacher-learners to become more aware of the opportunities for language learning afforded during dialogic interactions.

Teachers' Roles in Second Language Learning:
Classroom Applications of Sociocultural Theory, pp. 99–118
Copyright © 2012 by Information Age Publishing
All rights of reproduction in any form reserved.

I plan collaborative activities to give students the chance to interact and ask each other questions, but I'm still trying to figure out how I should step in, as their teacher, to push their thinking about language

(Interview with Ms. F, dual-language elementary teacher)

In the quote above, the teacher expresses a common concern among second-language teachers. Although teachers seem to understand the importance of student interaction in theory, many still wonder what teachers can do to mediate, participate, or intervene in these interactions. This chapter begins to address these questions by synthesizing lessons learned during a year-long ethnographic study observing three veteran teachers and their students in a dual language Spanish/English elementary school. This chapter offers insight to teachers through the analysis of student interactions and a synthesis of teacher mediational strategies that afford language learning opportunities in student-centered classrooms. Although the teachers in this study continued to have many questions, they provided helpful examples of teaching practices that successfully mediated and fostered language learning opportunities (as defined by sociocultural theory). While it is also important to recognize teachers' discursive and social practices that constrain language learning and often preclude students from further participation in learning activities, this chapter is intended to inform teachers who are seeking helpful strategies that can mediate learning; therefore, findings here focus on learning affordances (for a discussion of learning constraints, see Martin-Beltran, 2010b).

LITERATURE REVIEW

Interaction among learners has been a central topic of research in Second Language Acquisition (SLA), which has informed language education practices (see Gass, 1997; Hatch, 1992; Long, 1996; Mackey, 2007; Pica, 1994; Swain, 1985). This research, which began with an emphasis on cognitive or computational models of SLA that view interaction as activating individual, self-contained psycholinguistic acquisition processes (Ellis, 2005), has shifted to incorporate a sociocultural turn in our understanding of SLA (Block, 2003). Based on the work of Vygotsky (1978) who proposed a dialectic relationship between cognitive processes and social context (including the use of cultural artifacts such as language), there is a growing body of research that has given more attention to the social mediation of learning during interaction (Donato, 2000; Foster & Ohta, 2005; Lantolf, 2000; Swain, 2000, 2006; Swain & Deters, 2007; Swain,

Kinnear, & Steinman, 2010). Sociocultural theoretical approaches have opened up new perspectives of interaction research that shed light on *microgenesis* (Lantolf & Thorne, 2006; Vygotsky, 1978), or the moment-by-moment processes of language learning unfolding during the interactions. Much of this research applying a sociocultural theoretical lens has focused on the learners' mediation of learning for each other during interactions; with little attention to the teacher's role in these peer interactions. As Tocalli-Beller and Swain (2007) write, "Second language learning research informed by a sociocultural theory of mind situates second language learning in the dialogic interactions between learners and learners, learners and themselves and learners and the artifacts available in their world" (p. 145). The teacher's role in these interactions has often been neglected in this research; thus, it is evident that more research is needed to understand how teachers may be coparticipants or mediators in dialogic interaction among students. This chapter addresses this gap in the research by looking more closely at the teacher's role in the socially mediated learning processes that occur during interactions that, until now, have been peer-peer focused.

This study employs a sociocultural conceptual framework, influenced by the work of Vygotsky (1978) and scholars who have applied this work to second language educational contexts (Donato, 2000; Engeström, 1987; Foster & Ohta, 2005; Lantolf, 2000; Sannino, Daniels, & Gutierrez, 2009; Swain, 2000, 2006; Swain, Kinnear, & Steinman, 2010). This framework shifts the focus of SLA from the individual learner to the social activity of learning, situated in cultural and historical contexts. Thus, language learning, in this study, is conceptualized as a collaborative process and interaction is examined as an opportunity for learners and teachers to co-construct language competence.

In order to examine this interactional process, I draw upon theoretical constructs from sociocultural theory such as the zone of proximal development (Lantolf & Aljaafreh, 1995; Ohta, 1995; Vygotsky, 1978), Third Space (Gutiérrez, 2008), expansive learning (Engeström, 1987), co-construction (Foster & Ohta, 2005), collaborative dialogue (Swain, 2000), and languaging (Swain, 2000, 2006; Tocalli-Beller & Swain, 2007). To complement this framework informed by a sociocultural theory of the mind, I draw upon ethnographic work that has highlighted the importance of building upon learners' funds of knowledge (González, Moll, & Amanti, 2005; Moll, 2010) as part of the learning ecology. This social ecology is viewed not simply as the context for learning, but the source of learning (van Lier, 2000). It is not within the scope of this chapter to fully review the research that has developed each of these sociocultural theoretical constructs; rather, I will briefly operationalize these terms in order to explain how this conceptual framework guided this study.

The sociocultural concept of *funds of knowledge* acknowledges the experiences, practices and historically accumulated bodies of knowledge that exist in students' households, which are often undervalued at school (Gonzalez, 1995; Moll, 2010; Vélez-Ibáñez & Greenberg, 1992). Identifying and mobilizing funds of knowledge has been shown to shape teachers' perceptions and offer additive pedagogical practices that build upon what students bring to school (Moll, 2010; Moll, Amanti, Neff, & Gonzalez, 1992). This study builds upon this work and Smith's (2001) definition of linguistic funds of knowledge that focuses more specifically on what students know about their language(s).

As I discuss the examples of classroom interactions below, I draw upon the work of Gutiérrez (2008) and Engeström (1987) who expand the construct of zone of proximal/potential development (ZPD) to suggest that *expansive learning* can reach beyond a bounded zone, when participants construct new knowledge that doesn't exist at the onset of the activity. These scholars explain that the collective ZPD, or the *Third Space*, does not reside in any of the individual participants in the activity, but is a collective learning space that is constituted through interaction as participants co-construct knowledge together.

Related to this collective ZPD, I also draw upon research examining *collaborative dialogue* (Swain, 2000; Swain & Lapkin, 2000) as a window into the mediational processes of learners and teachers working together to co-construct knowledge about language. To analyze the interactional discourse in this study, I operationalize *co-construction* drawing upon Foster and Ohta's (2005) definition as:

> joint creation of an utterance, whether one person completes what another has begun, or whether various people chime in to create an utterance. Co-constructions are seen as allowing learners to participate in forming utterances that they cannot complete individually, building language skills in the process. (p. 420)

This study also applies Swain's (2006) construct of *languaging* to describe the ways the learners talk about language and use language as a sociocultural tool to mediate and enhance their learning. There is a growing body of research that examines the importance of languaging in the process of learning a second language (Knouzi, Swain, Lapkin, & Brooks, 2010; Swain & Deters, 2007), and this study will explore ways that teachers can encourage such languaging in their classrooms.

In sum, sociocultural research has suggested that languaging, co-construction of knowledge across peers, and the mobilization of learners' linguistic funds of knowledge may enhance language learning; yet, more research is needed to understand how teachers can support these processes in their classroom. In this study, sociocultural theory provides a lens to understand learners' microgenesis of language development during interactions and a lens to examine and guide teachers' participation in the interactions.

METHODOLOGY

Research Setting and Participants

The data presented in this chapter came from an in-depth year-long study carried out in a dual immersion bilingual school located in central California. The student body was 90% Latino (including recent immigrants and U.S. born children), 10% White and mixed heritage students, 75% English language learners, and 87% received reduced or free lunch. The school used a 90/10 dual language program where students began with 90% of their instruction in Spanish in kindergarten, and reached a 50/50 split of instruction in Spanish and English by the fifth grade, which was the focal grade for the data collection due to the equal time given to both languages for instruction.

In an interview with the school principal, he explained that qualified teachers were central to accomplishing the school's mission. All teachers were expected to be bilingual and were required to have their BCLAD[1] or an equivalent bilingual teaching credential. Teachers at each grade level were encouraged to plan in teams since they often shared the same students across different languages. The fifth grade class had three veteran teachers: two Spanish-model teachers (Mr. K and Ms. F) in the morning and an English-model teacher (Ms. G) in the afternoon. All teachers participated in on-going professional development to implement the dual language educational model at their school and expressed their commitment to developing bilingualism and biliteracy. Mr. K had ten years of teaching experience, Ms. F had 7 years of experience, and Ms. G had been teaching for over 20 years in linguistically diverse classrooms. Interviews with teachers revealed that they had chosen this school because of its strong bilingual program and commitment to improving the education of language minority students.

Data Collection

The research methodologies for this study were modeled after ethnographic and sociolinguistic studies that include participant observation, interviews and audio recordings of classroom discourse (Freeman, 1998; Harklau, 1994; Palmer, 2009; Valdés, 2001). Following guidelines for interpretive inquiry, ethnography and participant observation (Creswell, 2007; Emerson, Fretz, & Shaw, 1995; Hammersley & Atkinson, 1995; Miles & Huberman, 1994), fieldwork included intensive long-term participation in the school, careful recording and documentation (field notes, observation protocols, event maps, student work, transcription of digital audio and video recordings) as well as ongoing analysis during the data collection process.

I visited the school two to three times a week (staying most of the school day) from August to June (the academic year). Field notes included detailed descriptions of teacher and student interactions, and language related discussions were flagged (see definition of LREs below). I used event maps to track language patterns over time and across contexts (see Martin-Beltran, 2010b). To capture data at the whole class and small group level, audio recorders were placed on students' desks supplemented by a video camera in the corner of the room. All audio and video recordings were accompanied by detailed field notes (completed daily) and analytical memos, which served to identify areas for more detailed transcriptions and shape further data collection. Throughout the school year, I engaged in ongoing conversations with the teachers who shared their reflections about their teaching while I shared my observations and asked them how they would interpret the language related discussions that I had flagged in my field notes and transcriptions. I formally interviewed the teachers twice, at the beginning and end of the school year. At their second interview and in follow up e-mails, I engaged in member-checking of my preliminary findings and interpretations.

Data Analysis

I coded the transcriptions of classroom interactions for "language related episodes" (LREs), which Swain and Lapkin (1998) define as "any part of a dialogue where the students talk about the language they are producing, question their language use, or correct themselves or others" (p. 326). LREs served as a unit of analysis to link cognitive and sociocultural aspects of language learning by shedding light on sociocultural dimensions of communication successes, innovations and co-construction of language in interactions (Foster & Ohta, 2005; Tocalli-Beller & Swain, 2007). This analysis focused on LREs as *opportunities* or *contexts* for *potential* language learning, when language competence was explicitly discussed and simultaneously constructed. I found that the teacher played a key role mediating these opportunities for learning; therefore, I returned to the data set to look more closely at teachers' discursive moves within the LREs.

Teachers' meditational practices were the central phenomena to guide axial and selective coding (Creswell, 2009; Strauss & Corbin, 2008) of the larger data set of field notes and classroom discourse recordings. At the stage of axial coding, I identified patterns in teachers' practices of mediation that called attention to language. During selective coding I grouped these codes and examples of teacher practices into larger, thematic categories such as: (1) creating a classroom context, (2) modeling, and (3) intervention. The larger categories that emerged will be explained in the findings section below.

From my classroom observations and preliminary analysis of the audio recordings, I identified activities that promoted the most LREs, which usually involved the creation and revision of written text. The examples of dialogic interaction selected for this chapter come from a writing activity, and these examples represent the content and kind of speech from the larger sample of LREs found throughout my observations and include the teacher as the key interlocutor. The excerpts below are splices of interactions during a joint writing activity when students cowrote letters to a relative, one during English and the other during Spanish instructional time. The teachers required students to switch roles as the writer every couple of sentences, and encouraged students to "write out loud" so their writing partner could hear what they were writing during the composition process. After the letter writing activity, teachers asked students to complete self-evaluation rubrics about collaboration, which guided the students to reflect on their collaboration. For this chapter, I have chosen two excerpts from four students (2 dyads) who represent a range of language proficiencies and literacy levels. The first excerpt occurred with the English teacher during English instructional time, the second excerpt occurred with the Spanish teacher during Spanish instructional time.

FINDINGS

Throughout the school year, I observed several occasions where students and their teachers were successfully engaged in collaborative dialogue and languaging (Swain, 2006). In order to illustrate how languaging, teacher strategies of modelling, and intervention play out in the classroom, this chapter presents two excerpts from video recorded student and teacher interactions. These excerpts do not stand alone; rather, they were given meaning and importance by the utterances that came before and after (Bakhtin, 1981); and they provide a window into the classroom culture that was co-constructed by teachers and students throughout the year.

The examples below demonstrate the linguistic and metacognitive accomplishments of the students and their teachers as they cultivated a rich context for languaging and expanded opportunities for language learning. For the purposes of this chapter, I foreground the teacher's role and the context that afforded co-construction and recognition of learners' distinct linguistic funds of knowledge (Moll et al., 1992, Smith, 2001). I found that teachers were key mediators in this learning process by creating context, modelling, and intervention. The findings presented below first illustrate the microanalysis of moment-to-moment mediation occurring during two dialogic interactions and next, explain patterns of teaching mediation observed across the year.

Asking Questions Across Languages Inspires Co-construction and Transformation

The language related episode in *Excerpt 1* occurred when Daniel and Javier were discussing scary experiences related to their letter, and the teacher participated by asking further questions. As Daniel wrote the word "nightmares" and read it out loud, the students and teacher began languaging and co-constructing linguistic knowledge as they began to discuss the meaning and structure of words.

Example 1[2]

1.   **Daniel:** 'But he didn't have nightmares' [Daniel writes, reading out loud] ....Why do they call them nightmares if they're not - night mirrors?

2.   **Ms. G:** That's a good question!

3.   **Javier:** That's a scientist ::[inaudible overlap]...mirror::

4.   **Daniel:** Yeah, I've been thinking since like 5 years old... mirrors

5.   **Ms. G:** Do you think they're like a mirror of what you've seen all day?

6.   **Daniel:** Yeah...

Once I watched a movie and... there was this garden and this lady wanted to save the kids... the movie was called 'The Haunting'. In the garden she saw somebody hanging from the top, the kid... and she was like [drops his jaw, slaps his hands on cheeks] @@

7.   **Javier :** @@

8.   **Daniel:** And then all the other people were like ahh! ... And when I went to sleep I had a nightmare. You know how flashing stuff like... scares you?

9.   **Javier:** Oh flashing like... flashing through your eyes?

10.   **Daniel:** Like shoom, shoom, that happened to me and I was like sweating!

11.   **Javier:** Ok, My turn my turn!

One time, at night it was the middle of the woods or something

12.   **Daniel:** Oooooh [pretending to be scared]

13.   **Javier:** I was hiding. Here's like the tree, I was hiding like that [with the pencil demonstration and the eraser behind the tree]

there was a ghost floating like that.... I turned back , he said boo! I ran but I couldn't run that fast because it was an escalator. Then some dead people rised up from the ground and I waked up... It was like one in the morning and I could not sleep anymore! It was a bad nightmare!

14.   **Ms. G:** That sounds scary. So it's called nightmare in English. How do you say it in Spanish?

15.   **Daniel:** Un neetmare [trying to use Spanish phonology]

16.   **Javier:** No no.... *"Sueño mal"*   {bad dream} or something like that... or pesa... oh yeah, ::*"pesadilla"*:: [overlap with Daniel]

17.   **Daniel:** *Pensamiento?* {thought}

18.   **Javier:** No, *pesadilla* {nightmare}

19.   **Daniel:** Oh yeah, *"pesos"*... Oh I know *"pesa"* like your *"día"* was *"pesado"*

{Oh yeah *"weights"* Oh I know like *"to weigh"* like your *"day"* was *"hard/heavy"*}

20.   **Javier:** *"Dia"* like hard day, *"pesado dia"* like *"pesa...dia"*

{*"Day"* like hard day, *"heavy day"* like *nightmare*}

21.   **Daniel:** Oh! ...I think I know what 'mare' means, it's like a schmare... is like something scary that doesn't really happen, but you believe in it!

22.   **Both:** @@@ [they both laugh]

In this excerpt we can see how *languaging*, recognition of learners' linguistic funds of knowledge, and co-construction of language expertise unfolds in this interaction between students and teacher. First, the teacher recognized and affirmed Daniel's rhetorical question about nightmares as a "good question," despite the fact that this could be considered off-task behavior. Javier joined the teacher's affirmation when he described his partner as a "scientist." This comment was linked to previous classroom discourse. I observed Ms. G and Ms. F repeatedly emphasizing that good scientists ask good questions, which is a key strategy these teacher used to create a context for languaging and learning in their classrooms across the school year. Ms. G's validation of Daniel's question opened a space for language play, and she followed up with further questioning to deepen his semantic and etymological analysis. The teacher allowed the students to elaborate their understanding of the word nightmare with their vivid descriptions of personal experiences, and she expanded the space for language play across languages when she asked them to draw upon their linguistic funds of knowledge in Spanish.

When the teacher asked them how to say nightmare in Spanish, the boys collaboratively engaged in word analysis, co-constructing their knowledge across languages. They used Spanish and English as mediational tools and objects for analysis (Vygotsky, 1978). For example, they began by breaking down the word "*pesadilla*" into smaller parts for analysis. Together the students deduced that *pesadilla* must come from the words, "*pesado*" and "*dia*" and transformed this into the phrase for "hard day." In this interactional space, Daniel verbalized his analysis (and externalized his learning) and his partner, Javier, extended this analysis. Daniel and Javier's back and forth storytelling and animated discussion illustrated many instances of co-constructions as defined by Foster and Ohta (2005).

The teacher supported this Third Space (Gutiérrez, 2008; Gutiérrez, Baquedano-López, & Tejeda, 1999) for expansive learning when they crossed over into Spanish to engage in metalinguistic analysis and returned to English with new observations and hypotheses about word meaning. They invented a new word to represent an abstract concept that seemed beyond words, as they described "something scary that doesn't really happen, but you believe in it." The teacher allowed for expansive learning (Engeström, 1987) and nurtured this Third Space to play with language, in which students had time to elaborate and build upon their curiosity about language to generate new, unexpected knowledge.

This excerpt also illuminates the ways that teachers can mobilize students' diverse funds of knowledge within one classroom activity. Daniel brought his expertise and curiosity about English when he began to analyze the word nightmare, and he drew upon his prior classroom experiences searching for cognates to try to apply these rules to produce "neetmare." Javier drew upon his funds of knowledge in Spanish to correct Daniel's translation as he provided the more precise word, *pesadilla*, embedded in a meaningful context, which led to further co-construction of language knowledge. Without Javier's expertise, Daniel would not have expanded his Spanish vocabulary to include *pesadilla*, nor would they have reached their new level of insight about the word nightmare. The students

[handwritten margin note: letting/encouraging students to figure out together]

[handwritten margin note: students scaffolding each other's learning]

combined their funds of knowledge to generate new understanding, argu-
ably greater understanding than either could have accomplished alone.

In sum, this excerpt illustrates how the teacher created a context where
linguistic funds of knowledge are mobilized as she modeled curiosity
about language. The teacher's questions or intervention served as scaffolding within their ZPD directing students' attention to language and co-
constructing knowledge with them. The teacher afforded space for students to ask each other, rather than simply providing the words for them.
This was an unexpected opportunity for language learning that was not in
the teacher's lesson plan. Instead, the teacher allowed for a transformation of the goals of the activity as she was aware of the students' language
acquisition process on the fly (or in the microgenesis in the moment) and
attended to the ways that students asked questions. When reflecting on
this lesson, the teacher explained that she had not planned to use Spanish
nor had she planned for students to compare root words across languages, but the students showed curiosity and the teacher played a key
role nurturing that curiosity. The teacher seized this opportunity that
emerged from the students and pushed them into the upper limits of
their collective ZPD.

[Handwritten margin notes: teacher role, support, allow, go where lesson takes you.]

Inspiring Deeper Thinking about Word Choice and Expanding the ZPD

In the next excerpt the two boys were re-reading the letter that they
had co-written to Johnny's cousin. As Lorenzo began reading aloud, he
initiated an LRE when he paused and turned to his partner and teacher
to ask if they should refine their word choice. The teacher plays a key role
in this interaction as she expanded her students' collective ZPD.

Excerpt 2

Original Utterance	English Gloss (when needed) [actions and comments in brackets]
1. **Lorenzo:** 'Querido Miguel'	'Dear Miguel' [Reading the written letter aloud]
Estimado mejor ¿no?	Better to say esteemed, no?
2. **Ms. F:** Depende de … ¿qué crees?	*It depends … what do you think?* [looking at Johnny]

(Excerpt 2 continues on next page)

Excerpt 2 continued

Original Utterance	**English Gloss (when needed)** [actions and comments in brackets]
3. Lorenzo: ¿Lo quieres mucho, mucho, mucho? … … o 'estimado'	*Do you really, really, really love him?*… [asking Johnny] … Or … *'esteemed'*
4. Johnny: Estimado	*Esteemed*
5. Ms. F: ¿Por qué? Tu crees que estimado es más como--?::	*Why? Do you think esteemed is more like…?*
6. Johnny ::I don't know.	
7. Lorenzo: Porque querido suena como más…. Como…	*Because dear sounds more like … like…*
8. Ms. F: ¿Con quien usas querido?	*With whom do you use 'dear'?*
9. Lorenzo: Como querido … como con ::tu mama::	*Like dear … like with your mom*
10. Johnny: :: Como con alguien que quieres? ¿O amo? ::	*Like with someone you like ? … or I love?*
11. Ms. F:::: ¿Con tumamá?::	*With your mother?*
12. Johnny I <u>like</u> my cousin!	
13. Ms. F: Entonces ¿Martín es un primo querido para ti?	*So, Martin is a dear [close] cousin for you?*
14. Lorenzo: Mejor … xxx	*Better..xxx*
15. Johnny: Yeah	[Jonny nods and they decide to leave 'querido' on paper. Lorenzo goes on to read the next sentence]

The student initiated this LRE as he reflected on his partner's word choice and asked his teacher if they should change the word. To promote further languaging, the teacher did not give a simple yes/no response that might have precluded any further discussion. Instead, she brought forward the idea of contextual dependence of word choice, when she said, "it depends … what do you think?" Ms. F promoted co-construction of knowledge between the peers when she redirected the question to Lorenzo's peer, Johnny. The teacher's model of asking questions seemed to inspire Lorenzo to ask further questions about context and the author's relationship with the intended audience of the letter. At first Johnny was quick to agree with Lorenzo and simply accept his revision to "*estimado.*" However, once again, the teacher intervened to ask more reflective questions about language usage and appropriateness. When Johnny responded, "I don't know," Ms. F continued to encourage Johnny to participate as she pushed out the boundaries of this collective ZPD. This interaction illustrated how "determining a learner's ZPD is an act of negotiated discovery that is realized through dialogic interaction between learner and expert. In other words, the learner and expert engage each other in an attempt to discover precisely what the learner is able to achieve without help and what the learner can accomplish with assistance" (Lantolf & Aljaafreh, 1995, p. 620). As the teacher built upon Jonny's knowledge, she mediated his learning when she scaffolded or rephrased her question. Since Johnny could not answer her first probing question, she tried adjusting her question to one she knew he could answer. Rather than simply accept Johnny's "I don't know" as a failed response, she offered other mediating tools to think through this linguistic problem together.

[handwritten margin note: to mediating learning through questioning]

Although the text was not modified, their discussion about language afforded a learning opportunity to analyze word choice and consider the ways that language signifies social relationships. The teacher was a key mediator to push forward this collaborative dialogue that raised all participants' awareness of the connection between language and social context. Without the teacher's intervention in this interaction, it is unlikely that the boys would have engaged in *languaging* or social analysis, co-constructed in this moment. The teacher drew upon these students' funds of knowledge to create an opportunity to learn about what word choice may signal, and how to evaluate appropriateness. This was also an example of a collaborative ZPD (Gutierrez, 2008) that was not dependent solely on teacher knowledge, but was co-constructed with the students who were able to draw upon their own prior experiences in social communication outside the school, not available in many traditional, monolingual classrooms.

Patterns in Teaching Practices that Mediate Language Learning Opportunities

The excerpts analyzed above are representative of interactions observed throughout the year that inspired LREs and languaging. From field notes and recordings collected across teaching and learning contexts, I identified patterns and features of teaching practices that created affordances for languaging. In analyzing the pedagogical value of interactional contexts, I coded teaching practices that cooccurred with LREs and therefore cultivated a space for enhanced language learning. This section of the chapter synthesizes the findings from this analysis from which three broad categories of teacher meditational practices emerged: (1) creating a context, (2) modeling, and (3) intervention (see Table 6.1). Table 6.1 was generated as a heuristic to illustrate how sociocultural theory is applied in teaching practices, focusing specifically on social mediation of language learning. In the second column definitions of teachers' meditational practices are operationalized, and the third column offers concrete examples of teaching practices from findings to show how teachers can apply principles of sociocultural theory to their practices as they seek to mediate student learning. The examples of teaching discourse in the third column include quotes excerpted from field notes and composites of recorded teacher discourse found in transcripts.

Table 6.1.   Teaching Strategies That Mediate Students' Language Learning Opportunities

Teacher Practices of Mediation	Description	Examples of Teaching Practices & cLassroom Discourse
1. Creating classroom context for languaging	• Encourage the use of students' home languages (and target languages) as tools for academic problem solving • Recognize students' distinct linguistic funds of knowledge • Position students as experts, potential teachers, and ongoing learners • Cultivate curiosity about language • Create a space for language play across multiple languages • Promote co-construction/ collaboration as part of the classroom culture	• Create learning experiences that require multiple voices and encourage participants to draw upon their different strengths in different languages • Arrange students in flexible, collaborative groups to engage in learning activities that require co-construction among students with diverse linguistic funds of knowledge • Create language-rich environment with comparisons across languages (i.e. ongoing cognate lists posted on bulletin board) • Use bilingual discourse and recognize students who draw upon bilingual resources • Create group-worthy activities and establish guidelines for collaboration
2. Modeling	• Ask questions about language • Ask students for help with language • Show how mistakes can be opportunities to learn • Model co-writing and revision processes (manipulate text and try out different language) • Model "think alouds" about language	*Examples of teacher discourse* • I wonder why this language is....? • How would you say...? • I made a mistake here, could you help me learn how to correct it? • I don't think this sounds right, how could I say this better? • I noticed that we say ___ in English, in my home language we say___ • I wonder why we should use this kind of language here

| 3. Intervention in peer interactions | • Ask students to think about cross-linguistic comparisons in pairs

• Ask reflective questions about language usage and appropriateness as students produce language

• Encourage students to listen and paraphrase what their peers say

• Redirect questions to peers

• Offer strategies to solve linguistic problems

• Evaluate student collaboration explicitly | *Examples of teacher discourse*
• How would you and your partner say this in your home language/target language?

• When/why do you use that word?

• How else could you express that?

• Can your partner help with this?

• Show your partner what you mean (use gestures or drawings to inquire about language)

• Use rubrics that highlight collaboration as part of self- and teacher-evaluation |

The first category, *creating classroom context for languaging,* describes the ways that a teacher creates a culture of collaboration and multilingualism in her classroom. This category is based on the sociocultural proposition that the social context is not only the setting but also a source for learning (Vygotsky, 1978; van Lier, 2000). The excerpts described above were made possible within a context that afforded peer collaboration and co-construction. For example, the teacher provided guidelines for collaboration during peer revisions, required students to evaluate their group's learning and cooperation, and she also placed priority on cooperation during her own evaluation of student work. A teacher constructs a context for languaging as she makes choices about the language of instruction and the languages that are sanctioned for use among students. The teacher who supports languaging uses multiple languages as academic tools, recognizes students' distinct language expertise, and creates activities that allow for co-construction. Valuing languages as resources is also reflected in the environmental print and use of languages to mediate academic learning. For example, the teachers I observed posted ongoing lists of cognates on their bulletin boards that were co-constructed with students. Other instructional decisions, which constitute this context, include creating group-worthy tasks (Cohen, 1994) that require students to draw upon their diverse linguistic funds of knowledge. For example, I observed most opportunities for languaging when students coauthored texts, used bilingual resources to solve problems, and played with both languages to compare meaning.Flexible grouping that allowed students multiple opportunities to be positioned as both experts and learners offered greater affordances for language development (see Martin-Beltran, 2010b). Research has shown that using and hearing more than one language to engage in academic tasks offers additional language learning affordances, as languages become tools for mediation and analysis in cross-linguistic comparisons (Martin-Beltran, 2009, 2010a).

The second category of teacher strategies for mediation, *modeling*, captures the ways that teachers encourage languaging by engaging in languaging themselves. Findings demonstrated that when teachers publicly asked questions about language, positioning themselves as learners, students were more likely to engage in languaging with each other (see Martin-Beltran, 2010a). For example, by using "think alouds" teachers modeled their metacognitive processes or metalinguistic analysis of language, and they often framed mistakes as opportunities to learn. Teachers who showed curiosity about language as a constant topic of inquiry in the classroom engaged students in more instances of languaging. Throughout the year, I observed the teacher asking questions about language and drawing upon students' funds of knowledge thereby legitimizing students as co-constructors of knowledge.

The third category of teacher mediation, *intervention in peer interactions*, identified different ways that teachers play a part in the co-construction of knowledge during dialogic interaction, often pushing students forward in their zone of proximal development. Even in a student-centered classroom where peer interaction and peer feedback is emphasized, teacher intervention is important to redirect or call attention to language learning affordances that students' may overlook. Teachers in this study were found to be key mediators between students who were learning languages from each other. As students were involved in joint activities, teachers asked questions and redirected peers to ask questions of each, often stretching the students' collective zone of proximal development. Knowing when *not* to intervene in interactions was also important to allow students the space to problem solve and co-construct knowledge with their peers, thus amplifying language learning opportunities for both expert and novice students. A teacher's choice to remain silent during student interactions was often as important as her interjections in the dialogue.

IMPLICATIONS FOR RESEARCH AND PRACTICE

This study contributes to the field of second language education research by applying a sociocultural lens to shed light on the ways that teachers can create a classroom context and be involved in student interactions to guide and promote language learning opportunities. This study has implications for teachers who seek concrete teaching practices that can support sociocultural principles of second language learning. The analysis of student and teacher interactions presented in this chapter provides a window into the complex process of languaging (Swain, 2006), co-constructing knowledge (Foster & Ohta, 2005), and expanding the collective ZPD (Engeström, 1987; Gutiérrez, 2008). Although much SLA research has discussed the importance of peer interaction for language learning (Long, 1983, 1996; Mackey, 2007) and scholarship has suggested instructional methods that incorporate interactive learning activities (Brown, 2007; Long & Doughty, 2009; Richards & Rodgers, 2001), little research has provided a close analysis of how teachers may intervene or play a mediating role in that interaction. Findings from this chapter fill that gap and contribute to second language teachers' knowledge base.

The micro-analysis of learner and teacher interactions and patterns identified in teacher practices over time presented in this chapter offer teachers insights about how to create a context for language learning, how to model languaging, and how to decide when and how to intervene productively in peer interactions. Findings from this study can inform teacher education as we apply a sociocultural theoretical lens to encourage teacher-learners to become more aware of the opportunities for language learning afforded during dialogic interactions. The findings synthesized in Table 6.1 offer a framework for analysis or point of departure for further discussion and questions about teaching practices that apply sociocultural theory. During teaching practicum, teacher educators can inspire teacher-learners to engage in close analysis of their own discursive practices similar to the data analysis presented here, attending to the co-construction of knowledge with students, and brainstorming more way to create a context that affords languaging. Future research is needed with teachers engaged in inquiry of their own practices to further investigate the ways that teachers can play a key role mediating second language learning among learners.

NOTES

1.   At the time of this study, teachers providing instruction to English learners in California needed to be credentialed through the CLAD (Crosscultural Language and Academic Development), BCLAD (Bilingual, Crosscultural Language and Academic Development) and/or a test-based certification process. The CLAD and BCLAD required extra coursework beyond the K-6 credential, which included courses on second language acquisition, policy, and teaching methods for ELLs. The BCLAD credential prepared a teacher to provide instruction to English learners in a language other than English, in this case, Spanish.

2.   In this excerpt English translations are inserted in {curly brackets} only when needed.

REFERENCES

Bakhtin, M. (1981). Discourse in the novel (M. Holquist & C. Emerson, Trans.). In M. Holquist (Ed.), *The dialogic imagination* (pp. 259-422). Austin, TX: University of Texas Press.

Block, D. (2003). *The social turn in second language acquisition.* Washington DC: Georgetown University Press.

Brown, D. (2007). *Teaching by principles: an Interactive approach to language pedagogy.* New Jersey: Pearson.

Cohen, E. G. (1994). *Designing group work: Strategies for heterogeneous classrooms* (2nd ed.). New York, NY: Teachers College Press.

Creswell, J. W. (2007). *Qualitative inquiry and research design: Choosing among five approaches.* Thousand Oaks, CA: SAGE.

Cresswell, J. W. (2009). *Research design: Qualitative, quantitative, and mixed methods approaches* (3rd ed.). Thousand Oaks, CA: SAGE.

Donato, R. (2000). Sociocultural contributions to understanding the foreign and second language classroom. In J. Lantolf (Ed.), *Sociocultural theory and second language learning* (pp. 27-50). Oxford, England: Oxford University Press.

Ellis, R. (2005). Principles of instructed language learning. *System, 33*(2) 209-224.

Emerson, R. M., Fretz, R. I., & Shaw, L. L. (1995).*Writing ethnographic fieldnotes.* Chicago, IL: University of Chicago Press.

Engeström,Y. (1987). *Learning by expanding: An activity theoretical approach to developmental research.* Helsinki, Finland: Orienta-Konsultit.

Foster, P., & Ohta, A. S. (2005). Negotiation for meaning and peer assistance in second language classrooms. *Applied Linguistics, 26,* 402–430.

Freeman, R. (1998). *Bilingual education and social change.* Clevedon, England: Multilingual Matters.

Gass, S. (1997). *Input, interaction, and the second language learner.* Mahwah, NJ: Erlbaum.

Gonzalez, N. (1995). The funds of knowledge for teaching project. *Practicing Anthropology, 17 (3),* 3-6.

González, N., Moll, L., & Amanti, C. (2005). *Funds of knowledge: Theorizing practices in households, communities and classrooms.* Mahwah, NJ: Erlbaum.

Gutiérrez, K. D. (2008). Developing a sociocritical literacy in the third space. *Reading Research Quarterly, 43*(2), 148–164.

Gutiérrez, K., Baquedano-López, P., & Tejeda, C. (1999). Rethinking diversity: Hybridity and hybridlanguage practices in the third space. *Mind, culture, and activity, 6,* 286–303.

Hammersley, M. & Atkinson, P. (1995). *Ethnography: Principles in practice* (2nd ed.). London: Routledge.

Harklau, L.A. (1994). Tracking and linguistic minority students: Consequences of ability grouping for second language learners. *Linguistics and Education, 6,* 221-248.

Hatch, E. (1992). *Discourse and language education.* Cambridge, England: Cambridge University Press.

Knouzi, I., Swain, M., Lapkin, S., & Brooks, L. (2010). Self-scaffolding mediated by languaging: Microgenetic analysis of high and low performers. *International Journal of Applied linguistics*, *20*(1), 23-49.

Lantolf, J. P. (2000). *Sociocultural theory and second language learning*. Oxford, England: Oxford University Press.

Lantolf, J. P., & Aljaafreh, A. (1995). Second language learning in the zone of proximal development: A revolutionary experience. *International Journal of Educational Research*, *23*, 619–632.

Lantolf, J. P., & Thorne, S.L. (2006). *Sociocultural theory and the genesis of second language development*. New York, NY: Oxford University Press.

Long, M. H. (1983). Native speaker/non-native speaker conversation and the negotiationof comprehensible input. *Applied Linguistics*, *4*(2), 126-141.

Long, M. (1996). The role of linguistic environment in second language acquisition. In W. Ritchie & T. Bhatia (Eds.), *Handbook of second language acquisition* (pp. 413-468). London: Academic Press.

Long, M. H., & Doughty, C. J. (Ed.). (2009). *Handbook of language teaching*. Oxford, England: Blackwell.

Mackey, A. (Ed.). (2007). *Conversational interaction in second language acquisition: A collection of empirical studies*. Oxford, England: Oxford University Press.

Martin-Beltran, M. (2009). Cultivating space for the language boomerang: The interplay of twolanguages as academic resources. *English Teaching: Practice and Critique*, *8*(2), 25-53.

Martin-Beltran, M. (2010a).The two-way language bridge: Co-constructing bilingual language learning opportunities. *Modern Language Journal*, *94*, 254-277.

Martin-Beltran, M. (2010b). Positioning proficiency: How students and teachers (de)construct language proficiency at school. *Linguistics and Education*, *21*, 257-281.

Miles, M., & Huberman, A. M. (1994). Data management and analysis methods. In N. Denzin & Y. Lincoln (Eds.), *Handbook of Qualitative Research* (pp. 428-444). Thousand Oaks, CA: SAGE.

Moll, L. (2010). Mobilizing Culture, Language, and Educational Practices: Fulfilling the Promises of Mendez and Brown. *Educational Researcher*, *39*, 451-460.

Moll, L. C., Amanti, C., Neff, D., & González, N. (1992). Funds of knowledge for teaching: Using a qualitative approach to connect homes and classrooms. *Theory into Practice*, *31*(2), 132-141.

Ohta, A. S. (1995). Applying sociocultural theory to an analysis of learner discourse: Learner-learner collaborative interaction in the zone of proximal development. *Issues in Applied Linguistics*, *6*, 93-121.

Palmer, D. (2009). Middle-class English speakers in a two-way immersion bilingual classroom: "Everybody should be listening to Jonathan right now...." *TESOL Quarterly*, *43*(2). 177-202.

Pica, T. (1994). Research on negotiation: What does it reveal about second-language learning conditions, processes, and outcomes? *Language Learning*, *44*, 493-527.

Richards, J. C., & Rodgers, T. S. (2001). *Approaches and methods in language teaching* (2nd ed.). Cambridge, England: Cambridge University Press.

Sannino, A., Daniels, H., & Gutiérrez, K. D. (2009). *Learning and expanding with activity theory.* New York, NY: Cambridge University Press.

Smith, P. H. (2001). Community language resources in dual language schooling. *The Bilingual Research Journal, 25*(3), 252-280.

Strauss, A., & Corbin, J. (2008). *Basics of qualitative research techniques and procedures for developing grounded theory* (3rd ed.). Thousand Oaks, CA: SAGE.

Swain, M. (1985). Communicative competence: Some roles of comprehensible input and comprehensible output in its development. In S. Gass & C. Madden (Eds.), *Input in second language acquisition* (pp. 235-253). Rowley, MA: Newbury House.

Swain, M. (2000). The output hypothesis and beyond: mediating acquisition through collaborative dialogue. In J. Lantolf (Ed.), *Sociocultural theory and second language learning* (pp. 97-114). Oxford, England: Oxford University Press.

Swain, M. (2006). Languaging, agency and collaboration in advanced second language learning. In H. Byrnes (Ed.), *Advanced language learning: The contribution of Hallidayand Vygotsky* (pp. 95-108). London: Continuum.

Swain, M., & Deters, P. (2007). "New" mainstream SLA theory: Expanded and enriched. *Modern Language Journal, 91,* 820-836.

Swain, M., Kinnear, P., & Steinman, L. (2010).*Sociocultural Theory in Second Language Education: An Introduction through Narratives.* New York, NY: Multilingual Matters.

Swain, M., & Lapkin, S. (1998). Interaction and second language learning: Two adolescent French immersion students working together. *Modern Language Journal, 82,* 320-337.

Swain, M., & Lapkin, S. (2000). Task-based second language learning: The uses of the first language. *Language Teaching Research, 4,* 251-274.

Tocalli-Beller, A., & Swain, M. (2007). Riddles and puns in the ESL classroom: Adults talk to learn. In A. Mackey (Ed.), *Conversational interaction in second language acquisition: Empirical studies.* Oxford, England: Oxford University Press.

Valdés, G. (2001). *Learning and not learning English: Latino students in American schools.* New York, NY: Teachers College Press.

van Lier, L. (2000). From input to affordance: Social-interactive learning from an ecological perspective. In J. Lantolf (Ed.), *Sociocultural theory and second language learning* (pp. 245-259). Oxford, NY: Oxford University Press

Vélez-Ibáñez, C. G., & Greenberg, J. B. (1992). Formation and transformation of funds of knowledge among U.S.-Mexican households. *Anthropology and Education Quarterly, 23*(4), 313-335.

Vygotsky, L. (1978). *Mind in society.* Cambridge, MA: Harvard University Press.

PART II

CULTURAL PERSPECTIVES

CHAPTER 7

TEACHER'S USE OF FUNDS OF KNOWLEDGE TO PROMOTE CLASS PARTICIPATION AND ENGAGEMENT IN AN EFL CONTEXT

Hoe Kyeung Kim and Soyoung Lee

There have been a growing number of native speaker English teachers at Korean universities as a big emphasis is placed on improving oral communication skills. Some of these foreign-born teachers are having struggles with their Korean students due to their lack of understanding in students' culture, language and learning styles. The purpose of this study is to examine the case of a Canadian language teacher who taught a College English course at one Korean university. The study was grounded in the frame of sociocultural theory (Landtolf, 2000; Vygotsky, 1978). The study was conducted throughout one semester and the data were collected through videotaped classroom observations and interviews with the teacher as well as students. The findings suggested that the teacher used both his own funds of knowledge and his students' funds of knowledge as scaffolding to promote students' participation and engagement.

Teachers' Roles in Second Language Learning:
Classroom Applications of Sociocultural Theory, pp. 121–134
Copyright © 2012 by Information Age Publishing
All rights of reproduction in any form reserved.

In 2009, I (the first author) was in a meeting with Soyoung (the second author), a Korean faculty who works for the College English program of a Korean university. As we both were in the English education field, we were talking about the immense wave of teaching and learning English in Korea. Due to the big emphasis on improving oral communication skills in English, Korean schools and universities started hiring native speakers of English teachers and teachers with near-native fluency levels. Even in Soyoung's department, there were only three instructors who had Korean nationalities out of 20 full-time instructors. Most of the teachers in her English program were foreign-born such as American, Canadian, Australian and British. However, a significant number of foreign-born English teachers were having some struggles with their Korean students. Their lack of understanding in their students' culture, language, and learning styles did not lead to an effective teaching instruction.

Among many English teachers, Soyoung spoke highly of one Canadian teacher in her department. According to her, the teacher was not only well liked by his students but also respected by his colleagues in terms of the time and energy he put into his teaching. More interestingly, what I was told about him was that he was bilingual (French is his first language and English is the second language) and he had not majored in TESOL. He was learning Korean as his third language and well aware of the Korean culture. As I heard his story, I was very interested in his case and wanted to observe his teaching and if possible conduct a study on his successful teaching.

In this chapter, we report on a case study of a Canadian English teacher and examine his funds of knowledge and further his use of funds of knowledge in his teaching practices. The study was held throughout one semester and the findings were based on videotaped classroom observations and interviews with the teacher as well as students.

LITERATURE REVIEW

This study was grounded in the frame of sociocultural theory (Vygotsky, 1978). We used Moll and his colleagues' (1992, 2005) concept of funds of knowledge to understand the teacher's teaching practice and how the teacher supported students' learning.

Roles of the Teacher in Language Teaching

From the sociocultural perspective, teaching is a socioculturally and historically situated practice. Although other factors such as methodolo-

How do your funds of knowledge support students' learning?

gies, materials, teaching contexts and institutional rules shape teaching practices, teachers play an important role in interpreting and implementing these practices. It is the teacher who decides everyday decisions regarding teaching content, instruction strategies, students' assessment, student interaction, and classroom management. Thus, it is necessary to understand the role(s) of teachers and the influence of instruction strategies on students' learning.

Scaffolding is designed to assist students' Zone of Proximal Development (ZPD), which is responsive to students. The assumption behind this is that teachers are consciously aware of their students' prior knowledge and attempt to activate their knowledge and skills. Scaffolding supports the development of further complex skills and concepts (Tharp & Gallimore, 1989). Teachers' use of funds of knowledge in classroom can be an important and effective scaffolding tool.

Cultural Funds of Knowledge

The term, funds of knowledge, used by researchers Moll, Amanti, Neff, and Gonzalez (1992), is defined as the "historically accumulated and culturally developed bodies of knowledge and skills essential for household or individual functioning and well-being" (p. 133). Students' funds of knowledge refer to bodies of everyday knowledge learned through participation in home and community practices (Moll, 2005; Moll et al., 1992). This definition needs to be extended to include larger contexts in which the individual student can learn and acquire social knowledge through interacting with their community members. In English as a Foreign Language (EFL) settings where language teachers have different cultural backgrounds, students' funds of knowledge can be a critical factor. In understanding students' cultural resources, EFL teachers need to consider students' prior experience extending to their interactions with their communities.

Studies have shown that the use of students' funds of knowledge, such as the primary language and the knowledge and skills they learn outside of school, can be drawn on to support the development of new school-based skills and practices, including learning a second language and the use of more complex literacy skills (Gutiérrez, Baquedano-López, & Tejeda, 1999; Moll & Diaz, 1987). Thus, it is beneficial to recognize and capitalize on language learners' first language and literacy skills. Students express more complex ideas than those which are constructed when these funds are accessed and utilized (Gutiérrez et al. 1999; Moll & Diaz, 1987).

Research on EFL contexts shows that many native speakers of English teachers have struggled in understanding their students due to their lack of understanding students' culture. Most studies are focused on the difference between teacher and students' cultural practices and expectations in implementing teaching methods and methodologies developed in Western countries (e.g., Jin & Cortazzi, 2006; Li, 1998). This approach leads to a deficit model that believes that students are lacking the necessary competence, knowledge and skills, which makes teachers fail to support their strengths and resources they bring to class.

Classroom teachers need to understand and capitalize on their students' diverse cultures and languages, and funds of knowledge. In an EFL setting where students share the same culture and language, there is a gap between teacher's and the students' cultures. Often, native speakers of English teachers might not know their students' cultures and also the value of knowing it. In a language class, however, culture is always a critical factor that a teacher must be aware of. Culture is embedded in language and commonly practiced rituals that shape thinking. One of the powerful funds of knowledge that students bring into the class is culture and their living experience. Knowing students' cultural resources and linking their cultural funds of knowledge with instruction can be beneficial as it taps into their prior knowledge and ZPD.

The use of students' funds of knowledge for instructional purposes can be an important scaffolding tool. Teachers who lack knowledge of their students' home language and culture might not know students' hidden funds of knowledge. An alternative means of accommodating this limitation is to use the experiences of teachers who may have a similar experience of their students including backgrounds, professional experiences, and beliefs. Accordingly, they can draw on their own funds of knowledge in connecting with students' prior knowledge.

The research question that we developed was how the teacher used his own and students funds of knowledge to promote students' participation and engagement.

STUDY

EFL Settings

Korean students learn English in their middle and high schools. English counts as an important subject in their secondary education and on the Korean scholastic aptitude test for entering college. Besides the rigorous study at school, a majority of students go to institutes to get an edge on their English testing skills. Students take the standardized tests focusing on testing reading and listening comprehension, grammar, and vocabulary skills. Most questions on the test are multiple choice and students take English as a subject that they are tested on rather than as communicative skills. Once they enter colleges and universities they have to meet a certain minimum requirement in English.

At the university where we collected the data, students were required to take College English courses regardless of their majors during their freshman year. At the university where the participating teacher worked, students must complete 12 credit hours in English courses to graduate and some departments require official test scores. The goal at this university is to train for proficiency in the four communicative skills of reading, writing, listening, and speaking in an academic setting as can be seen by the following excerpt from the standardized College English syllabus:

> *College English* is the university's first-level English language course. It is designed to develop your English language proficiency in an academic setting and has a primary emphasis on reading and writing and a secondary emphasis on speaking and listening. This course includes the study of (1) reading skills and strategies required to understand challenging texts; (2) advanced paragraph writing and basic essay composition; (3) discussion skills to further extend oral competence; and (4) listening skills required in academic settings.

One of the challenges EFL students face is that they do not have enough input and interaction in English. A popular teaching methodology employed by many universities in Korea is a communicative language teaching approach, which emphasizes authentic and meaningful interaction. The content-based curriculum seems to be well matched with the limitation of EFL settings and supports the communicative language teaching approach.

The College English program that the participating teacher worked at implemented an immersion program which discouraged students' use of the home language, Korean. The program did not specify its curriculum type but it was obvious that both teachers and students had to use English only in classroom. On the course syllabus, it was stated explicitly under the participation section that students should use English only. The textbooks the program adopted across the campus were the *Northstar* series which focused on improving academic skills. The textbook series were based on content-based and communicative language teaching approaches.

All freshmen at the university were required to complete one semester of College English classes, and with the exception of a few majors, another semester of such classes were required of them. The College English and the following English classes were designed to make a transition from the secondary school English learning to a more authentic English academic setting.

As stated in the program curriculum, the College English program was implementing an English only policy and stressed oral exams and participation. The program hired 17 full time native speakers of English teachers, three full time Korean-English bilingual teachers and 23 part-time Korean teachers who had near native English fluency. Both full time and part time teachers were conducting entire classes in English. Their background was either TESOL or English Literature or English Language and most had some experience living and studying abroad.

Although there was much stress on improving speaking and communication skills, the grading criteria for students' performance on the course included four language skills of speaking, listening, reading, and writing and focused reading skills. In addition to one or two oral exams, students had to take their midterm and final tests on standardized pencil-and-paper tests. While the oral exams were counted for 10% and participation counted for 20%, midterm and final term reading tests and writing essay were counted for a total of 60%. In practice, it seems that most students achieved satisfactory grades for participation if they were able to complete homework, and perform well on the oral exam as well as contribute to the class orally. There were three required compositions, a paragraph, an essay, and an essay rewrite, which counted for a total of 20% and attendance was a strict requirement with each absence worth a 2 points out of 10% of the total grade.

Participant

The participant, Jay (pseudonym) came from Montreal, the French speaking part of Canada. His first language was French and he majored in English Studies in College and in graduate school. He was very fluent in English and had near-native speaker fluency. He was in his mid-30s and lived by himself in Korea. During the school break, he went back to his home country to see his family members and relatives.

He came to Korea to teach English 7 years ago. Prior to his teaching in Korea, he did not have any teaching experience. After receiving a BA in English studies, he came to Korea with the view of teaching English for only one year. However, after completing his MA, he came back to Korea in 2001 to study Korean at a university Korean language institute on a fellowship. He resumed teaching English in Korea in the year 2003, moved to his current college 3 years ago, and has continued learning Korean through language exchanges, participating in a local church, and watching Korean dramas.

At school, he is received by students as an "angel" who pays attention to his students' needs and treats weaknesses with care. Students commented that he tried to build students' confidence and make student comfortable in English learning. In explaining the writing process, he first considered how students' mind flowed and explained how sentences were organized and why. Some of the comments referred to his effort in learning Korean and Korea culture.

Data Collection and Analysis

The primary data consisted of interviews with the participating teacher, classroom observations, an interview with a focus group of students, and written documents. The interviews with the teacher were conducted before the class observation started in order to obtain the general background of the participating teacher such as educational background, teaching experiences and language profiles. The following two interviews were conducted during the observations. The interview questions were semi-structures focusing on the teacher's beliefs about language teaching, views about EFL teaching and language proficiency, and understanding of Korean students' language learning. Each interview lasted about 60 minutes and all the interviews were transcribed verbatim.

The classroom observations were done three times and videotaped during the semester. The lengths of each class were 75 minutes. The dates for the videotaped classroom observations were selected randomly; one at the beginning, in the middle and at the end. The focus of the videotaping and the field notes were how the teacher assisted students in promoting their learning.

At the end of the semester, three students from his class were interviewed to examine the teacher's teaching practice and assistive support for his students' learning. Also, it was done to triangulate the teacher's interviews and classroom observations. The selection of the focus group was made randomly. The focus group interview was done for about 30 minutes and audiotaped.

In addition, information on the participant's course related activities such as cyber campus, an online course management program, and E-Lounge tutoring service were collected. Written documents such as course syllabus, textbook, supplementary teaching materials were reviewed.

All the collected data were reviewed by both authors to increase the reliability. The transcribed interview data were reviewed to find the participant's use of funds of knowledge such as understanding of his students' culture and language as well as the use of his own experience as a language learner. The videotaped classroom observations were reviewed to identify the teacher's applications of fund of knowledge in his teaching practices.

His uses of Korean language, culture and scaffolding were identified and categorized to find the patterns.

FINDINGS

The participating teacher, Jay, used his linguistic and cultural knowledge of his Korean students to support his students' reading comprehension and engagement. He believed that EFL students' motivation was critical in improving language skills. As reflected on his course syllabus, interviews and his teaching practices, his view on participation was extended to include students "engagement" in class activities and homework assignments as well. Seemingly, students' engagement in learning contents and materials was regarded as active participation. During the class, Jay used Korean words and phrases as scaffolding and exemplified Korean culture and customs to assist his students' understanding of the reading materials. With heavy dependence on the standardized tests and students' concerns on grades, he believed that his students' main concern was to increase their reading comprehension and his assistance in reading the texts would lead them to active participation and engagement.

Using Linguistic Knowledge

Jay used his linguistic knowledge to support students' reading comprehension and engagement. As he was aware of his students' major concern, that is, the grades, he spent a lot of his time on preparing his teaching materials so that his students thoroughly understood and participated in the lessons. He usually scanned most of the reading texts presented in the textbook and put them on the screen in front of the classroom. He explained key vocabulary words and provided modified input. He highlighted the key vocabulary words in yellow to ensure that students understood the meaning. This was done mainly to prepare students for their midterm and final tests. He thought that Korean students were familiar with the close reading analysis method and preferred to be confident about every detail of the reading, from the organization to unfamiliar vocabulary items or expressions. Jay was well aware of such needs of his Korean students. The focus group students that I interviewed were satisfied with his teaching styles and acknowledged his care for students. When the researcher asked the students if they had any suggestions to improve the class, they answered nothing should be changed.

On the day the researcher observed the class, the topic of the lesson was about "the Chinese kitchen" and how to write a persuasive essay. The reading on the textbook was a personal essay written by a Chinese-American cook and cookbook author, and contained expressions that were personal and unique. The main idea of the reading was that a culture's food and customs reflected the cultural beliefs, and the author reminisced about her grandmother, father, and mother who had taught life's lessons through teaching her how to cook the Chinese dishes. A lot of preparation that went into the cooking reflected the love and wishes for good fortune that her grandmother or parents had for the family. He was first explaining the concepts and expressions used in the text in detail. While explaining the meaning of the word "leaning" in the text, Jay used his linguistic knowledge about Korean to scaffold his students' reading comprehension.

> T: "...something like leanings is tendencies. You can think of this word as somewhat similar to the Korean expression ..... 하는 편이다." (55:05-55:10)

The Korean expression "하는 편이다" has the meaning of "rather~, on the ~side." Knowing that to explain a difficult English word with other difficult English terms has its limitations, Jay emphatically used Korean to explain some abstract terms. By doing so, he ensured students' comprehension and made an effort to accept his students' language in the classroom. His students felt that it was okay to use Korean words for better understanding and acknowledged the the Korean language as a useful tool to promote their understanding. In some extent, his use of Korean language indicated that students were not the ones responsible to pick up the right terms, but that the teacher had once been in their place, knows their frustration and is willing to take the extra effort to help them out. Based on his knowledge of Korean language, he knew well what expressions or sentences Korean students had problems with, and tried to help them from their perspective. Unlike his colleagues, he called students by their Korean names and used Korean words when necessary. It was obvious that Jay tried to create a supportive and encouraging learning environment where his students were being welcomed and respected.

Using Students' Funds of Knowledge

Jay used students' funds of knowledge to foster students' class participation and engagement. He used his knowledge about Korean culture to scaffold his students' reading comprehension. As he was teaching the introduction to the above-mentioned reading, "The Chinese Kitchen," he used his knowledge of the Korean culture to link the reading's main ideas to students' understanding of their own culture. While he was explaining the food related to tradition, he used an example of the Korean Thanksgiving.

T: "Our food is inextricably linked with manners, with forms, with tradition, with history ... history so this is more specifically like the special dates, like on Chusok (추석) you eat the certain things or food is prepared in a certain way...." (57:11-57:16)

By relating the text content to the students' own culture, the teacher made the reading more relevant and meaningful to the students. Not only did he mention Chusok (추석) which is the Korean Thanksgiving holiday which falls on August 15 (the full moon of August) of the lunar calendar and is celebrated for at least three days, but the general examples he gave about the "manners, with forms, with tradition, with history" were actually referring to the Korean culture. For example, to explain the manners, he referred to the Korean culture where you are not supposed to leave the table until everyone was finished, of formality, he used examples of Korean formality saying "when you set up the table, the bowl goes there, the spoon goes there, and the chopsticks go there, and the tradition is about which days you eat certain food, and what you eat after what." The examples he used are from his detailed knowledge of the Korean culture so the whole readings' main ideas become open to his Korean students. They approached the reading activity with a prior understanding of how food is linked with culture as he tapped into students' funds of knowledge.

By constructing the context of comparing the knowledge of their own culture with the Chinese culture introduced in the reading, the students could encounter the reading more meaningfully and with confidence. Therefore, not only comprehension was enhanced but students' participation and motivation were triggered. Jay's use of students' funds of knowledge attempted to draw students' attention to their experience and connect them with the reading in the classroom. He provided students with contextual information as well as comparison of Korean cultures to ensure that students had the deeper meanings of the text and that they were able to make inferences. The complex layers of cultural experience were once opened to students as they associated and compared their layers of experience with those introduced in the reading. In fact, as the Chinese customs introduced in the reading were closer to the Korean customs, it became much easier for the students to relate to the cultural inferences being made.

Taking Up Students' Funds of Knowledge as Scaffolding

Jay made use of students' funds of knowledge as well as his own funds of knowledge as scaffolding. Jay tapped into students' prior knowledge, took up his students' funds of knowledge, and used it as scaffolding to

[handwritten margin note: —authentic connections to students' lives/ culture]

assist students' understanding, which resulted in increasing students' participation and engagement. In addition, he used his own knowledge about his students' culture. The following script from his class demonstrated how he used students' funds of knowledge to explain the word "hitch hiker" when explaining textbook materials.

Excerpt from video clip (29:20-29:56)

01   T: And lastly here, what is a hitch hiker?

02   Ss: (some students showing their thumbs up)

03   T: Right. (showing his thumb up) so…

04   Ss: (laughing)

05   T: Actually, I was wondering… Is it what you use in Korea (showing his thumb up) if you want to get a ride? (He looked around) No? Usually (He puts his thumb down and copied one student's gesture and put his both hands together). Usually like this?

06   Ss: (laughing)

07   T: You beg? (laughing and putting both of his hands together)

08   Ss: (laughing and nodding)

09   T: But actually, hitch hiking is not very popular in Korea, I think. But in a western country, if you want to ask somebody to give you a free ride if you are on the side of the road, if you do like this (showing his thumb up), they will, well, they may stop…

Not only did the teacher explain about hitch-hiking which was an integral part of understanding the reading text to the students unfamiliar with the custom, but by comparing how different gestures carry meaning, the teacher explained the cultural significance that gestures carry. In line 5, Jay noticed and recognized one student's begging gesture (putting both hands together) which was very different from his gesture (putting a thumb up). He knew that that putting a thumb up was not common in Korea and asking for a ride was not something one can request easily to a stranger. So when the student made a begging gesture, he took up that gesture and showed it to his students. He asked students whether they all knew the hidden meaning of the gesture (putting both hands together) in Korea and invited students to agree by asking "you beg?" The students' nodding and laughing in line 8 was their response to his invitation to active participation.

Jay's understanding of the Korean culture and students' ability to know about the American culture enabled him to ask significant questions that could bring in students' voluntary participation. Because he was familiar with the level of students' thinking, how much input they already have, and what they would identify easily with, he could bring out significant participation and interaction. His understanding and respect for students' funds of knowledge enabled him to build the scaffolding needed to support, promote, and encourage students' understanding. A true two-way interaction which involved students' voluntary participation and the opportunity to show their own knowledge developed, thanks to the teacher's respect and acquaintance with the culture and thoughts of his students.

Jay's effort to support his students' reading comprehension such as using scanned textbook materials, and attending to students' needs, especially in preparing exams, resulted in positive responses from students. His students perceived that his class was balanced and well designed to improve all the skills of speaking, listening, reading and writing. With his support on reading comprehension, his students' scores on midterm and final exams reached fairly high degree compared to other classes. He had tried to tailor to and make the best of students' established way of studying. Sensing students' need to reach out of the limits of the classroom, he encouraged students to use the E-lounge where students can go individually or in groups to practice their speaking skills with their instructors. This arrangement was specially done for students who need more speaking practice as class had limited time. He made announcements about the use of the E -lounge in class several times. He also opened his office hours for those who needed individual meetings. His active use of cyber campus, exchanging e-mails with students and posting learning materials demonstrated his effort to meet students' desire for meaningful engagement and to motivate his students' learning.

CONCLUSIONS AND IMPLICATIONS

The teacher used both his own funds of knowledge and students' funds of knowledge as scaffolding to promote students' participation and engagement. By incorporating the cultural knowledge he had of the students' culture, he put himself on equal terms with students, not as an authoritative figure. He did not position himself as a legitimate knowledge holder, but as a negotiator who seeks *the space* for reaching both parties' understanding. The students were not treated as being ignorant of the target culture and lacking something but as equals, having just different cultural and experiential assets. In this process, students felt respected and responded also maturely by engaging and communicating with the teacher. As a result, they were willing and ready to demonstrate their prior knowledge and add onto their funds of knowledge which was valued by the teacher.

Students participated and engaged greatly when the teacher's funds of knowledge matched with students' funds of knowledge. Learning to communicate in another language and culture is then the active exchanging of cultural assets, not the acquisition of what one lacks. As shown in the last examples on the hitch hiker, there was an active participation by students during the reading activity. While Jay's funds of knowledge and students' funds of knowledge were negotiated, he continuously demonstrated his scaffolding practice for his students' learning. Funds of knowledge is not only an entity or a body of knowledge but also the activation and capitalization of that knowledge.

For classroom teachers, it is important that teachers welcome and respect students' linguistic and cultural assets in the classroom. Further, teachers need to activate and capitalize these assets to support students' learning. Scaffolding is essential in promoting students' learning. The question for classroom teachers has been "how to scaffold the students" in their classroom. This paper showed one Canadian teacher's examples of how to scaffold effectively his students' learning using students' funds of knowledge in the EFL setting. The findings of study imply the benefits of learning students' language and cultures for classroom teachers. In addition, teachers' own language learning experiences could be a useful tool to understand their students' learning.

In the findings of the study stress teachers' awareness of the importance of students' background knowledge and their life experience in teaching. Teachers' awareness is the prerequisite of effective scaffolding practices. Instructional scaffolding further requires teachers' increasing awareness and connecting students' resources to the teaching content. These teaching skills need to be addressed and taught in teacher education programs for teacher candidates and future teachers to become effective in their practice.

REFERENCES

Gutiérrez, K. D., Baquedano-López, P., & Tejeda, C. (1999). Rethinking diversity: Hybridity and hybrid language practices in the third space. *Mind, Culture and Activity, 6*(4), 286-303.

Jin, L., & Cortazzi, M. (2006). Changing practices in Chinese culture of learning, *Language, Culture & Curriculum, 19*(1), 5-20.

Li, D. (1998). "It's always more difficult than you plan and imagine": Teachers' perceived difficulties in introducing the communicative approach in South Korea. *TESOL Quarterly, 32*(4), 677-703.

Lantolf, J. P. (2000). *Sociocultural theory and second language learning*. Oxford, England: Oxford University Press.

Moll, L. C., & Díaz, R. (1987). Teaching writing as communication: The use of ethnographic findings in classroom practice. In D. Bloome (Ed.), *Literacy and Schooling* (pp. 193-231). Norwood, NJ: Ablex.

Moll, L., Amanti, C., Neff, D., & Gonzalez, N. (1992). Funds of knowledge for teaching: Using a qualitative approach to connect homes and classrooms. *Theory into Practice, 31*, 132-141.

Moll, L. (2005). Reflections and possibilities. In N. Gonzalez, L. C. Moll, & C. Amanti (Eds.), *Funds of knowledge: Theorizing practices in households, communities, and classrooms* (pp. 275-287). Mahwah, NJ: Lawrence Erlbaum Associates.

Tharp, R. G., & Gallimore, R. (1989). Rousing schools to life. *American Educator, 13*(2), 20-25, 46-52.

Vygotsky, L. (1978). *Mind in Society: The development of higher psychological process.* Cambridge, MA: Harvard University Press.

CHAPTER 8

TEACHERS' ROLES IN FACILITATING NOVICE WRITERS FROM GENERATION 1.5

Paula M. Carbone

Academic writing instruction was studied with students from Generation 1.5 enrolled in a tenth grade remedial English class. Generation 1.5 students, who are bilingual and bicultural but maintain their heritage language, have been studied extensively in postsecondary settings, with little attention to their academic trajectories in secondary school. Two strategies using mediation are discussed that proved instrumental in promoting access and engagement with academic writing. First, students' funds of knowledge pertaining to literacy practices were identified and examined to highlight students' competencies as leverage for mediation to academic writing. Second, developing a topic for persuasive writing from students' narratives about their cultural backgrounds was mediated through whole-group and individual questioning from general to specific. The teacher's role emerged as actively valuing students' funds of knowledge and understanding their cultural backgrounds for leveraging to meet expectations of academic writing.

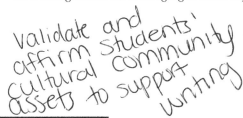
Validate and affirm students' cultural community assets to support writing

Teachers' Roles in Second Language Learning:
Classroom Applications of Sociocultural Theory, pp. 135–153
Copyright © 2012 by Information Age Publishing
All rights of reproduction in any form reserved.

When I was a secondary English teacher at a diverse urban school, a refrain often heard in the faculty lounge was, "these kids can't write." This anecdotal lore speaks to the frustration, what Delpit (1992) identifies as the "despair" that teachers face when confronted with writing from novice writers with linguistic and culturally nondominant backgrounds, including those students speaking English as a Second Language (ESL). Teachers' frustration and despair are very real, part of a complex problem in which they want to do a good job and are trying their best, but may not know how to tackle what seems an insurmountable issue, especially when students' "Funds of Knowledge" (Moll, 1998; Moll, Amanti, Neff, & Gonzalez, 2001) are not used for academic writing tasks. Because academic writing is rule-bound in conventions requiring specific skill-sets (Barnard & Campbell, 2005), second language writers (Kutz, Groden, & Zamel, 1993; Matsuda, 2006) may be unfamiliar with the expectations of academic writing in the target language, or unable to produce writing to meet those expectations due to language acquisition issues.

This chapter provides information on the teacher's role in mediating writing instruction for English Language Learners (ELLs)—specifically, students in Generation 1.5 (Rumbaut & Ima, 1988). Since the term was first introduced by Rumbaut and Ima, it continues to be used most frequently to describe foreign-born college students who received U.S. high school diplomas (Blumenthal, 2002), but has also been taken up to describe those youth who are fluent English-speakers familiar with U.S. culture due to their arrival at an early age (Singhal, 2004). In fact, Roberge (2003) argues the term should be more expansive to include "native-born non-native speakers." This group varies in the degree of biculturalism and bilingualism each adopts, but primarily they have strong linguistic and emotional connections to their homeland (Blumenthal, 2002; Harklau, Losey, & Siegal, 1999; Ortmeier-Hooper, 2008) that many second-generation students no longer maintain. Due to their young age upon arrival, they often speak English (L2) without an accent and use the slang and colloquialisms of their native-speaker peers, yet they maintain their heritage language (L1) at home and in the community. This language characteristic is an issue not shared by ESL students in general; 1.5G may sound and behave so similarly to their mainstream, native English-speaking peers that they can be misunderstood as native speakers, and their language acquisition issues ignored or misrepresented as lack of competence. By applying this term to a group of students that has been traditionally underserved in secondary academic contexts (Forrest, 2006), I draw attention to their unique issues and discuss strategies to facilitate their academic writing.

THEORETICAL FRAMEWORK

Sociocultural theory highlights the robust literacy competencies 1.5G students engage in outside of the classroom, helping teachers perceive writing as a social practice (Moll, Sáez, & Dworin, 2001), drawing on the experiences and knowledge of language and literacy use from family, social, and community interactions. Teachers can leverage these outside-of-classroom writing competencies for instruction in academic writing. Moll (1998) advances using the concept of students' everyday knowledge as leverage for academic tasks, adding the critical distinction of cultural backgrounds, or funds of knowledge. He argues that if students' funds of knowledge are ignored or devalued, learning of academic concepts is impaired.

If teachers are not aware of the funds of knowledge that ELLs, including 1.5G, draw upon when they write, and think of writing as an individually based skill, they tend to expect the same type of writing mainstream, native English speakers produce. What may not be apparent to some teachers is that the cultural practices, understanding of academic expectations, and experiences necessary for academic writing proficiency that mainstream students have acquired and internalized are often masked, embedded in English instructional discourses with which they are familiar from years of schooling, as well as their family and community literacy practices supporting strategic understandings of academic writing (Echevarria & Graves, 2007). Their higher-level thinking about academic writing tasks have been internalized and are used in a seemingly effortless manner.

However, for students in 1.5G, the funds of knowledge they bring to their acquisition of academic writing in most cases do not emerge from previous experiences with academic writing, but are grounded in everyday writing for their own purposes. Writing instruction with 1.5G that is inclusive of their funds of knowledge with writing provides "ample cultural and cognitive resources with great, *potential* utility for classroom instruction" (Moll et al., 2001, p. 134) and leads to leveraging those experiences and practices for mediation between them and academic writing (Lee, 2000). Students, including ELLs, *can* write and *are* writing for their own purposes—just not always to meet the expectations of academic writing. This chapter examines the teacher's role leveraging from everyday writing to academic writing in a classroom of novice 1.5G writers.

RELEVANT LITERATURE REVIEW

Teachers often misunderstand novice writers as incapable writers (Rose, 2006). Though not widely used in secondary settings, the term "novice writers" is a powerful descriptor that shifts the lore of "students can't write" to the appropriate role of the teacher in facilitating writing instruction. Students in 1.5G are novice writers of academic English; traditional approaches used for teaching L1 writing are laden with cultural practices so normalized that the difficulty 1.5G might have in accessing them is not transparent (Atkinson & Ramanathan, 1995).

Many of the instructional strategies for ESL students are applicable to 1.5G. Strategies for correction and feedback such as limiting the errors on which to focus, explicating detailed steps for revision, assisting the L2 writer in finding and correcting their own mistakes through grammar mini-lessons (cf. Shin, 2002) all apply to 1.5G. However, while ESL students may have poor listening skills impeding verbal instruction, 1.5G's listening skills are excellent due to their acquisition of English aurally, or by the ear (Reid, 1998). Their limited experience with academic expectations is more of an impediment (Harklau, Losey, & Siegal, 1999).

Transfer in writing ability shown between L1 and L2 writing (e.g., Olson, 1999) is often lacking with students in 1.5G, who may enroll in U. S. schools with little or no experience in academic literacy skills in their heritage language (Blumenthal, 2002; Gawienowski & Holper, 2006; Ortmeier-Hooper, 2008; Reid, 1998). Research on 1.5G and college writing shows they need awareness of structural demands to transform information into expected rhetorical conventions (Grabe & Kaplan, 1996; Swales, 1990) as well as exposure to varied writing tasks (Hartman & Tarone, 1999) before entering college. Yet with 1.5G, viewed as low-performing native-speakers of English (Asher, Case, & Zhong, 2009) and enrolled in low-tracked classes, literacy practices are limited to rote, lower-level tasks such as fill-in-the-blanks and drills (Harklau, Losey, & Siegal, 1999). This approach, focusing on decontextualized skills-based instruction, has no empirical, evidence-based substantiation that it will help students meet expectations of academic writing (Hillocks, 2008; Street, 2005).

An alternative instructional approach to provide advancement for 1.5G in academic writing begins with students' cultural and social funds of knowledge using everyday literacies. The connection between academic achievement and the valuing of students' heritage language and everyday writing practices in classrooms is well documented (cf. Gee, 2004; Valdés, 2004). Pérez (1998) notes teachers of ELLs need to "find out about [students'] lives and culture, and to make space for their literacy practices" (p. 251). This is a starting point for new approaches in writing instruction to meet the needs of students in 1.5G.

The evidence-based findings reported are part of a larger study examining an instructional intervention to facilitate academic writing using qualitative formative design research (Reinking & Bradley, 2008). The larger study focused on studying the intervention, with the primary research question of: How does a writing pedagogy facilitate students' choices in using the elements of persuasion in academic writing? This chapter will examine the teacher's role in identifying and analyzing students' everyday literacy practices and leveraging them for instruction in academic writing. There is a wealth of information noting the importance of valuing students' funds of knowledge, but little on what that looks like in practice, especially in secondary writing instruction. This chapter provides information to fill that gap.

METHODOLOGY

The data reported here were collected over several days in a tenth-grade, Language Skills Class, which was compulsory for students who scored "below basic" on the state-mandated standardized test. Students were required to pass this course before enrolling in 10th-grade English, and received no credits towards graduation for the course. Participants included 20 students from a total of 31 and their classroom teacher, Mariana.

The youth in this study lived in an urban neighborhood that has long been a working class Mexican American community, despite being gentrified by whites to the east and bordering a city to the north of affluent whites. The gang problems that plague the area, intensifying in the 1970s and continuing today, may in part explain the lack of gentrification. The high school in which the study took place is comprised of 93% "Hispanic" students, which is not surprising given that the neighborhood is 83% Latino/a, with 63% speaking Spanish at home. All participants were identified as 1.5G due to their immigration to the U.S. at an early age and oral fluency in English; all identified as Latino/a. (The 11 students not participating showed close alignment with the participants.)

Mariana and I worked together on other research projects during her student teaching and first year of teaching. When I asked her to participate in this study, she stated her goal was to promote students' development in literacy, and she agreed the study would develop this goal. We discussed countering the reductive practices favored in remedial classes (Rose, 2006), which bar access to the scientific concepts of literacy and limit experiences with academic writing.

Mariana grew up not far from the school site, but had a very different academic trajectory than her students. She was bussed to high-performing secondary schools across town in White neighborhoods that were more racially, socially, and economically diverse than the research site. She attributed her ability to interact with teachers and students from different backgrounds to influencing her academic success, and often referred to her role in providing the same access to academic achievement she experienced for the students enrolled in her classes. When the study took place, Mariana was a second-year teacher.

The data reported here include field notes, transcripts from audio-taped classroom talk, select student work-products, and transcripts of informal interviews. They were analyzed using grounded theory (Strauss & Corbin, 1990) to identify patterns occurring during instruction, which could then be further analyzed and categorized. I also drew from discourse analysis for its ability to examine the affordances of the classroom context (Bloome et al., 2008) from a sociocultural perspective. The intent was to systematically study the teacher's role in scaffolding the relationship between students' everyday writing and expectations of academic writing.

Through recursive reading and re-reading of the written-up fieldnote, transcripts, and student work samples for patterns, the general categories of *students' competency/self-efficacy* and *leveraging/scaffolding* emerged. Within those categories, the codes of "building competency, identifying competency, telegraphing competency (high expectations)" developed within the category *students' competency/self-efficacy,* and "bridging, probing, foregrounding" developed within *leveraging/scaffolding*. The coded data were then further analyzed for relationships that provided insight on the teacher's role.

FINDINGS

Findings showed the teacher's role as actively identifying and leveraging students' funds of knowledge provided an important context for writing instruction. First, the teacher's role in identifying and mediating between students' everyday literacies and academic expectations is demonstrated, followed by reporting of direct instruction in guiding students' development of topics for a persuasive essay.

Mediating Between Students' Funds of Knowledge and Academic Literacy

Students completed an Activity Log, listing their activities over the past 24 hours with the purpose of identifying their funds of knowledge. Mariana began a whole-class discussion asking students, "what were some of the things you guys listed?" She wrote their activities on the board as they shared them; everyday literacy activities included watch TV, do homework, read, take tests, use computer, use MySpace, listen to music, and play video games. When student suggestions tapered off, she paused and asked, "anything else? (*pause*) OK, look at all these different things you guys did—all these different things over the course of 24 hours and other things."

Mariana used the pause in students' responses to begin mediating. She noted the "things" students did, saying, "look at all these different things," positioning students' activities as being varied and expansive. She continued by asking, "Most of these involved what? (*pause*). You have to be able to what?" Mariana shifted from asking for students to repeat the activities they wrote down to *how* they performed them. She began mediating the process of guiding students to discern how their literacy practices required skills, and that those skills were aligned to skills needed for schooled tasks.

In answer to her question, a student said, "technology" and another added, "You have to use technology." To which Mariana answered, "OK, technology, iPod (*previously mentioned by a student*), when you use an iPod— if I gave an iPod to my mom she wouldn't know what to do with it." Amidst laughter, she continued,

> You have to teach her, right? Do you need to know how to use it? You need to know what to press to turn it on, how to play the music, you have to know how to use a computer, right? And to be able to understand how to download a song.

Through comparison to her mother, who did not know how to use an iPod or computer, Mariana took up technology here as being a skill the students not only used effortlessly, but had acquired and developed.[1] She started to break down the aspects of the task that they practiced automatically by modeling her thinking out loud about the skills needed to use an iPod.

At another point in the discussion, Mariana pushed students to think about the everyday literacies they practiced competently. Students had listed using MySpace as an activity, and Mariana asked them what they did on MySpace. Students shared that they "talk to people" "write" and "chat." Mariana then asked if anyone had designed their own MySpace page, and a few students raised their hands and said yes:

Mariana:	how do you know how to do that?
Female Student:	there is—there's codes. You go to a website and there's code
Mariana:	who taught you to do that?
Male Student:	myself
Female Student:	I taught myself

Mariana mediated how students acquired their abilities to interact with MySpace. These discussions took place before connecting students' personal and collaborative technological literacy practices to school tasks. Mariana first made their practices explicit through questioning. She followed a student's answer "you talk" with the question, "do you talk to them" to make their literacy practice of writing explicit. Then, she continued to lead students in examining just how detailed and complex their literacy practices were by asking, "who designed their MySpace page?" After two students revealed they looked for the code and taught themselves, the discussion led to video games, and how students learned to play and knew how to find the "cheat sheets" to get to the next levels. One student said he read the manual, and that "practice makes perfect." Mariana had facilitated the discussion to allow students to reveal their capabilities. She continued to press on that idea.

Mariana noted, "I want you to look at these things – these are things that you guys already do every day, right? Do you need to know how to either read something or interpret something to do these things?" She repeated that they knew how to search and read the codes for MySpace, video games, get music and use iPods, and find answers to help them with technology. She continued:

Mariana:	You guys are doing a lot—you're doing a lot of?
Male Student:	Thinking
Mariana:	thinking, right? You're doing a lot of – you're interpreting a lot of things. You were reading. You're already doing a lot of reading. But you guys don't think of it that way do you?
Several voices:	No
Mariana:	when you're working on your MySpace page and chatting with people do you think oh look I'm reading and writing?

Mariana first elicited that students are using thinking skills as they engage in these activities. She then named the thinking skill as "interpreting." She used critical thinking terminology for their everyday literacy practices, and to show connections between their everyday reading to the reading they might encounter in their classes. She asked students what kinds of reading and writing they did in school. Students listed the activities they normally were asked to complete in school, such as read math problems, read books, write essays, and take tests. Mariana then explicitly mediated how their literacy practices were linked to expectations of academic tasks:

Mariana: What are you doing at school? and what are you doing at home?

Female Student #1: the same thing

Mariana: do you consider the reading and writing that you do outside of school to be as important as school literacy?

Several voices: No

Female Student #2: it's wrong

Mariana: what do you mean it's wrong?

Female Student #1: because you speak it wrong you have to speak it the right way—because teachers grade you on how you speak.

Mariana: is it wrong or is it just (*pause*) not what?

Male Student #1: it's not proper

Mariana: not proper for what

Male Student #1: for school

Mariana: for school. OK it's a different setting ... do you—are you going to write the same way you write to your friends that you write in school?

Female Student #4: no

When Mariana asked the two questions about home and school, positioning them together telegraphed her expected response from students. She was perhaps more stating the obvious conclusion she had been leading them towards than attempting to elicit new information. Mariana engineered the trajectory of the discussion by first guiding the discussion to how students learned and developed literacy practices, then to examine literacies they were required to use in school, and to connect the literacies as using skill sets from their funds of knowledge that were similar, when Mariana asked, "do you think, oh look I'm reading and I'm writing?" She showed that students' everyday literacies were so automatic they did not need to stop and think about them; they performed with competence and without assistance.

[handwritten margin note: students doing for the grade, rather than for learning]

This mediation was important in the students' school-going culture; labeled "remedial students," they were conditioned to low teacher-expectations, continual failure, and years of reductive practices (FN). After making it out of "the ESL ghetto" (Valdés, 2001, p. 145) they were never afforded access or meaningful experience with academic writing. One student noted this collective background when she said, "I turn in all my work," noting she expected an A for completing assignments, as opposed to demonstrating learning.

Mediating Students' Cultural and Social Backgrounds and Experiences

During a pilot study of the intervention, students (predominantly from 1.5G) had difficulty choosing topics for their persuasive essay. For 1.5G, because they often enter the country with little schooling from their homelands (Blumenthal, 2002; Gawienowski & Holper, 2006; Ortmeier-Hooper, 2008; Reid, 1998), they may have less extensive background knowledge leading to more limited content for writing (Gawienowski & Holper, 2006). This might explain the struggle to develop a topic; for the study discussed here, developing their funds of knowledge shored up their choices for topics emerging from their cultural and social experiences.

Student narratives were assigned to gain further knowledge of students, to build on their identification of literacy practices and competencies, and to scaffold instruction for persuasive writing through use of their funds of knowledge. The instruction discussed here focused on selecting a topic from which students would develop a stance. The narrative detailed an important incident in their cultural backgrounds, noting a time they experienced unfairness; they chose varied topics, such as their entry to the U.S. and visiting an older brother in prison.

Mariana used the narratives as a scaffold to develop a topic for a persuasive essay. Many students wrote about their school experiences, and the struggles they had encountered to maintain passing grades over the years of their enrollment. It was not surprising when one student suggested "schools" as a topic associated with unfairness. Mariana did not merely accept the topic and move on after that suggestion, but mediated how to turn a general topic into a persuasive stance. She also provided students an opportunity to discuss perceived cultural biases:

Mariana:	Schools, very good. What about schools?
Male Student #1:	they're corrupt—corruption
Mariana:	where do we see corruption?
Male Student #1:	like in our school, the budget, cutting supplies and stuff
Male Student #2:	oh yeah that's so unfair because we don't get the stuff we need
Mariana:	you don't have what you need for a quality education. Like a school in (neighboring city) has everything they need
Male Student #3:	it's cuz we're Mexican, and they don't like us, it's racism

Female Student #1: it's racist, so racist

Male Student #2: yeah, there's a lot of racism and also we don't get the money, like to fix the bathrooms

Mariana: you guys are always complaining about the bathrooms, about how they're always dirty

Male Student #2: yeah it takes like a week to fix them

Mariana: this whole topic is a huge area that affects you—so how would this be persuasive?

Female Student #2: we need stuff

Mariana: how is that persuasive?

Female Student #2: tell them to give us better stuff

Mariana: you mean supplies, or something else?

Female Student #2: yeah, stuff like better books and desks, like that

Mariana: who are you talking to, who do you need to persuade?

Male Student #4: the district

Mariana: what does that mean the district? And what if they don't have any money?

Female Student #3: so write to the governor, to give us what we need

Mariana asked questions to mediate how the topic of schools could be narrowed to a persuasive stance, including identifying an appropriate audience. She also brought in what could be viewed as a counter-argument when she asked, "and if they (the district) don't have any money?" Students' comments before that were made from a single perspective, and while institutional racism may have been an accurate assessment of why the school did not have adequate supplies, the study took place as the district was tightening its budget due to decreased funding. Mariana's question interjected an important alternate perspective, which illustrated the complexity of persuasion and the importance of multiple perspectives in constructing an argument. (The use of counter-arguments and multiple perspectives was taken up many times through the course of the intervention; Mariana introduced it briefly here.) Mariana mediated a large, vague topic into a specific purpose: resources for the school are lacking. A nascent stance was suggested, but in this part of the discussion, it was not developed. Mariana noted and promoted the importance of students' cultural backgrounds and educational resources through comparison to a wealthier, predominantly white school district and questions taking up students' complaints. The discussion continued through several other topics, all mediated through similar questioning.

From this discussion, students wrote their topics, and identified their audience and purpose. To illustrate how students' choice of topics was further mediated, I use an example from Marvin's work. He first identified his topic as "racism"—below [errors intact]:

> I want to persade to think about that racism is wrong and that they should stop it cause you hurt other people. I think that racism needs persuasion to give people so they all think about it what are doing wrong stuff they need to stop it. My audience will be all the world because in the world every where there's always racism.

Marvin did not demonstrate internalization of the concepts from Mariana's whole class mediating. His topic was expansive, and his stance clear but naïve in its attempt to persuade "all the world." Individually, Mariana mediated the topic with him, providing additional assistance. She asked Marvin how he chose that topic. Marvin answered, "you don't ever see Latinos like you see white people" and that "the immigrants are always just in the fields or living bad, somehow they never seem to get the same things." Mariana asked him "what do you want to happen, if you persuade people about this?" After thinking about that question, Marvin said he thought he really wanted to talk about immigrants, not just racism. Mariana said, "explain, and think about how we discussed topics together to focus on important issues" and he replied, "I want to have immigrants here have licenses." His answer was more specific than what he wrote about racism, by choosing an issue he associated with racism. As Mariana mediated through his interest in how racism was harmful, the issue of racism became applied to a group with which he affiliated, being an immigrant himself. Mariana asked if his audience would remain the same, and he said, "no, it's the governor who gives the licenses and decides about it." With brief mediation, Marvin's topic, purpose, and audience were revised and strengthened to: "I want to give license to the immgrants but the governor is being cruel with that idea." His topic was directly related to his cultural background as an immigrant, something Mariana helped leverage.

Marvin produced five drafts of his essay. While his final draft still showed gaps in skills regarding spelling and grammar (e.g.: "imagene" for imagine, run-ons), and had lapses in persuasive logic (e.g.: "if undocumented people leave … the world's economy would get weaker & weaker"), he showed elaboration in his means of persuasion (e.g., "I see Mexicans & central Americans go to work pick fruit, garden, and do nasty work."). He and the other participants were still novice writers. But they had a meaningful experience with academic writing, summed up by one student who spoke of his teacher the year before always failing him, because he never knew what to do, but saying that Mariana explained everything so he knew how to do it.

DISCUSSION

Conley (2008) notes that explanation, modeling, and guided practice are "essential elements of cognitive strategy instruction" (p. 95). The two examples of mediation discussed here fall in that category—Mariana used strategies to mediate between everyday literacies and the cognitively demanding task of academic writing. The mediation took place within classroom activities—classroom experiences designed to construct and support student learning. These activities (inquiring about students' backgrounds and selecting a topic for persuasion) are not new or even unique in their classroom application, and have no guarantee of leading to student learning. As mediated by Mariana, however, they facilitated academic writing through explicit, verbal guided participation (Kozulin, 2003).

There are three areas in which the importance of the teacher's role beyond merely assigning activities was revealed:

1. accessing and valuing students' everyday literacies;
2. questioning for discovery; and
3. focusing on what students' *can* do to provide assistance with what they cannot do on their own.

Students' everyday literacies were identified within the context of an academic task, and given considerable time through the assignment and the class discussion. Mariana not only identified students' literacy competencies in an immediate, engaging way, but she communicated that those competencies were important and valued by making time to uncover them (Fleckenstein, 2003). When the student discussed speaking "the right way," she revealed a dichotomized view of academic tasks and everyday literacies. Other students shared this view by answering in unison to Mariana's question if reading and writing outside of school was as important as in school with a loud, "No." Mariana began to bring together students' outside of school and schooled literacies, helping them to see that their capabilities in acquiring skills to perform complex everyday literacies made them capable to perform schooled literacy tasks such as writing an academic essay. With knowledge of students' everyday literacies, teachers can provide the needed assistance for mediation between those literacies and academic writing. Knowing how students engage in literacy practices, including writing, for their own purposes also provides valuable information about competencies, or funds of knowledge, students possess, which can inform future instructional choices.

An integral part of revealing students' competencies was questioning, not for evaluation, but for assistance. Tharpe and Gallimore (1988) note that "questions call up the use of language and in this way assist thinking" (p. 59). Mariana did not judge students' answers, but used questioning to engage them in thinking beyond their initial responses. For example, Mariana asked Marvin how he chose the topic, which led to his thinking through his topic to develop a more viable stance. When she asked students what they had to be able to do in order to practice the literacies they described, she assisted them in thinking metacognitively, to think about the "processes involved in learning" (Livingston, 2003, p. 3) by shifting from recall of tasks to thinking about the processes required to perform them.

The mediation of students' choice of topic emerged directly from students' backgrounds and experiences, written in their narratives. Mariana had to instantaneously assess students' gaps in understanding how a topic for persuasive writing is developed. Using a sociocultural perspective to inform her practice, Mariana did not "tell" or transmit knowledge. She guided students' exploration of a topic; students provided suggestions for how to narrow and focus it within the social interactions of a guided discussion. Students called out words such as "gangs" and "violence" when Mariana asked for topics from their narratives. Mariana mediated each suggestion from the broad, overly general topic to a specific issue on which a stance could be taken. Mariana modeled the process several times during discussion, using questioning to assist students and provide experiences in developing topics of importance they could not accomplish on their own. She then provided assistance as needed individually, illustrated with Marvin, while the students worked on their topic, audience, and persuasive stance. Mariana scaffolded support for the students and provided assistance as a more knowledgeable other.

The activities were designed to build students' confidence in academic writing. Graves and Rueda (2009) note that motivation is in part "a set of task-specific beliefs, which include perceived competence" (p. 226). Mariana explicitly noted the skills students brought to their everyday literacy practices, mentioning more than once how they could "do all these things." For students enrolled in a class they knew was for "failures" this was an important stage in writing instruction. Mariana engaged in a discourse of persuasion to convince students of the value and worth of their abilities as well as their capability to learn challenging literacy tasks. Importantly, the roles Mariana took up during this instruction were not enacted separately, but were often enmeshed and used simultaneously during her "in the moment" responses to students.

Instruction in academic writing was interdependent with students' everyday writing, foregrounding students' cultural and linguistic experiences, and emerging organically from those experiences. The two strategies focused on here show instruction informed by sociocultural learning theory. Both provided mediation for students between their backgrounds, experiences, and competencies for access to academic writing. Mariana's mediation was beneficial for these novice writers as an important precursor to academic writing. Through mediation of their known skills and competencies, Mariana was focused on what they could do and where they needed assistance. This approach counters traditional approaches that identify students' gaps in skills—foregrounding what they might lack, rather than what they were capable of accomplishing.

IMPLICATIONS

The findings discussed here stress the potential of using mediation, detailing what it looked like in practice. Explicit instructional strategies for writing to help students understand the process to produce writing meeting academic expectations were not only respectful of students' cultural and social backgrounds and the complex funds of knowledge they possess, but through mediation, leveraged those funds to capitalize on students' abilities.

Sociocultural theory kept instruction focused on appropriate assistance, as opposed to reverting to a deficit view focusing on what the students are lacking. Knowing the background of students from 1.5G was important to promote their academic literacy development. If teachers are unaware of their language acquisition and academic literacy backgrounds, they may not see this group advance academically when using strategies for mainstream native-English speakers. Generation 1.5 may not have had the experiences to develop academic literacy, and therefore should not be viewed as lacking competency. Sociocultural perspectives promote understanding that 1.5G are competent and willing to engage with academic writing if they are given access and experiences to meet expectations. Assistance of a more knowledgeable other defines the role of the teacher as being actively engaged in the mediation of literacies.

The strategies illustrated use students' cultural, social, and linguistic competencies and experiences as a starting point for academic writing. The two strategies described here were more than applications of activities—they both involved mediation of complex social interactions. The first strategy, identifying and valuing students' funds of knowledge, was a crucial starting point in re-mediating students' self-concepts of "failures." The activity chart was a means to have students begin to identify their many competencies, competencies most often ignored or devalued in academic settings. The chart on its own would not promote students' self-efficacy, but paired with Mariana's mediation delving into *how* students enacted those skills, students were allowed to identify their strengths and use them to access academic writing.

The second strategy relied on students' cultural experiences as they wrote of a situation that was significant in their lives due to unfairness. The topics that emerged were mediated via questioning to stances from which students could develop a persuasive essay. Group discussion modeling that process, followed by individual intervention where needed, was important to this strategy. Both strategies directly involved students in social situations to promote collaborative learning, two key aspects of sociocultural theory, which 1.5G may not experience in traditional, remedial classrooms.

It may seem the strategies and activities used here apply to all novice writers, and are not specific to 1.5G, or even L2 writers. To a certain extent, I would agree. Perhaps it is not so important to isolate instructional strategies and target their use with one group but not another—but to have a wide repertoire of strategies from which to choose, and use strategies appropriate for a given context. They might be adapted to contexts other than instruction for 1.5G, but as described here, they foregrounded students' cultural and linguistic histories and celebrated their rich funds of knowledge. The teacher's role in mediation should disrupt the monolithic discourse of academic writing by promoting those histories and leveraging those funds of knowledge, not reverting to skills-based instruction or telling and assigning without instructional support.

NOTE

1.   Based on writing surveys students completed, 18 participants had computers and an Internet connection at home, and the two who did not have access at home reported using the Internet at friends' homes, the library, and school at least three times a week.

REFERENCES

Asher, C., Case, E., & Zhong, Y. (2009). Serving generation 1.5: Academic library use and students from non–English-speaking households. *College and Research Libraries, 70*(3), 258-272.

Atkinson, D., & Ramanathan, V. (1995). Cultures of writing: An ethnographic comparison of L1 and L2 university writing/language programs. *TESOL Quarterly, 29,* 539-568.

Barnard, R., & Campbell, L. (2005). Sociocultural theory and the teaching of process writing: The scaffolding of learning in a university context. *University of Waikata Research Commons.* Retrieved from http://researchcommons.waikato.ac.nz/handle/10289/433

Bloome, D., Carter, S. P., Christian, B. M., Otto, S., & Shuart-Faris, N. (2008). *Discourse analysis in classrooms: Approaches to language and literacy research.* New York, NY: Teachers College Press.

Blumenthal, A. (2002). English as a second language at the community college: An exploration of context and concerns. *New Directions for Community Colleges, 117,* 45-53

California Commission on Teacher Credentialing. (2011). *Standards: Educator preparation.* Retrieved (July 2, 2011) from: http://www.ctc.ca.gov/educator-prep/STDS-prep-program.html

Conley, M. W. (2008). Cognitive strategy instruction for adolescents. *Harvard Educational Review, 78*(1), 84-106.

Delpit, L. (1992). Acquisition of literate discourse: bowing before the master? *Theory into Practice, 31*(4), 296-302.

Echevarria, J., & Graves, A. A. (2007). *Sheltered content instruction: Teaching students with diverse needs* (3rd ed.). Los Angeles, CA: Allyn & Bacon.

Fleckenstein, K. S. (2003). *Embodied literacies: Imageword and a poetics of teaching.* Carbondale, IL: Southern Illinois University Press.

Forrest, S. N. (2006). Three foci of an effective high school Generation 1.5 literacy program. *Journal of Adolescent & Adult Literacy 50*(2), 106-112.

Gawienowski, M. F., & Holper, K. (2006). A portrait of generation 1.5 students. In C. Machado (Series Ed.) & A. Blumenthal (Vol. Ed.), *Perspectives on community college ESL series: Vol. 2. Students, mission, and advocacy* (pp. 117-130). Alexandria, VA: Teachers of English to Speakers of Other Languages, Inc.

Gee, J. P. (2004). Language and identity at home, Chapter 3. *Situated language and learning: A critique of traditional schooling.* New York, NY: Routledge.

Grabe, W., & Kaplan, R. B. (1996). *Theory and practice of writing: An applied linguistic perspective.* New York, NY: Longman.

Graves, A. W., & Rueda, R. (2009). Teaching written expression to culturally and linguistically diverse learners. In G. A. Troia (Ed.), *Instruction and assessment for struggling writers: Evidence-based practices,* (pp. 213-242). New York, NY: Guilford

Harklau, L., Losey, K. M., & Siegal, M. (1999). Linguistically diverse students and college writing: What is equitable and appropriate? In L. Harklau, K. M. Losey, & M. Siegal (Eds.), *Generation 1.5 meets college composition: Issues in the teaching of writing to U.S educated learners of ESL* (pp. 1-14). Mahwah, NJ: Lawrence Erlbaum Associates.

Hartman, B., & Tarone, E. (1999). Preparation for college writing: Teachers talk about writing instruction for Southeast Asian American students in secondary school. In L. Harklau, K. M. Losey, & M. Siegal. (1999). *Generation 1.5 meets college composition: Issues in the teaching of writing to U.S.-educated learners of ESL* (pp. 99-118). Mahwah, NJ: Erlbaum.

Hillocks, G. (2008). Writing in secondary schools. In C. Bazerman (Ed.), *Handbook of research on writing: History, society, school, individual, text* (pp. 311-330). New York, NY: Lawrence Erlbaum.

Kozulin, A. (2003). Psychological tools and mediated learning. In A. Kouzlin et al., (Eds.), *Vygotsky's education theory in cultural context,* (pp. 15-38). New York, NY: Cambridge University Press.

Kutz, E., Groden, S., & Zamel, V. (1993). *The discovery of competence: Teaching and learning with diverse student writers.* Portsmouth, NH: Boynton/Cook.

Lee, C. D. (2000). Signifyin' in the zone of proximal development. In C. Lee and P. Smagorinsky (Eds.) *Vygotskian perspectives on literacy research: Constructing meaning through collaborative inquiry,* (pp. 191-225). Cambridge, England: Cambridge University Press.

Livingston, J. A. (2003*). Metacognition: An overview.* (Report No. 034 808). Buffalo, NY: University of Buffalo. (ERIC Document Reproduction Service No. ED 474 273).

Matsuda, P. K. (2006). Second-language writing in the twentieth century: A situated historical perspective. In P. K. Matsuda, M. Cox, J. Jordan, & C. Ortmeier-Hooper (Eds.), *Second-language writing in the composition classroom* (pp. 14-30). Boston, MA: Bedford/St. Martin's.

Moll, L. C. (1998, February). *Funds of knowledge for teaching: A new approach to culture in education.* Keynote address: Illinois State Board of Education.

Moll, L. C., Amanti, C., Neff, D., & Gonzalez, N. (2001). Funds of knowledge for teaching:Using a qualitative approach to connect homes and classrooms. *Theory into Practice, 31,* 132-141.

Moll, L. C., Sáez, R., & Dworin, J. (2001). Exploring biliteracy: Two student case examples of writing as a social practice. *The Elementary School Journal, 101*(4), 435-449.

Olson, S. (1999). Errors and compensatory strategies. *System, 27,* 191-205.

Ortmeier-Hooper, C. (2008). English may be my second language, but I'm not ESL. *College Communication and Composition, 59*(3), 389-41.

Pérez, B. (1998). Making decisions about literacy instructional practices. In B. Pérez (Ed.), *Sociocultural contexts of language and literacy,* (251-276). Mahwah, NJ: Lawrence Erlbaum Associates.

Reid, J. (1998). "Eye" learners and "ear" learners: Identifying the language needs of international students and U.S. resident writers. In P. Byrd & J. Reid, (Eds.), *Grammar in the composition classroom* (pp. 3-17). New York, NY: Heinle & Heinle.

Reinking, D., & Bradley, B. A. (2008). *Formative and design experiments: Approaches to language and literacy research.* New York, NY: Teachers College Press.

Roberge, M. (2003, March). *Generation 1.5 immigrant students: What special experiences, characteristics and educational needs do they bring to our English classes?* Presented at the 37Annual TESOL Convention, Baltimore, MD.

Rose, M. (2006). Two case studies. In M. Rose (Ed.), *An open language: Selected writing on literacy, learning, and opportunity* (pp. 28-55). Boston, MA: Bedford Books of St. Martin's Press.

Rumbaut R. G., & Ima, K. (1988). The adaptation of Southeast Asian refugee youth: A comparative study. *Final Report to the Office of Resettlement.* San Diego, CA: San Diego State University.

Shin, S. J. (2002). Understanding ESL writers: Second language writing by composition instructors. *Teaching English in the Two-Year College, 30*(1), 68-75.

Singhal, M. (2004). Academic writing and Generation 1.5. *The Reading Matrix, 4*(3), 1-13.

Strauss, A., & Corbin, J. (1990). *Basics of qualitative research: Grounded theory procedures and techniques.* Newbury Park, CA: SAGE.

Street, B. V. (2005). Introduction. In B. V. Street (Ed.), *Literacies across educational contexts: Mediating literacy and teaching* (pp. 1-21). Philadelphia, PA: Caslon.

Swales, J.M. (1990). *Genre analysis: English in academic and research settings.* Cambridge, England: Cambridge University Press.

Tharpe, R. G., & Gallimore, R. (1988). *Rousing minds to life.* Cambridge, MA: Cambridge University Press.

Valdés, G. (2001). *Learning and not learning English: Latino students in American-schools.* New York, NY: Teachers College Press

Valdés, G. (2004). The failure to educate immigrant children. In O. Santa Ana, (Ed.) *Tongue Tied: The Lives of Multilingual Children in Public Education* (pp. 111-117). Lanham, MD: Rowman & Littlefield.

CHAPTER 9

THE TEACHER'S CULTURAL INCLUSIVITY AND ENGLISH LANGUAGE LEARNERS' PARTICIPATION IN LANGUAGE AND LITERACY ACTIVITIES

Bogum Yoon

Grounded in sociocultural theory, the purpose of this chapter is to examine a regular classroom teacher's teaching approaches to promote English language learners' (ELLs) interaction and participation in language and literacy activities. The data of this case study, which was conducted in a middle school setting, include interviews, classroom observations, and artifacts from the teacher and the two ELLs. The study suggests that the teacher's awareness of ELLs' cultural and social needs, cultural inclusivity approach, and utilization of ELLs as a cultural resource contributed to the students' learning. The findings of the study provide significant implications for regular classroom teachers who work with ELLs in the mainstream classroom.

Teachers' Roles in Second Language Learning:
Classroom Applications of Sociocultural Theory, pp. 155–169
Copyright © 2012 by Information Age Publishing
All rights of reproduction in any form reserved.

Through a case study method, the central purpose of this chapter is to discuss a regular classroom teacher's teaching approaches to assist English language learners' (ELLs) participation in language and literacy activities. In the course of one semester, I observed the classrooms of three English language arts teachers who had ELLs in their classrooms (For the detailed analysis of the three classrooms, see Yoon, 2008). Among these regular classrooms, the ELLs in Mrs. Young's (all names are pseudonyms) class looked more comfortable and participated more actively in language and literacy activities as the days went by. In her classroom, Mrs. Young promoted ELLs' participation by accommodating their cultural differences. Given that the ELLs were quiet and silent in the beginning of the semester, their different participant levels were conspicuous. The ELLs' interaction with their mainstream peers became more active compared to the ELLs in the other two classrooms.

One of the most noticeable features in Mrs. Young's classroom was that the mainstream peers' attitudes toward these ELLs were entirely different from those of the other classes. Mrs. Young's students treated their ELLs in a more favorable manner than the students of the other classes who showed strong resistance or indifference towards them. These classroom dynamics led me to focus on Mrs. Young's teaching approaches. Sociocultural theory (Vygotsky, 1978, 1981, 1986) provides an important theoretical lens to analyze Mrs. Young's roles and her impact on ELLs' interaction with their peers in the classroom.

SOCIOCULTURAL PERSPECTIVES AND THE TEACHER'S ROLE

According to Vygotsky (1978, 1981), learning is a social practice and it occurs through interaction between people. Vygotsky views that learning is a joint activity between a more knowledgeable person and a less knowledgeable person in social contexts. The process of arranging for such learning to occur in joint activity is known as scaffolding (Bruner, 1975). Scaffolding or mentoring means that more experienced people guide learners to reach the level of independent problem-solving through interaction. Scaffolding is not the carrying out of a specific task for children, but facilitating children's cognitive thinking in "the zone of proximal development" (Vygotsky, 1978, p. 86). Teachers play a role in providing scaffolding as they offer opportunities for students to participate in learning activities (García, Pearson, Taylor, Bauer, & Stahl, 2011). Scaffolding does not mean that teachers simply transmit knowledge or do activity on behalf of students. Moreover, it does not mean that teachers are active and students are passive in interacting for mental process as students play active roles in interpersonal activity.

Sociocultural theory implies the significance of teachers' roles for maximizing students' learning. The role of the teacher is one of mediation, to borrow Vygotsky's term. By helping children create the zone of proximal development—"development achieved and developmental potential" (Lantolf & Thorne, 2006, p. 206), teachers mediate experience. When teachers mediate learning, it is important to know students' current level. According to students' current level, teachers can provide different types of support, by adjusting and modifying their speaking modes such as strategic or referential statements. In this mediating process, students' emotionality is crucial (DiPardo & Potter, 2003; Tappan, 1998). As DiPardo and Potter (2003) pointed out, individuals' emotions "develop in concert with the whole of a person's cognitive and social life, continually constructed through social interaction and progressively internalized" (p. 320). Since students' emotion is inseparable from their thought, sociocultural theory endorses that it is important for teachers to consider these concepts of mind and emotion together to help their learning.

In addition, sociocultural theory emphasizes cultivating talk in the process of mediation (Britton, 1993). Articulate talk is significant to inquiry, to collaborative learning, and to assimilating knowledge in meaningful ways (Boyd & Rubin, 2002). Articulate talk is a way to literacy, as students learn first in speech techniques for manipulating larger portions of discourse into coherent texts. This idea applies to ELLs. As Boyd and Rubin claimed, ELLs need to have opportunities to develop talk in the classroom because classroom talk serves ELLs the same purposes that does for native English speaking students. The difference between the meaning of talk for ELLs as compared with that for native English speakers is that through talk, which is a vehicle for acquiring both speech practices and linguistic structures, they come to notice and consolidate structural properties of English—their target language (Pica, 1994).

Vygotskian theory furthermore provides insights as to what regular classroom teachers need to do for facilitating ELLs' learning in classroom settings. For example, teachers need to encourage collaboration between peers. In particular, new comers who do not understand English well tend to remain silent and feel isolated in mainstream contexts. In such situations, mainstream students might view these silent students as "inferior" and not want to approach them (Miller, 2000). In this context, the teacher's role is vital in having them interact with each other. In other words, teachers need to consider how they can use native-English speaking students as language resources for ELLs. Moreover, they need to take into consideration how they can use ELLs' cultural resources for mainstream students.

Tudge (1990) addresses that "interaction with a more competent peer has been shown to be highly effective in inducing cognitive development"

(p. 159). Tudge applies cognitive thinking development by linking Vygotskian ideas to second language learning. As Vygotsky theorized, learning is a social process and subsequently so is learning a language. Faltis and Hudelson (1998) pointed out that

> learning and language acquisition overlap to a great extent in the sense that both are social, contextual, and goal-oriented. That is, individuals learn both content and language as they engage with others in a variety of settings and to accomplish specific purposes. (p. 85)

This social view of learning applies to all learning, including learning a second language. In a second language environment, non-native English speakers can receive help from native English speaking peers. For example, native English speaking students can be more knowledgeable about linguistic skills. However, ELLs might have more cultural resources. In this case, peer collaboration between native English speaking students and ELLs works to support and facilitate learning. Through interaction, students are involved in the cognitive process by sharing their ideas, co-constructing meaning, negotiating their perspectives, linking their ideas to their life experiences, and reshaping their ideas in meaningful social contexts. Through these activities, they are in the learning process.

Sociocultural theory contributes to our understanding of how children learn and how teachers mediate their learning. It also contributes to deepen our understanding of the importance of culture and context on human development (Lee & Smagorinsky, 2000). However, there is little research on how the theory is actualized in the classroom where regular classroom teachers work with ELLs. Therefore, in this study the practical issue is examined through one regular classroom teacher's teaching practices for ELLs' language and literacy learning.

METHODOLOGY

Data Collection and Analysis

I collected data at Mrs. Young's middle school over one semester, which is located in a first-ring suburban area in New York State. The school served a wide range of students of Bolivian, Chilean, Indian, Japanese, Korean, Nigerian, Pakistan, Puerto Rican, Russian, and Ukrainian descent. As point of departure, I began by contacting the English as a Second Language (ESL) teacher in the school to find out who was teaching ELLs in their English classes. There were four teachers: two sixth grade teachers, one seventh grade teacher, and one eighth grade teacher. Three teachers were willing to be my participants, and Mrs. Young was one of them. I visited the school and Mrs. Young's classroom almost every day, Monday through Friday.

This study subscribed to a case study method (Merriam, 2009; Yin, 2003). Yin stated that a case study is "the preferred strategy when 'how' or 'why' questions are being posed, when the investigator has little control over events, and when the focus is on a contemporary phenomenon within some real-life context" (p. 1). A case study was a preferred tool to examine how the regular classroom teacher's teaching approaches formulated the ELLs' interaction and participation within the contemporary classroom dynamics.

Data sources included interview transcripts, field notes and audiotaped transcripts of classroom observations, research logs, interview memos, and documents such as the teacher's lesson plans as well as Dae's and Ana's classroom projects. The primary form of data was in-depth interviews with Mrs. Young and the two ELLs, and extensive observations in the classroom. At least, four 1-hour-long formal interviews and several informal interviews with Mrs. Young were conducted. Two formal interviews and several informal interviews were completed with Dae and Ana. To capture the dynamics of Mrs. Young's classroom, focusing on her practices and the students' interaction and participation in learning activities, I took field notes. Furthermore, I audiotaped classroom conversations and cross-checked them with the field notes. All of the classroom observations and audio-taped interviews were labeled and transcribed.

For data analysis, Corbin and Strauss's (2008) coding strategies and Spradley's (1980) taxonomic analysis were employed. The categories were guided by sociocultural theory (Vygotsky, 1978, 1981) which provides insights to the teacher's role as a mediator and the ELLs' learning as a social practice. In particular, the key concepts of the zone of proximal development, mediating, emotionality, and interaction were used as important frameworks for the analysis.

Profile of Mrs. Young and Focal Students

Mrs. Young is a European American in her late 40s. She has approximately six years of teaching experience in her middle school. The teacher received her bachelor's degree in elementary education (K-6) and a master's degree in reading. She taught two classes (A & B) of sixth graders ELA/reading/social studies in a block schedule where each block lasted about 2 hours. All sixth grade ELLs were assigned to Team I, in which the teacher belonged. In her class B, which this chapter will focus on, there were 26 students: 18 European American, 6 African American, one Russian, and one Korean. Among them, there were six special education students and two English language learners: Dae and Ana.

Dae is from South Korea. At the time of the study, Dae had lived in the United States for one year. Before coming to the United States, Dae attended an elementary school in a rural area in South Korea. The other student, Ana, is from Russia. She had 3 years of schooling in Russia, in addition to the 1 year in New York City. Both students' English level is in its beginning, according to the standardized test and the ESL teacher's decision. Both Dae and Ana received two periods of ESL program a day. Except for these two periods, they stayed in the mainstream classroom and received the same instruction with other children.

Researcher's Role

The role of researcher was different according to the situation. I functioned as a nonparticipant observer when Mrs. Young was conducting her lesson. During the lesson, I wrote field notes while sitting in the corner of her classroom. However, I played the role of a more participatory observer when some students asked for help by looking at me and raising their hands while the teacher was busy helping other students. In observation of the classroom, I witnessed Dae and Ana from a close distance when they did small group work or pair work. Sometimes, I observed them from a remote distance while they interacted with their peers and the teachers. Overall, I sought to balance my research role as a passive participant observer and a moderate participant observer (Spradley, 1980) according to situations at the teacher's and the students' requests.

FINDINGS

In this section, the teacher's role to promote her ELLs' participation and interaction with their peers is discussed. Three themes include: (1) Awareness of ELLs' status in the mainstream classroom, (2) Cultural inclusivity approach, and (3) Impact on ELLs' interaction and participation.

Teachers' Awareness of ELLs' Current Status

Mrs. Young, who stated that she is a "teacher of children," viewed that teaching ELLs in her classroom is her responsibility. She seemed to be aware of how her ELLs might feel isolated in the regular classroom in the beginning of the semester. In an interview, Mrs. Young described her opinion of ELLs' feelings and status in the mainstream classroom. She claimed that her experience working with ELLs for over six years taught her that ELLs wanted to belong to a mainstream culture:

> You want to assimilate. You want not to be different. I hear that a lot from the kids. They feel different. And so if you can celebrate those differences, I think we are ahead of the game. I think that's where we need to go.

The interview data from Dae and Ana support Mrs. Young's statements about ELLs' feelings in the mainstream classroom. In the first interview with Dae and Ana focusing on their opinions about regular classes including Mrs. Young's class, they mentioned that they like being in the ESL classroom better because they feel more comfortable there. Dae stated, "I feel more comfortable in the ESL classroom. I can talk there." Ana said, "I like being in ESL class. There are people don't speak English very well. Everybody is same. My friends are there. But in other classes, everybody looks at me. I don't like it." Their responses show that their comfort level comes from their familiarity with friends and the environment. They feel different in the regular classroom than in the ESL classroom.

Mrs. Young expressed that ELLs need careful consideration and caring in order for them to adjust to a new culture successfully. Her understanding of ELLs' difficulties facilitated this role:

> When you are in the situation where you don't know things, you feel uncomfortable and self-conscious. I think about how would I feel if I were in their shoes. They need a friendship and support and they need to know that they can count on someone. I hope they feel that they count on me.

She mentioned that when ELLs are assigned to her class, she approaches them and asks them questions, such as their reason for coming to the United States, length of stay, first language, and family backgrounds. She explained, "I try to get background on them when they first come in."

After obtaining basic information about ELLs, Mrs. Young works to assist ELLs' learning in the classroom. Mrs. Young considered ELLs' cultural and social issues to support their academic needs. In an interview, Mrs. Young emphasized her role as a supporter: "I am supportive of their learning. They have to know I am approachable. They have to see me as someone who is willing to help them and able to move them forward."

As shown in the interview data, Mrs. Young is conscious about ELLs' cultural and social needs in the new context. Mrs. Young's priority is to know about her ELLs' comfort level, which she believes is the first stage for their academic success. This finding references the emotional aspects in learning.

Teacher's Cultural Inclusivity

Mrs. Young's awareness of her ELLs' current level is the foundation for her to implement diverse instructional approaches for the students. She utilizes the concept of cultural inclusivity in her approach. She appears to value and respect her ELLs' cultural and social identities and wants them to retain their identities while living in the United States:

> I am putting value on their lives and their cultures. I think that helps them to retain their heritage and their pride and their identity because that can be lost when you are in another culture. Socially I think we need to celebrate differences.

To help them sustain their heritage, she did many "intentional" things. For instance, she called on ELLs as often as other students for having them produce their opinion. Based on my observations, she sometimes called on their names first before other students. When Dae and Ana were hesitant to answer due to their lack of command of English or for some other related reasons, she adjusted her questions to be easier so that they could answer even just by saying yes or no. Moreover, she reminded other students how hard it would be if they were to go to other countries and study a language which is totally new. By having non-English language learners understand ELLs' difficulties and by giving them the impression that the problem is not their ability but their language obstacle, she helped ELLs feel comfortable and confident in learning contexts.

Mrs. Young used her ELLs as an important resource. Her intention of celebrating ELLs' differences is not only for the benefit of ELLs, but also for non-ELLs. In other words, by using ELLs as a cultural resource, Mrs. Young's intentional approaches benefited both of the groups. In order to utilize ELLs as cultural resources, she asked them many questions:

> Every time I say in the classroom, how do you do that? What's the norm in your country? How do you celebrate that or how do people feel about this? What are your traditions? I want non-ESL kids to know that their beliefs and their cultures are different. I want them to understand and to enjoy and appreciate those things. If we don't, we are in a big trouble. I don't want American children to think that Americans are better than Iraq or Iraqi children. Because that is not true.

My classroom observation supports Mrs. Young's statements. For example, as Thanksgiving Day approached, the students in her classroom were reading *The Thanksgiving Visitor* by Capote (1997). Mrs. Young asked her ELLs whether they celebrated it in their countries. Dae said "Yes" in an excited voice and explained how Korean people eat "Songpyun," which is

[Handwritten margin notes: "- opportunities for ELL students to participate in any way possible", "- making them feel comfortable, embracing differences"]

rice cake. By encouraging ELLs to present their culture and traditions, she assisted her other students in broadening their ways of thinking and to develop their critical thinking. In other words, by using ELLs as a resource, she promoted her students to consider an additional cultural dimension:

> I appreciate and enjoy other people and wanted to expose them to that, part of which is why I really enjoy having all the ESL kids on our team. It adds a dimension that we would not have otherwise.

Mrs. Young appreciated that ELLs were on her team. To Mrs. Young, teaching ELLs was not a frustration, but a useful resource. She was concerned about ELLs but not frustrated because of them.

The other approach that she employed, the concept of cultural inclusivity approach, was to expose her students to various multicultural literature. She often brought to her class multicultural literature written by minority groups in the United States, such as African-American, Asian, and Hispanic literature. She said, "What I try to do is to expose kids to lots of different writings. We read Puerto Rican pieces or Black pieces." By using multicultural literature as one of the main resources for her teaching, Mrs. Young stated that she wanted to have her ELLs feel connected to the literature and wanted to play a role in broadening her students' way of thinking towards the world.

Teacher's Impact on ELLs' Interaction and Participation

Mrs. Young's cultural inclusivity approach, based on the celebration of differences and using ELLs as a cultural resource, influenced the behaviors of Dae and Ana. Their participation and interaction with peers in class changed as time passed. Visible differences between the beginning of the first semester and the end indicate that Mrs. Young's approaches worked in helping them to feel comfortable and to join their group of American peers. When I started my observation at the beginning of the school year, her ELLs were very quiet, and rarely participated in classroom discussion. Although Mrs. Young tried hard to engage them in class, they did not seem to feel comfortable. When most of the students sat on a rug for discussing or listening to the teacher, Ana and Dae usually sat at the end of the rug, not in the middle. Otherwise, they simply sat on their chair without joining the rest of the group on the rug. Both Ana and Dae usually sat in the corner and listened while other peers discussed. When Mrs. Young asked, they simply answered yes or no or in a simple phrase. For example, when Mrs. Young asked Dae and Ana, "How did you feel when you came to America?" he answered, "I don't know," and she said, "O.K." Most of the time, Dae seemed to be attentive. Ana, however, often looked away through the window while playing with her hair by curling it or biting her fingernail.

Although the students had feelings of isolation in their mainstream classroom at the beginning of the semester; toward the end of semester, their participation and interaction with their peers seemed to be more active. Mrs. Young's approaches, calling on their names and asking them questions about their culture, are perceived positively in this matter:

> Dae: I feel good when she asks me about my country. I think she is interested in other cultures. My American friends like to ask me about my country.
>
> Ana: My ELA teacher wants to know many things about my country. I like that. I feel good when I can answer, but I feel bad when I cannot answer.

Their statements prove that they perceive Mrs. Young's cultural interest in their countries positively. The students' positive perception of Mrs. Young is shown in their actions. For example, Ana was not hesitant to approach Mrs. Young. She talked about personal details, such as her family members. One day, during a break, she approached Mrs. Young and told her that her mother "screamed" at her because she did not want to eat much. Both Mrs. Young and Ana laughed while they were talking. Her mother was concerned about her daughter, who she thought only cared about her "slim" body without considering her health. In fact, I observed that Ana usually ate fruits or salad for her lunch. In her writing about what she wants to change about herself, she expressed that she wants "to be very tall, be thin, beautiful and to be very clever".

With these positive perceptions of Mrs. Young, the two students' participation and interaction with their American peers were promoted. For example, I could see more smiling on their face, talking, and laughing with their partners. They seemed to be more confident than before. Dae, in particular, took initiative in choosing a partner, and found the partner easier to work with. However, in the beginning he could not do that. He passively waited for a partner to approach him. Ana was also quiet in the beginning of the semester, but her elevated comfort level was shown in her participation. Ana often raised her hand to present her opinions and, sometimes, she almost stood up from the chair, waving her hand, to be called on by Mrs. Young to talk about her stories and opinions.

In addition, their comfort level working with non-ELLs seems to be increasing, as shown in their interview responses, which were obtained at the end of the semester:

Dae: I can ask anyone. They are nice. They answer me when I ask questions.

Ana: They [American peers] are friendly and nice. Even though they don't understand me, they say, it is ok. They don't laugh at me.

These statements show Dae's and Ana's growth in their confidence and their positive feelings for the regular and ESL classrooms. Their confidence seemed to affect their participation in learning activities.

The increase in their participation seems to be largely due to Mrs. Young matching them with American peers, who sat next or near to them. Mrs. Young elaborated her approach to utilize mainstream students to assist ELLs:

pairing w/ strong students

I use other students to help them. I try to partner them up with children who are strong in one area so that I am not the only person going around to help. They have somebody next to them who can help them. It is nice when a peer understands and can help another child. Child-to-child that builds the friendship also, so that's positive. Whoever we think is kind and understanding, who is very friendly, we will pair up, so that's a resource.

According to close observation, her ELLs sat with friendly and academically strong students. My interview transcripts indicated that Dae and Ana in Mrs. Young's class seemed to feel comfortable sitting with them and did not seem to hesitate to ask questions. Dae said, "I ask them when I need a help and they help me." Ana told me, "Sandy is my second best friend. She is nice."

American peers' interest and encouragement played a major role for these ELLs in participating and engaging more in class. For instance, Mrs. Young asked about school differences in Korea and America. Dae talked about his school in Korea, which does not take school fighting seriously. He said that teachers expect the students who are involved in fighting to solve the problem by themselves. After hearing that, some students said, "Wow, it is cool. I want to go to Korea." Being excited by his peers' interest, Dae talked exuberantly to his learning group who wanted to hear more about it.

Another example of American peers' positive attitude towards these ELLs is when Dae received 83% on a Social Studies test, which was a good score for him. He usually got under 70 or sometimes worse. His American partner encouraged him by saying, "Wow, you did a good job." When I asked him later why he said it to Dae, his answer was: "He is Korean. English is not his language, but he did a wonderful job. It is amazing." His response indicates that he understands Dae's difficulties as a non-English speaking person. Mrs. Young's American students are friendly to Ana as well. For instance, Ana's partner, who was sitting next to her, saw that Ana did not "scotch" tape her twenty vocabulary cards on the file folder as her social studies homework well enough. As soon as Ana's partner saw this, she brought a tape from the teacher's desk and helped Ana tape them firmly. In an additional occurrence, one of Ana's American peers approached her and asked whether she could come to her birthday party. Ana responded to her with a smile that she would ask her mother.

These examples indicate that ELLs' American peers are friendly to them and they are accepted as a part of the community. In sum, my findings indicate that Mrs. Young's active approach, grounded on her philosophy of celebrating ELLs' differences, improved their interaction with mainstream kids, without losing their identity as English language learners. Their interaction was fostered by their peers, who have positive attitudes and understand their difficulties in a new culture as a result of Mrs. Young's careful and caring approaches. In short, Mrs. Young's approaches seem to affect both groups of the students and assist their learning as they work together. Her pluralistic model encouraged her ELLs to sustain their identity and feel more proud of themselves while enabling them to work with their American peers more cooperatively.

DISCUSSION

This chapter discussed one regular classroom teacher's roles and teaching approaches for her ELLs' language and literacy learning. Research shows that many regular classrooms do not consider that they have a responsibility of teaching ELLs (Duff, 2001; Fu, 1995; Yoon, 2008). However, the case of Mrs. Young refines the existing literature. Mrs. Young, who assumed a strong responsibility to work with ELLs, shows a positive example that regular classroom teachers might consider when they work with ELLs. Mrs. Young's practices reflect several basic characteristics that sociocultural theory suggests for students' learning.

First, Mrs. Young, who viewed that her work is to support her ELLs to meet their cultural, social, and academic needs, played an active role in assisting her ELLs by implementing cultural inclusivity in her approach. Vygotsky (1978) emphasized the importance of the teacher's understanding of the student's current level through the concept of zone of proximal development. The findings of this study show that Mrs. Young was implementing Vygotsky's concept by being aware of her ELLs' cultural and social needs in the new context. Realizing that the students might feel isolated and different in the mainstream context, this teacher first attempted to establish a personal relationship with them. With this foundation, the teacher supported their academic needs and assisted them to reach their potential levels.

One noticeable point is that Mrs. Young, who is a regular classroom teacher, extended her role to teach all children including ELLs. She did not dichotomize her role as a specialized area teacher or as a teacher for regular classroom students only. Mrs. Young assumed the responsibility of teaching ELLs and did not relinquish the responsibility to someone else (Compton-Hall, 2004). Before approaching the students' academic task promptly, their emotional features were her priority. As Vygotsky (1978) stresses human relations in learning, Mrs. Young implemented this idea in her classroom. By building a relationship and trust through personal connection, and by utilizing every possible means, Mrs. Young was actualizing sociocultural theory that endorses Noddings's (2003) caring concept for her ELLs' language and literacy learning. The affective aspects that Mrs. Young considered seemed to play a key role for her ELLs to participate in learning.

Second, Mrs. Young used her ELLs as a cultural resource which helped them to participate in learning activities and which contributed to other mainstream students' learning as well. She utilized "funds of knowledge" (González, Moll, & Amanti, 2005) that the ELLs brought to classroom for all students' learning. By using the notions of "interpsychological plane" and "intrapsychological plane," Vygotsky (1978) underscores the importance of interaction for learning. He claims that learning takes place first on the social plane between people in social contexts and then moves to the intrapsychological plane to become part of the individuals. Mrs. Young appeared to implement this concept of interpsychological plane to assist ELLs for their learning. She promoted ELLs' interaction with their mainstream peers by allowing them to sit together and to help with each other. As Freeman and Freeman (2001) claimed, language is learned best when students are focused on content and meaning rather than on aspects of language itself. Mrs. Young attempted to help ELLs learn language and literacy in meaningful and authentic contexts by encouraging them to work with mainstream students.

Finally, Mrs. Young utilized the concept of joint activity by working as a mediator. Vygotsky (1978, 1981) views that learning is a joint activity between more knowledgeable adults and less knowledgeable children in social contexts. This joint activity involves mediation between the teacher and the student. Although Mrs. Young might be a more knowledgeable person in terms of English language and literacy, she did not position herself as an authority figure of knowledge to her ELLs in the classroom. Rather, she positioned herself as a learner who was willing to learn cultural knowledge from her ELLs by calling on them and by asking questions about their culture. Mrs. Young did not position her ELLs as "containers that must be filled with knowledge and skills by teachers (Kozulin, 2003, p. 16). She actualized that learning is a mutual constructive process between individuals. She utilized her ELLs' cultural and historical experiences that are inseparable from their learning experiences.

In sum, several key concepts of sociocultural theory (Vygotsky, 1978, 1981, 1986) provide important frameworks to analyze Mrs. Young's roles and approaches to ELLs. Mrs. Young's cultural inclusivity approach promoted her ELLs' participation in language and learning activities. Mrs. Young who was aware of the students' cultural and social needs in the mainstream context attempted to promote ELLs' interaction with their mainstream peers through careful consideration. Given that learning is related to how students position themselves and how they are positioned by others through interacting, Mrs. Young's awareness of this positioning relationship in the classroom was significant to promote ELLs' participation in learning. Through her teaching approach, Mrs. Young models that efforts to specially educate ELLs create learning opportunities for all students in the classroom.

REFERENCES

Boyd, M., & Rubin, D. L. (2002). Elaborated student talk in an elementary EsoL Classroom. *Research in the Teaching of English*, *36*, 495-530.

Britton, J. (1993). *Language and learning*. Portsmouth, NH: Heinemann.

Bruner, J. (1975). From communication to language: A psychologcal perspective. *Cognition*, *3*, 255-287.

Capote, T. (1997). *The Thanksgiving visitor*. New York, NY: Scholastic Inc.

Compton-Hall, M. (2004). Establishing a culture of acceptance: "This kind a stuff don't happen everywhere." *National Reading Conference Yearbook*. Chicago, IL: National Reading Conference.

Corbin, J., & Strauss, A. (2008). *Basics of qualitative research: Techniques and procedures for developing grounded theory*. Thousand Oaks, CA: SAGE.

DiPardo, A., & Potter, C (2003). Beyond cognition: A Vygotskian perspective on emotionality and teachers' professional lives. In A. Kozulin, B. Gindis, V. S. Ageyev, & S. M. Miller (Eds.), *Vygotsky's educational theory in cultural context* (pp. 15-38). New York, NY: Cambridge University Press.

Duff, P. A. (2001). Language, literacy, content, and (pop) culture: Challenges for ESL students in mainstream courses. *Canadian Modern Language Review*, *58*(1), 103-132.

Faltis, C., & Hudelson, S. (1998). *Bilingual education in elementary and secondary school communities*. Boston, MA: Allyn and Bacon.

Freeman, D. E. & Freeman, Y. S. (2001). *Between worlds: Access to second language acquisition*. Portsmouth, NH: Heinemann.

Fu, D. (1995). *My trouble is my English: Asian students and the American dream.* Portsmouth, NH: Heinemann.

García, G. E., Pearson, P. D., Taylor, B. M., Bauer, E. B., & Stahl, K. A. D. (2011). Socio-constructivist and political views on teachers' implementation of two types of reading comprehension approaches in low-income schools. *Theory into Practice, 50*(2), 149-156.

González, N., Moll, L. C., & Amanti, C. (2005). *Funds of knowledge: Theorizing practice in households, communities, and classrooms* (Eds). Mahwah, NJ: Erlbaum.

Kozulin, A. (2003). Psychological tools and mediated learning. In A. Kozulin, B. Gindis, V. S. Ageyev, & S. M. Miller (Eds.), *Vygotsky's educational theory in cultural context* (pp. 15-38). New York, NY: Cambridge University Press.

Lee, C. D., & Smagorinsky, P. (2000). Introduction: Constructing meaning through collaborative inquiry. In C. D. Lee & P. Smagorinsky (Eds.), *Vygotskian perspectives on literacy research: Constructing meaning through collaboration inquiry* (pp. 1-15). New York, NY: Cambridge University Press.

Lantolf, J. P., & Thorne, S. L. (2006). *Sociocultural theory and the genesis of second language development.* New York, NY: Oxford University Press.

Merriam, S. B. (2009). *Qualitative research: A guide to design and implementation.* San Francisco, CA: Jossey-Bass.

Miller, J. M. (2000). Language use, identity, and social interaction: Migrant students in Australia. *Research on Language and Social Interaction, 33*(1), 69-100.

Noddings, N. (2003). *Caring: A feminine approach for ethics & moral education.* Berkeley and Los Angeles, CA: University of California Press.

Pica, T. (1994). Research on negotiation: what does it reveal about second language learning conditions, processes, and outcomes? *Language Learning, 44,* 493-527.

Spradley, J. P. (1980). *Participant observation.* Philadelphia, PA: Harcourt Brace Jovanovich College.

Tappan, M. (1998). Sociocultural psychology and caring pedagogy: Exploring Vygotsky's "Hidden Curriculum." *Educational Psychologist, 33*(1), 23-33.

Tudge, J. (1990). Vygotsky, the zone of proximal development, and peer collaboration: Implications for classroom practice. In L. C. Moll (Ed.), *Vygotsky and education: Instructional implications and applications of sociohistorical psychology* (pp. 155-172). New York, NY: Cambridge University Press.

Vygotsky, L. S. (1978). *Mind in society: The development of higher psychological processes.* Cambridge, MA: Harvard University Press.

Vygotsky, L. S. (1981). The genesis of higher mental functions. In J. Wertsch (Ed.), *The concept of activity in Soviet psychology* (pp. 144-148). Armonk, NY: M. E. Sharpe.

Vygotsky, L. S. (1986). *Thought and language.* Cambridge, MA: MIT Press.

Yin, R. K. (2003). *Case study research: Design and methods* (3rd ed.). Newbury Park, CA: SAGE.

Yoon, B. (2008). Uninvited guests: The influence of teachers' roles and pedagogies on the positioning of English language learners in regular classrooms. *American Educational Research Journal, 45*(2), 495-522.

CHAPTER 10

WORKING WITH PRESCHOOL ENGLISH LANGUAGE LEARNERS

A Sociocultural Approach

Joyce Bezdicek and Georgia Earnest García

This chapter shows how a monolingual English-speaking preschool teacher draws from sociocultural theory to validate the home languages and cultures of the English language learners in her multilingual/multicultural preschool classroom. It also illustrates how the teacher used sociocultural theory to support the children in their English language acquisition. Para-educators were hired to work with the children in their home languages in the classroom and to make home visits. In addition, the teacher collaborated with the para-educators to implement a multicultural curriculum that reflected the languages and cultures of the children. By incorporating home languages and cultural features into her classroom instruction and curriculum, the teacher integrated the familiar with the less familiar, making her classroom instruction linguistically and culturally relevant.

A small group of pre-school English language learners are looking at books in the book center in a multilingual preschool classroom in which English is the common language. Two Pakistani girls, Radhwa and Safa, are sitting together. Radhwa is pretend reading a book of shapes, first in Urdu, her

Teachers' Roles in Second Language Learning:
Classroom Applications of Sociocultural Theory, pp. 171–188
Copyright © 2012 by Information Age Publishing
All rights of reproduction in any form reserved.

home language, then in English. Radhwa says in English, "Brown square, blue circle." Kalam, a Pakistani boy, joins the two girls. Radhwa moves away from the two children, and holds up the book as if reading to them. Radhwa then says to the English-speaking teacher, Joyce, "I can read this in my language." Joyce responds, "I can hear you while you are reading. I like it! I never have heard anyone read in Urdu before." Radhwa continues to pretend read her book in Urdu.

The above vignette illustrates how an English-speaking preschool teacher, Joyce, implemented sociocultural theory in her instruction of 16 English language learners (ELLs). By creating a book center, and facilitating the children's engagement with books in their home languages and English, she gave them the opportunity to actively engage in literacy activities, at the same time that she validated their home languages and helped them to further their acquisition of English.

Preschool educators in the United States often ask how they should organize early childhood instruction for young ELLs. According to Kindler (2002), 44% of the ELL population is enrolled in pre-K-3. Although precise numbers of preschool ELLs are not available, 30% of all Head Start and Early Head Start participants are ELLs (National Clearinghouse for English Language Acquisition [NCELA], 2011). Yet, national policy on the appropriate type of instruction for preschool ELLs is essentially nonexistent. Experts in bilingual and ESL education point out that effective preschool instruction should validate children's home languages and cultures at the same time that it promotes children's acquisition of English and long-term ability to learn through the medium of English (NCELA, 2011). The purpose of this chapter is to explain how an English-speaking teacher drew from sociocultural theory to organize and implement her instruction so that it (a) validated the children's home cultures and languages and (b) helped them to acquire English.

THEORETICAL FRAMEWORK

Sociocultural theorists view human development and learning from a cultural perspective (Rogoff, 2003; Vgotsky, 1934/1986). Rogoff explains that learning is shaped by humans' participation in the everyday cultural practices and traditions that characterize the communities in which they live. According to Vygotsky, humans acquire and internalize knowledge with the guidance of a more expert peer or adult as they socially interact and collaboratively share their interpretations. The instructor's role is not to transmit knowledge but rather to provide scaffolding as she/he creates opportunities for participants to collaboratively problem solve, participate, and develop their interpretations of new events (García, Pearson, Taylor, Bauer, & Stahl, 2011). Moll (2005) points out that school personnel should build on children's home languages and cultural experiences because these are "their most important tools for thinking" (p. 276).

Young children's views of the world, approaches to school, interpretations of school events, and learning are all rooted in their home cultures, languages, and families. For example, when preschool children enter school, they bring with them the cultural knowledge, language, and experiences of their family and community. In the United States, the instruction of White, middle-class, monolingual, English-speaking children often includes the children's home and community knowledge because it is the same knowledge shared by their White, middle-class, monolingual, English-speaking teachers (García, 1992). When students bring different types of cultural knowledge, experiences, and languages to school, then it often is difficult for teachers to recognize and utilize these in their classroom instruction or integrate them into their curriculum (García, 1992; Moll, 2005). Similarly, when the school setting does not recognize children as dynamic learners who have valuable perspectives to share, then it often is difficult for the children to be engaged in their own learning, and to self-identify themselves as school learners.

The *funds of knowledge* approach espoused by González, Moll, and Amanti (2005) is rooted in a sociocultural approach to learning. In collaboration with ethnographers, teachers use ethnographic techniques to understand the everyday cultural practices of families (i.e., funds of knowledge), and later incorporate these practices into their curriculum. Although the funds of knowledge approach has been used with diverse groups (McIntyre, Rosebery, & González, 2001), González et al. explain that the approach initially was implemented with low-income Latina/o students and their families. In this case, the teachers collaborated with university researchers and family members in an after-school laboratory to integrate some of the funds of knowledge (e.g., talents and household skills) into their classroom instruction and curricula. As teachers learned about the strengths of the families, they began to ask why the educational system had not recognized the knowledge and skills of low-income families and incorporated them into school practices. Moll (2005) credits this disposition to question the U.S. educational system for deepening the teachers' understanding of social class and schooling. According to González et al., the funds of knowledge approach improved the instruction of low-income Latina/o students because it "alter[ed] [the teachers'] perceptions of working-class or poor communities" (p. x). They argue that the major contribution of the approach is its development of "a relationship of trust with the families so that they can tell us about their lives

[handwritten margin note:] building relationships with families, seeing what strengths they have, building relationships as a positive resource

and experiences ... [resulting in] a deep appreciation of how people use resources of all kinds, prominently their funds of knowledge, to engage life" (p. xi).

Moll (2005) emphasizes that a critical component of the funds of knowledge approach is the opportunity for teachers to share their ideas, perspectives, and questions in a forum. For example, in the González et al. (2005) work, it was during this scheduled time of discussion, that teachers challenged their previous thinking, supported each other, and shared their thinking. Moll explains that the sociocultural processes enacted by the teachers in the forum duplicated the same types of sociocultural processes that the teachers were encouraged to facilitate with their students in the classroom.

RELATED LITERATURE

Although all children benefit when learning moves from the familiar to the unfamiliar, the latter principle especially is important for ELLs. As newcomers to U.S. classrooms, ELLs and their families often have different cultural expectations, behaviors, interpretations, and customs than those valued by U.S. educational personnel (Carger, 1996; Igoa, 1995). To ease the transition of ELLs into the U.S. educational system, it is especially important for teachers in general, and preschool teachers in particular, to recognize cultural differences, validate them when possible, and accommodate such differences, so that ELLs are comfortable in mainstream classrooms and identify themselves as capable learners (Schecter & Cummins, 2003).

Several researchers have identified cultural mismatches between teacher expectations and those of children from diverse backgrounds in terms of student participation and teacher authority (Au & Jordan, 1981; Philips, 1972). Researchers also have recorded the important changes in student engagement and academic learning that occur when teachers acknowledge the students' home and community knowledge and use it to shape their instruction and/or integrate it into their classroom curriculum (Au & Jordan, 1981; Erickson & Mohatt, 1982; Kahn & Civil, 2001). For example, Kahn & Civil report on a gardening unit that was part of the funds of knowledge project previously described. When Kahn, a fourth/fifth grade teacher in a multiethnic community, made home visits, she observed that many families had flower and vegetable gardens. She decided to approach the study of mathematics through a gardening theme. Kahn sent a survey to the families inquiring about materials they could contribute. Families not only sent plants, pots, soil, seeds, and books, but they also assisted by helping to plant the garden and by building wire enclosures to keep out *javelinas*, or boars that were known to destroy gardens in the community. As Kahn and her students worked in the garden, the students measured plant growth and explored the concepts of area and perimeter, strengthening their mathematical skills and engagement.

Children's home languages also are an important feature of their home cultures. Many parents use the home language to convey cultural values, customs, and practices to their children. Fillmore (1991) reported the difficulties that often occur when young ELLs acquire English without continuing to develop and use their home language. Due to the children's loss of the home language, parents who do not speak English well are not able to communicate with their children, are severely limited in their transmission of cultural values and practices, and cannot help their children with their school adjustment or school work. Providing ELLs with opportunities to use their home language at school also facilitates their continued development of the home language, helping them to realize the potential of cross-linguistic transfer, or the ability to use what has been learned in one language to approach learning in a second language (Cummins, 1989). The continued development of children's home language, as they acquire English, is essential so that ELLs continue to develop cognitively and emotionally and are not delayed in their learning until their English proficiency is high enough for them to learn new material through it (Echevarría, Vogt, & Short, 2008).

How to best access and support children's home cultural knowledge and languages when teachers are not from the same cultural or language background is still an unresolved question. Several sets of researchers recommend the funds of knowledge approach (González et al, 2005; McIntyre et al., 2001). Rueda and DeNeve (1999) recommend an alternative approach, in which part-time employees (para-educators) from the children's cultural and language backgrounds are hired as teacher aides or assistants to help ELL children in the classroom adjust to U.S. classroom practices and to make the school practices more culturally relevant.

METHODS

Our findings are drawn from a year long ethnographic study of the first author's (Joyce's) preschool classroom, which met from 9 A.M.-11:30 A.M., 5 days per week during the academic year. Sixteen preschool children between the ages of 3-5 were enrolled in Joyce's classroom. They spoke a variety of home languages (Chinese, Russian, Urdu, French, and several African languages), and were in the process of acquiring English-as-a-sec-

[handwritten margin note: what if one doesn't have access to aide like this?]

ond language (ESL). At the time of the study, Joyce was certified in early childhood education, had limited knowledge of Spanish, and had completed some coursework in bilingual/ESL education. She only spoke with the children in English. In addition to Joyce, there was a bilingual (Chinese-English) teacher's aide, who also served as the Chinese family coordinator (explained below). The bilingual aide spoke Chinese with the Chinese-speaking children, who represented the largest language group in the classroom ($n = 6$), and English with the other children. Other adults, known as family coordinators, periodically participated in the classroom. Joyce hired them with grant funds to work on an hourly basis. We discuss their roles under the findings section below.

The second author (Georgia) is a professor in bilingual and ESL education at a local university. Joyce invited Georgia to collect data in her classroom on the type of literacy, multicultural, and multilingual instruction she provided to the children. Georgia collected data in Joyce's classroom across the academic year by taking field notes of classroom instruction, making video-recordings of classroom instructional activities 2 to 3 days/week, and reviewing and collecting the weekly lesson plans. Georgia and Joyce met weekly to discuss the instruction that was being observed.

Joyce and Georgia analyzed the instructional data according to Activity Setting Theory (Tharp & Gallimore, 1988), in which key instructional events are identified and coded according to who participates in the activity or instruction, when an instructional event occurs, its focus, how it occurs, and why it occurs. In addition, we coded the events according to whether the children's home cultural knowledge and home language were evident and to what extent they were exposed to English and/or used English. We used data triangulation and the constant-comparative method (Strauss & Corbin, 1990) to identify connections among the coded data, arriving at interpretive themes (e.g., family coordinators as cultural and linguistic brokers, integration of home cultural features into everyday practices), which help us to explain the teacher's classroom instruction.

FINDINGS AND DISCUSSION

In the discussion of the findings below, we first show how the classroom teacher (Joyce) drew from sociocultural theory to organize and implement her instruction so that it validated ELL children's home cultures and languages. Next, we discuss how she drew from sociocultural theory to help the children acquire English.

Validating ELLs' Home Cultures and Languages

Working with para-educators. Although researchers have noted the importance of drawing on home cultures and languages (González et al., 2005), one question that has not been addressed is how to do this when ELLs from a variety of language and cultural backgrounds are in the same classroom. Joyce was in this situation. She did not know her children's home languages, nor did she have the expertise and time to conduct ethnographic research in her children's homes. Instead, she chose to follow Rueda and DeNeve's (1999) recommendation by hiring para-educators who knew the children's home languages and who were from the same or similar cultural backgrounds as the children. Rueda and DeNeve point out that para-educators from the same cultural and linguistic communities as students often are able to strengthen the students' relationship to school by relating to them and their parents in culturally and linguistically appropriate ways.

To help establish strong relationships with her preschool children and their families, Joyce hired bilingual community members from the children's respective cultural backgrounds (African, Chinese, Pakistani, and Russian) to work as family coordinators. Prior to hiring them, Joyce and the program coordinator wrote and posted job descriptions, which specified the family coordinators' responsibilities, the frequency with which they were to work in the classroom and meet with Joyce and the families, and rate of pay. Their responsibilities included working with the respective children and their families 5 to 7 hours per week. They worked with the children in their home languages in the classroom at least once per week, made monthly home visits and assisted Joyce with the incorporation of the children's home languages and cultures into her instruction and curriculum.

The family coordinators met monthly as a group with Joyce. In keeping with a sociocultural approach to learning, the nature of the meetings was collaborative, with the family coordinators sharing and building on each other's contributions, problem solving why miscommunications between Joyce and the children or families sometimes occurred, and helping Joyce to build on the children's cultural and linguistic knowledge. How well these meetings served their purpose sometimes depended on the questions Joyce asked. For example, when Joyce met with many of the Chinese parents during parent-teacher conferences, neither she nor the parents seemed satisfied with their communication. Joyce could not articulate her uneasiness, so did not ask her Chinese family coordinator/teacher aide about the situation. Upon further reflection, Joyce suspected that she had been approaching the conferences from an American perspective. In the conferences she shared positive information about the children and their strengths, while many of the parents wanted to know the areas in which their children needed to improve and how they could help them.

Using the family coordinators as cultural and linguistic brokers. Although Joyce did not have the opportunity to participate in the type of teacher/ethnographer collaboration that characterized the funds of knowledge approach (Gonzáles et al., 2005), she was able to use the family coordinators as cultural and linguistic brokers. All the family coordinators had immigrated to the United States, so they understood the acculturation processes that the families were undergoing, and how such processes affected families' dynamic funds of knowledge and everyday lived practices. They spoke the families' respective home languages, and when Joyce was present, translated for her. Because none of the parents were native-English speakers, Joyce encouraged them to call their family coordinators when they had questions or concerns.

However, before Joyce could use the family coordinators as cultural and linguistic brokers, it was important for her to let the family coordinators and families know the roles that she wanted them to play. Joyce did this by accompanying each of the family coordinators on an initial home visit to each of the families. During these visits, Joyce met the children and their families, learned which languages the families spoke, and which features of the home cultures were present in the families' lives in the U.S. Joyce and the family coordinators spent time working with the families to complete a questionnaire on children's language use and parents' expectations for their children in terms of performance and behavior. Joyce also gave the families a parent handout (translated into their home language), which explained the family coordinator's role (excerpted below):

> The family coordinator is a model home language speaker for your child. She works with your child to maintain the home language and to develop concepts in the home language. When she speaks to your child in the home language in the classroom, it is our way of showing to your child the importance of the home language at school as well as at home.
>
> The family coordinator also works with you and our staff so that your child's culture and language may become a part of our studies in the classroom. In this way, we show your child that we respect and value his/her culture. Your culture is an essential part of who your child and family are.

During the other monthly home visits, the family coordinators acquired cultural information that could be integrated into the classroom or curriculum as well as shared school information with the family. Because the family coordinators were from the same cultural and linguistic communities as the families, they were able to establish trustworthy and respectful relationships with the families, similar to the types of teacher-family relationships that occurred in the funds of knowledge study reported by González and her colleagues (2005). In fact, Joyce considered the home visits, conducted by the family coordinators, to be an important way for the immigrant parents to contribute to her classroom instruction and curriculum. For example, when the Chinese family coordinator/teacher aide told the Chinese parents that Joyce was going to introduce the children to emerging writing in English, the parents voiced concern that their children were not learning the basic Chinese characters expected of preschoolers in China and Taiwan. Joyce responded by working with the Chinese family coordinator/teacher aide and parents so that the Chinese children would be taught the basic Chinese characters, as shown in the vignette below.

> Four Chinese-speaking children and the Chinese family coordinator/teacher aide are sitting at a table in the writing center. The aide is sharing Chinese characters that the children's parents previously wrote on notecards. She also is showing the children how to write several of the individual characters. Two of the children have sheets of paper in front of them on which they have written some of the simpler characters. Two other children from other language and cultural groups (Russian and Urdu) also are participating.

Integrating funds of knowledge into everyday classroom practices. From a sociocultural perspective, just as communities have cultural everyday practices, so do classrooms (García, 1992). Moll (2005) points out that classrooms are "characterized by certain historically developed, socially mediated, cultural practices, and funds of knowledge" (p 283). One of Joyce's goals was to make the children feel part of the classroom culture by integrating features of their home languages and cultures into her everyday classroom practices. For example, to welcome the children and their families, the family coordinators created welcome signs in the children's home languages, which they displayed in the classroom doorway. Joyce also purchased books in the children's home languages, which she placed in the book center. The family coordinators worked with the families to create books in their home languages, such as, photo books of the families or of cultural events that took place in the community. They then laminated the books, and Joyce placed them in the book center.

When the family coordinators worked in the classroom on a weekly basis, they used their home language in centers throughout the classroom. In the art center, the family coordinators recorded children's dictations in the home language about their paintings or artwork, and posted the artwork along with their dictations in the classroom. In the music center, the family coordinators sang in their home languages as they and the respective children played with the instruments characteristic of the children's home cultures and those from the United States.

The children demonstrated a keen sense of awareness about which languages were being used in the classroom. They were aware of multiple languages, and learned when to use which language with which person. For instance, Jaio, a Chinese child, spoke English with Annakiya, an African child, and Chinese with Ju, a Chinese child. Another African child, Ayize, accurately identified a Chinese record when she said to a group of children. "That's a Chinese song. Your mommy teaches you?" When a different song was played, the child asked, "Is that another Chinese song, too?"

After Joyce learned that all the Chinese families had rice cookers in their homes, she purchased a rice cooker to use for preparing snacks. She also purchased Chinese dishes, chopsticks, a small steamer, and a wok, which she placed in the dramatic play center. The Chinese family coordinator/teacher aide then used these items as she engaged the Chinese children in dramatic play. For example, they made Chinese dumplings out of play doh and put them in the steamer to pretend cook.

Creating and implementing a multicultural curriculum. Another way that Joyce worked to implement a sociocultural perspective was through a multicultural approach (Banks, 2010), which involved the purposeful integration of multiple cultural perspectives into her curriculum. Each month the bilingual family coordinators met with Joyce and the program coordinator for planning meetings. At these meetings, Joyce presented an outline of the topic the children would be studying, and led a discussion of what was known about the children's understanding of the topic. The family coordinators then shared how they thought the families would interpret the topic, and what cultural information could be incorporated into the curriculum so that the topic bridged U.S. culture and the children's home cultures. For example, when Joyce and the children pursued a project on airplanes, the family coordinators shared information about the trips the families had made to their home countries. Joyce purposefully planned the project so that family members and the family coordinators helped the children make passports in their home languages, which the children subsequently used as they role-played flying between their home countries and the United States.

Features of Joyce's early childhood instruction were very similar to the type of instruction emphasized in much of the sociocultural literature. For example, Moll, Amanti, Neff, and González (2005) supports an inquiry approach to learning, in which the "teaching and learning [are] motivated by the children's interests and questions" (p. 74), and thematic cycles that cut across various domains (e.g., mathematics, literacy, science). Joyce often began her instruction with a general theme, such as, our bodies/our clothing, which cut across domains. She also followed the project approach (Katz & Chard, 2000), by giving the children the opportunity to explore and conduct in-depth investigations of topics for which they raised questions or displayed considerable interest. Two examples of multilingual and multicultural curricula observed in Joyce's class, are described below: our bodies/our clothing and the post office.

Joyce initiated the unit on our bodies/our clothing because the unit concepts provided an important academic foundation for the children's entrance to elementary school and supported the children's vocabulary development in both the home language and English. The unit also lent itself to considerable family participation. One family from Pakistan donated a boy's "salwar kameez" (baggy pants and loose tunic) for dress up play. Other families made clothing with fabrics, thread and materials that had been purchased for them. One grandmother made a Chinese dress for the children for dress-up play, while another parent made a Chinese jacket, typically worn by babies in the winter, for the dolls. Joyce purchased a supply of flannel in a variety of colors and skin tones, and the African mothers chose skin tones, created body shapes, and made traditional and everyday clothing representative of their children and families for the flannel board.

Joyce also designed center activities so that the children learned the names of body parts and clothing in the home language and English. For example, the dramatic play center had a collection of multicultural dolls. Family coordinators reinforced the names of body parts and clothing in the home languages as they joined the children in play. Play doh in multicultural skin tones was made for the art center. A grandmother of one of the Chinese-speaking children helped her grandson make a body out of play doh while she named the body parts in Chinese.

[margin note: providing many opportunities to incorporate primary languages/culture into instruction]

Each month families were invited to participate in a night of family activities. When the children were working on the bodies/clothing unit, families were given large sheets of paper and asked to trace their children's bodies. They then labeled the children's body parts in the respective home languages, and these body tracings later were displayed in the classroom.

The post office project began as the children were studying the topic of families. The family coordinators shared with Joyce that all the families wrote letters to family members and had some experience with a post office, either in the U.S. or in their home countries. The project was initiated in the children's homes, with family members working with their children to write letters in the home language to extended family members. When families completed the letters, they sent them to school in their children's backpacks. At school, the children worked with their family coordinators to write letters to their parents, also in the home language. When all the children had completed their letters, the class took a field trip to the post office to mail the letters.

The field trip to the post office gave the children the opportunity to learn more about the work that takes place in a U.S. post office. They learned about the weighing of mail to determine the amount of postage required, how mail is sorted and transported, and how mail is loaded in trucks and delivered. While the tour took place in English, the children were encouraged to talk together in English or the home language. Parents and family coordinators were available to interpret information for the children as well as assist the children in asking questions.

When the class returned to school, the post office project continued. Photos of the field trip were displayed in the classroom, and the children were invited to make their own post office by looking at the photos. In addition, to creating a post office with large motor blocks, they created trays from cardboard boxes for sorting and transporting the mail and a gurney from a toy shopping cart. Joyce introduced items from the post office (stamps, overseas package forms, a scale, etc.) to the children during large group time, and the items became part of the children's post office play. A desk also was set up in the dramatic play center and stocked with writing materials. Play continued between centers as children wrote letters individually or with friends in English or their home languages, and then mailed them in the classroom post office. Joyce and the teacher aide assisted the children in creating a U.S. mailbox, and the children and family coordinators created mailboxes representing the children's countries. Children, who enacted the role of the mail carrier, then delivered the letters, created in the classroom, to the mailboxes.

Toward the end of the post office project, some children began to receive letters, along with photos, from family members in the home countries who had written in response to the letters the children had sent earlier. The children presented the letters and photos to the class during large group time, and they were displayed in the classroom.

Supporting the Children's English Language Acquisition

Joyce also used sociocultural theory to facilitate the children's acquisition of English. English was the medium of instruction in the classroom and the common language of all the participants. In keeping with sociocultural theory, Joyce did not provide explicit English instruction, but rather presented opportunities for the children to acquire English as they responded to each other and communicated with Joyce and other adults in the classroom. Because the children were in the process of acquiring ESL, it was important for Joyce to use second-language sheltering techniques to assist their understanding.

Making the English classroom comprehensible. Joyce employed a wide variety of ESL techniques. For example, photos of the children were hung on the front of the children's lockers. When the children first came to school, they were shown their photos as they placed their backpacks in their lockers. The children soon learned that the way to find their lockers was to look for their photos. Photos also were pasted above the children's names on their individual nametags. During center time, children took their nametags and hung them on a set amount of hooks in a center to identify the center where they chose to play. If all the hooks were full, they had to choose a different center.

Multiple modalities (integration of reading, writing, listening, speaking) were employed. Directions were presented visually to the children. For example, the snack center was set up so that children, once they learned the routine, could independently help themselves to a snack during center time. Snack items (cups, bowls, napkins, spoons, etc.) were placed on shelves near the snack table. Each day the teacher aide created a sign in English, showing the children what the snack was and how much of the snack they were to serve themselves. For example, one day they were told they could have two scoops of popcorn. Children also were encouraged to create their own signs for the classroom. One day the children built a large construction of blocks in the block center. During clean up time they shared their concern that the construction might get broken. Joyce helped the children write a sign that said, "Do not break," and the children hung the sign on the block construction.

Videos and music also assisted the children in learning English. After Joyce introduced a thematic project, and taught related vocabulary, she frequently showed an English video to the children. Joyce scaffolded the children's comprehension of the video by interrupting the video to highlight major points or to ask questions. Children from the same home language were allowed to sit together so that their family coordinator could respond to their questions or translate their responses to Joyce. As the children developed their English, many of them responded to Joyce in English.

Using music in the classroom not only helped the children to learn English but also helped them to recognize and participate in the daily classroom routines. Joyce taught the children to sing a hello song to initiate the school day, a book pick-up song, and a clean-up song: "Time to clean up. Time to clean up. Time to clean up. Put your toys away." The children joined Joyce in singing as they cleaned the classroom.

At the beginning and end of each day the children joined Joyce in singing fun, catchy songs, accompanied by motion. Many of these songs had repetitive verses that helped the children to learn the songs and English. The children often were observed humming or singing parts of the songs, and parents reported that they heard their children singing these songs at home. Some parents asked for the English words, so they could help their children learn the songs and sing with them at home.

English for authentic communication. When children from diverse home languages played in the centers, they communicated by using the English they knew. Often Joyce and her teacher aide supported the children in their use of English by explicitly providing them with the words they needed for appropriate social interactions. For example, when a child was trying to join others in center play, Joyce told the child the appropriate words, "Ask her, can I play?" Similarly, Joyce intervened by telling children what to say when their classroom rights were violated. For example, when a child was being teased or a toy was taken away, Joyce provided the child with words, such as, "Stop" or "Stop. I don't like it." By teaching the children such basic phrases in English, she assisted them in playing together and helped them to learn the essential English phrases and sentences that were important for classroom life.

Written English was a visible part of the classroom. Joyce often used the Language Experience Approach to let the children dictate to her in English what they had learned from various fieldtrips, such as going to the post office or taking a walk outside to look at fall leaves. After the post office field trip, Joyce invited each child to look at the post office photos and talk about what they had seen. Joyce recorded the children's comments in English, and posted the comments with the photos. Other charts in English also were displayed. For example, during the study of families, Joyce kept a chart that recorded the number of people in each child's family. Another chart recorded children's responses to the question, "What do you like to do with your family?"

Books in English were read at the beginning and end of each class session. Some of the books became favorites, such as, *It's just me, Emily* (Hines, 1987), a repetitive story about a little girl who surprises her mother. The repetitive nature of the book, along with illustrations that matched the print and the thematic project on families, helped the children to understand the book. The children chimed in on the sentence that was repeated throughout the story, "It's just me, Emily." Other books that Joyce used were books with photographs, especially when talking with the children about projects they were investigating. The photos helped to visually support the children's understanding of the English text and discussion. For example, when the children worked on the post office project, Joyce read and led a discussion about photos in an informational text on the post office, as illustrated in the transcript below (J = Joyce; Cs = children; C1, C2, C3 = indicate the different children participating):

J: (Sits and holds the book so it is facing the class. Points to the pictures). What's this girl doing?

Cs: Putting her letter in the mailbox.

J: What are the people doing?

Cs: Putting a stamp.

C1:   Joyce, what's a zip code?

J: (Explains zip code; returns to reading)

J: And here's the mail. What is she doing with the box?

C2:   Weighing the box.

C1:   He's taking out the mail.

C3:   The mail. The truck driving and I said goodbye. (Begins to explain what he saw on the fieldtrip to the post office).

J: They are doing what we saw yesterday. Look at this. All the mail they have to sort.

Cs: Wow!

CONCLUSIONS AND IMPLICATIONS

Our findings illustrate how a classroom teacher used sociocultural theory to organize and inform her instruction for preschool ELLs. With the help of para-educators, which she called family coordinators, the teacher created a multicultural and multilingual classroom community that validated ELL children's home cultures and languages at the same time that she introduced the children to U.S. classroom culture and English. In keeping with sociocultural theory, the children participated, interacted, and shared their interpretations with each other as they internalized their learning in their home language and English (Vygotsky, 1934/1986). By incorporating home languages and cultural features into her classroom instruction and curriculum, the teacher integrated the familiar with the less familiar, making her instruction more meaningful.

Learning about the funds of knowledge and cultural interpretations of children and families from diverse cultural and linguistic backgrounds can be a daunting and overwhelming task for many teachers. Although early childhood educators recommend that teachers develop and implement multicultural curricula in their classrooms (Ramsey, 2004), many teachers are unsure of how to develop or implement these type of curricula. Others with limited cultural information are concerned about being stereotypical in their approach. We believe that it is important for teachers to begin with the resources that are available to them—the children in their classrooms and their families.

One way to access the funds of knowledge of the families is through para-educators, as described in this paper. When the teacher is a monolingual, native-English speaker from the United States, and has children from a range of languages and cultures in her classroom, she cannot be the sole source of instruction. In this chapter, the teacher resolved this issue by hiring and organizing the work of para-educators. However, due to the power differentials that automatically exist between classroom teachers and para-educators, we strongly recommend that teachers establish set roles and scheduled meetings, so that the para-educators understand that the teacher really wants to know their perspectives and those of the families they represent. In a study of other preschool teachers who had access to para-educators, the teachers did not integrate cultural and linguistic information from the children's homes into the curriculum or classroom environment because there was no regularly scheduled time for the teachers and para-educators to meet to work on the integration (Bezdicek, 2008).

Many teachers may not fully understand the important role that home language and culture play in helping ELL children make meaningful connections to the curriculum and in learning English. When small numbers of ELLs are placed in mainstream preschool classrooms, finding out about ELLs' cultural and linguistic knowledge often is not a priority. Bezdicek (2008) reported that mainstream teachers with small numbers of ELLs in their preschool classes felt it would be easier to integrate home language and culture if they had more ELLs from specific language groups in their classrooms. Given the above finding, it may be important for ELL children to be placed together in one classroom with a classroom teacher who can use a sociocultural approach to access and integrate children's cultural and linguistic resources. In an ideal world, to best meet the needs of ELL children, this teacher would be certified in bilingual and/or ESL education.

Clearly, we need much more research on early childhood education and ELL preschoolers. We not only need to understand how preschool teachers work with ELL children, but we also need to understand what they are using to inform their decision making, priorities, and curriculum. Once we know more about preschool teachers' questions and concerns, we will be in a much stronger position to aid them in their use of a sociocultural approach to instruct ELL preschoolers.

[handwritten margin note: not always possible to have these resources... alternative approaches?]

REFERENCES

Au, K. H.-P., & Jordan, C. (1981). Teaching reading to Hawaiian children: Finding a culturally appropriate solution. In H. T. Trueba, G. P. Guthrie, & K. H.-P. Au (Eds.), *Culture and the bilingual classroom: Studies in classroom ethnography* (pp. 139-152). Rowley, MA: Newbury House.

Banks, J. A. (2010). Approaches to multicultural curriculum reform. In J. A. Banks & C. A. McGee Banks (Eds.), *Multicultural education: Issues and perspectives* (7th ed., pp. 233-256). Hoboken, NJ: John Wiley.

Bezdicek, J. (2008). *Learning from teachers serving preschool English language learners: Perspectives in integrating home language and culture* (Unpublished dissertation). University of Illinois at Urbana-Champaign, Champaign, IL.

Carger, C. L. (1996). *Of borders and dreams: A Mexican-American experience of urban education*. New York, NY: Teachers College Press.

Cummins, J. (1989). *Empowering minority students*. Sacramento, CA: California Association for Bilingual Education.

Echevarría, J. J., Vogt, M. J., & Short, D. J. (2008). *Making content comprehensible for English Learners: The SIOP model* (3rd ed.). Boston, MA: Pearson/Allyn & Bacon.

Erickson, F., & Mohatt, G. (1982). The cultural organization of participation structures in two classrooms of Indian students. In G. Spindler (Ed.), *Doing the ethnography of schooling: Educational anthropology in action* (pp. 133-174). New York, NY: Holt, Rinehart & Winston.

Fillmore, L. W. (1991). When learning a second language means losing the first. *Early Childhood Research Quarterly, 6*(3), 323-346.

García, G. E. (1992). Ethnography and classroom communication: Taking an "emic" perspective. *Topics in Language Disorders, 12*(3), 54-66.

García, G. E., Pearson, P. D., Taylor, B. M., Bauer, E. B., & Stahl, K. A. D. (2011). Socio-constructivist and political views on teachers' implementation of two types of reading comprehension approaches in low-income schools. *Theory into Practice, 50*(2), 149-156.

González, N., Moll, L. C. & Amanti, C. (Eds.). (2005). *Funds of knowledge: Theorizing practices in households, communities, and classrooms*. Mahwah, NJ: Lawrence Erlbaum.

Hines, A. G. (1987). *It's just me, Emily*. New York, NY: Clarion Books.

Igoa, C. (1995). *The inner world of the immigrant child*. Mahwah, NJ: Lawrence Erlbaum.

Kahn, L. H., & Civil, M. (2001). Unearthing the mathematics of a classroom garden. In E. McIntyre, A. Rosebery & N. González (Eds.), *Classroom diversity: Connecting curriculum to students' lives* (pp. 37-50). Portsmouth, NH: Heinemann.

Katz, L. G., & Chard, S. C. (2000). *Engaging children's minds: The project approach*. Stamford, CT: Ablex.

Kindler, A. L. (2002, October). *Survey of the states' limited English proficient students and available educational programs and services 2000-2001 summary report*. Washington, DC: Office of the English Language Acquisition, Language Enhancement and Academic Achievement for Limited English Proficient Students.

Moll, L. (2005). Reflections and possibilities. In N. González, L. C. Moll & C. Amanti (Eds.), *Funds of knowledge: Theorizing practices in households, communities, and classrooms* (pp. 275-287). Mahwah, NJ: Lawrence Erlbaum Associates.

Moll, L., Amanti, C., Neff, D., & González, N. (2005). Funds of knowledge for teaching: Using a qualitative approach to connect homes and classrooms. In N. González, L. C. Moll, & C. Amanti (Eds.), *Funds of knowledge: Theorizing practices in households, communities, and classrooms* (pp. 71-81). Mahwah, NJ: Lawrence Erlbaum Associates.

McIntyre, E., Rosebery, A., & González, N. (Eds.) (2001). *Classroom diversity: Connecting curriculum to students' lives*. Portsmouth, NH: Heinemann.

National Clearinghouse for English Language Acquisition [NCELA]. (2011, January 28). *Key demographics and practice recommendations for young English learners*. Retrieved October 28, 2011 from http://www.ncela.gwu.edu/files/uploads/9/EarlyChildhoodShortReport.pdf

Philips, S. U. (1972). Participant structures and communicative competence: Warm Springs children in community and classroom. In C. B. Cazden, V. P. John & D. Hymes (Eds.), *Functions of language in the classroom* (pp. 370-394). New York, NY: Teachers College Press.

Ramsey, P. G. (2004). *Teaching and learning in a diverse world: Multicultural education for young children* (3rd ed.). New York, NY: Teachers College Press.

Rogoff, B. (2003). *The cultural nature of human development*. New York, NY: Oxford University Press.

Rueda, R., & DeNeve, C. (1999). How paraeducators build cultural bridges in diverse classrooms. *Community Circle of Caring Journal, 3*(2), 53-55.

Schecter, S. R., & Cummins, J. (2003). *Multilingual education in practice: Using diversity as a resource*. Portsmouth, NH: Heinemann.

Strauss, A., & Corbin, J. (1990). *Basics of qualitative research: Grounded theory procedures and techniques*. Newbury Park, CA: SAGE.

Tharp, R. G., & Gallimore, R. (1988). *Rousing minds to life: Teaching, learning, and schooling in social context*. New York, NY: Cambridge University Press.

Vygotsky, L. (1986). *Thought and language* (A. Kozulin, Ed.) Cambridge, MA: MIT Press. (Original work published 1934)

PART III

SOCIAL PERSPECTIVES

CHAPTER 11

TEACHER DISCOURSE AND PEER INTERACTION IN LINGUISTICALLY DIVERSE CLASSROOMS

Ester J. de Jong

This study examined how two first grade teachers in a two-way immersion program structured their instruction to enable pair work between native and nonnative speakers of the instructional languages, Spanish and English. Using videotaped, observational data, the analysis showed that the teachers enacted four important roles: helping students negotiate the activity providing access to the content, providing access to language, and encouraging students to extend their language production. Importantly, the strategies that scaffolded the activity, the content, and the language demands were more teacher-fronted in nature whereas the strategies that encouraged student language use were in response to student and interactional needs. The findings stress the importance of tending to language demands in addition to the cognitive and social expectations of cooperative learning. They also point to the importance of balancing macro- and microscaffolding strategies in linguistically heterogeneous classrooms.

Teachers' Roles in Second Language Learning:
Classroom Applications of Sociocultural Theory, pp. 191–212
Copyright © 2012 by Information Age Publishing
All rights of reproduction in any form reserved.

Peer (native/nonnative speaker) interaction plays an important role in providing second language learners with meaningful opportunities to use their new language while at the same time receiving appropriate scaffolding from more capable peers. Teachers play a central role in specifically structuring their classroom for such peer interactions (Cazden, 2001). Successful pair or small group work in the classroom requires specific efforts by the teacher (Gillies, Ashaman, & Terwel, 2007; Webb et al., 2009). Despite a long tradition of second language acquisition research on native/nonnative speaker interaction and students' interactional processes during small group work (e.g., Mackey, 2007), less is known about how teachers facilitate peer interaction beyond the selection and implementation of cooperative learning activities and specifically what role they play in encouraging meaningful interactions between native speakers and second language learners in PK-12 classroom settings.

To examine this question, this study was designed to explore how teachers who worked in linguistically heterogeneous (including native speakers and second language learners) classroom settings structured their classroom interaction to encourage peer interaction. The study took place in a two-way immersion program, a bilingual education program that enrolls native English speakers and native Spanish speakers with the purpose of developing high levels of bilingualism and biliteracy for all students.

THEORETICAL FRAMEWORK

Language and language development are social phenomena. Context and the nature of interaction among participants in a particular event constantly shape the what, where, how, and why language(s) are learned and by whom. It is through interactions with others that learners internalize the linguistic practices of the various speech communities in which they may be participating (Johnson, 2004; Lantolf, 2000). Access to opportunities to use language in a wide range of authentic learning contexts and for meaning making thus greatly influences second language (L2) development.

Scaffolding plays a mediating role in structuring classroom interaction. Scaffolding refers to a complex phenomenon of teachers structuring their interactions with students to match the skills and needs of their students in such a way that it optimizes their learning (Gibbons, 2002; Hall, 2010). It provides supports for students that are just beyond their ability to complete a task independently (Sharpe, 2006; Waqui, 2006). Simply put, then, scaffolding can be defined as "task-specific support, designed to help the learner independently to complete the same or similar tasks later in new contexts" (Hammond & Gibbons, 2005, p. 8). Scaffolding can be provided by teachers as well as peers.

PEER INTERACTION AND THE ROLE OF TEACHERS

One of the implications of a sociocultural perspective for teaching and learning is an increased awareness of the importance of providing opportunities for students to interact with one another. Peer interaction is an important resource for L2 learning, in addition to carefully scaffold teacher-student interaction. In particular, studies have underscored the importance of L2 learners' interaction with native speakers who can provide them with a 'more expert' language model, in addition to the teacher (Lantolf, 2000; Swain, Brooks, & Tocalli-Beller, 2002). Research suggests that interactions with other learners can provide access to comprehensible input, create opportunities to negotiate for meaning through language (Long & Porter, 1985; Pica, Lincoln-Porter, Paninos, & Linnell, 1996), and offer ways to actively use the L2 (Jacob, Rottenberg, Patrick, & Wheeler, 1996; Kagan, 1986; McGroarty, 1989; Swain, 1995).

Premised on the assumption that knowledge is socially constructed, cooperative learning (CL) has been proposed as a key strategy to encourage peer interaction in an organized way. CL activities involve specifically designed instructional tasks that encourage students to collaborate and interact as they complete the task (Johnson & Johnson, 2003; Kagan, 1986). Much research has focused on the nature of interaction processes among students during CL small group work (Cohen, 1994; Cohen & Lotan, 1997; Slavin, 1985). The role of teachers in structuring peer interaction has received significantly less attention, although there is increased interest in this particular area of research (Gillies, Ashaman, & Terwel, 2007; Webb et al., 2009).

The studies that have been conducted to explore the role of teachers during small group work have noted that teachers' explicit modeling of expected academic and cooperative behavior plays an important role in ensuring that students engage in these behaviors, such as asking probing questions that encourage students to explain their thinking and problem solving and explicitly addressing features of collaborative or helping behavior (Gillies & Boyle, 2005; Meloth & Deering, 1999; Naughton, 2006; Webb et al., 2009). They also suggest that teacher interventions while students are working in small groups may affect student behavior in those groups. Cohen and Lotan (1985), for example, noted that less teacher supervision and guidance was particularly important in the case of open-ended, divergent thinking tasks.

These studies provide some insights into teachers and their roles, particularly as it relates to facilitating the social and cognitive aspects of cooperative learning activity. One aspect that has received minimal attention is how teachers negotiate linguistic diversity as part of their efforts to structure interaction among students. There are some classroom-based studies which suggest that without teacher intervention, students' language proficiency may negatively affect L2 learner participation during small group work (de Jong, 2006; Lotan, 2006; Valdés, 2001; Wiltse, 2006). These findings point to considering the role of the teacher in mediating not only the cognitive demands of CL work but also differences in language proficiency levels. If teachers are unable to implement CL activities so that participation opportunities will be distributed equitably within the small group, opportunities to learn content as well as the academic language needed to successfully negotiate school may be diminished for L2 speakers (Valdés, 2001).

One optimal context to examine the role of teachers in structuring peer interaction is a two-way immersion (TWI) program. TWI represents a model of bilingual education where language majority students and native speakers of a minority language are educated together for most or all of the day, and receive content and literacy instruction through both the majority and the minority language. The goals of TWI are academic achievement, additive bilingualism and biliteracy, and cross-cultural competence for all students. Due to the dual target population of the program (native English and native minority language speakers), peer interaction among native (fluent) and nonnative (less fluent) speakers is viewed as an important resource for L2 development (de Jong & Howard, 2009). Like the general CL research, most studies on peer interaction in TWI have focused on student behavior during pair or small group work, that is, students' use of language when interacting with their partner(s). These studies richly describe the way that students discursively help each other learn content, language, and literacy (e.g., Angelova, Gunarwarneda, & Volk, 2006; Martin-Beltran, 2006; Potowski, 2004; Rubinstein-Avila, 2003). Other studies have considered how teachers encourage participation during whole group instruction (Montague & Meza-Zaragosa, 1999; Peregoy & Boyle, 1999).The role of the teacher in structuring interaction among students in TWI classrooms, however, remains largely unexamined. The purpose of this study was to fill this gap in the literature by considering how teachers in a TWI program structured their learning environments to encourage participation in cooperative learning activities between native and nonnative speakers of the language of instruction.

THE STUDY

This qualitative study used videotaped classroom observations and individual teacher interviews to gain insights into how teachers structured partner work between native speakers and L2 learners. The data presented here are part of a larger research study that explored teacher discourse in six classrooms across grade levels (first, fourth, and fifth grade) in the same TWI school. This analysis focuses on two first grade teachers, one teaching in Spanish (Sra. Esperanza) and the other teaching in English (Mrs. Moore).

Setting

The TWI program where the study took place has been a strand within the school since 1991 and is therefore a long-standing program. Four years ago the school became a TWI school. Sra. Esperanza and Mrs. Moore's (pseudonyms) first grade classrooms are part of a TWI school that currently implements a 80-20 TWI model, that is, all students (native English and native Spanish speakers) are initially taught 80% of their instruction through the minority language (Spanish) and 20% in English (English language development or ELD). Spanish is taught by one teacher and the ELD classes by another teacher. The amount of English instruction gradually increases to become 50% by third grade (and 50% Spanish). There are about 600 students in the school; half of them are Hispanic and about 40% are English language learners. About 86% are low-income or qualify for free/reduced lunch.

Data Collection

Data collection took place in Sra. Esperanza's Spanish classroom and during English language development (ELD) in Mrs. Moore's class during the 2009-2010 school year. A total of 20 lessons were videorecorded and audiotaped in Spanish during 2-week visits to the school in October, November, and December 2009 and January, May and June, 2010. The lessons observed with Sra. Esperanza included the daily Morning Message (10 observations) and Literacy block (10 observations). Each Morning Message (MM) was about 30 minutes. The MM was the opening activity of the day where students read the "message of the morning." It included greetings, reviewing of content previously learned and content and/or concepts to be learned. It also included reviewing grammar points such as subject-verb agreement, and Spanish accent rules. At the end of the MM, there were usually some specific language structures and one or two questions that served the purpose of getting students engaged and having them interact in pairs or groups. The literacy block lasted about 90 minutes and focused on the teaching of reading content and skills. It was organized around self-regulated centers, which targeted various skills, including independent reading, partner reading, creating their own books, reviewing vocabulary words, vocabulary and sight word development. While students rotated through the self-regulated centers, the teacher worked with a small group of students in the guided reading center, focusing on specific reading skill development.

Ten first grade ELD classes were observed in Mrs. Moore's classroom, lasting one hour each. These classes focused on teaching English through content (social studies and science). Five of the observed classes focused on social studies (families, pilgrims and native Americans, and Japan) and three classes focused on science (solids, liquids, and gas). Two additional classes were observed where the focus was on the individual assessment of the students' understandings of the properties of matter. During these lessons, students were working independently while the two teachers pulled students to conduct individual assessments. Given the assessment rather than content teaching focus of these classes, these latter two observations have not been included in this analysis. An important feature of the ELD classes was that the Spanish-language classroom teacher accompanied her students (native and nonnative speakers) and participated in the class (in English). The two-teacher model allowed for small group instruction with half the class, a structure that was applied frequently. A typical ELD lesson would begin with a whole group calendar review and introduction/review of the topic/theme of that day and vocabulary instruction. This would be followed by the Spanish-language teacher taking one half of the class and Mrs. Moore taking the other half of the class. Each teacher would first conduct an activity with her group and then they would switch students and repeat the same activity with the other group. Mrs. Moore planned the class, provided the other teacher with information about the activity on a clipboard at the beginning of each class, and prepared all the necessary materials. The audio recorder and video camera followed Mrs. Moore during this time block and only her data have therefore been included in this analysis.

Data Analysis

The analysis focused on those segments of the lesson where teachers explicitly encouraged peer interaction. Nonstructured, spontaneous peer interaction that occurred among students (e.g., during center time or interactions that took place informally before the school day started) as well as a few instances in which students rather than the teacher led an interactive activity (this occurred during calendar time at the end of the school year) were excluded. Pair work was the only peer interactive structure observed in Spanish. In English, pair work was the dominant interactive structure though small group cooperative work was also observed on three occasions. Only the segments where teacher—structured pair work took place were therefore included from both classes. This pair work was a CL structure akin to Think-Pair-Share (TPS) where teachers pose a question, ask students to think about it, share their answer with a partner and then with the whole group.

The TPS events took place during whole-group instruction and involved the teacher asking students to talk with a partner about a specific topic. Typically, the teacher would explicitly indicate the time for partner work and the topic ("turn to your partner and tell them ..."). The beginning of each TPS event was delineated by the lesson segment preceding and related to the topic the teacher indicated she wanted students to talk about with their partner and ended when students had shared with their partner and with the class. In both classrooms, the events unfolded in a predictable sequence consisting of four, relatively distinct, phases: a Preparation phase, a Direction phase, a Pair-Talk phase and a Sharing phase.

The Preparation phase was an introduction to the question or task given to the students to share. It was during this phase that teachers ensured that students had access to relevant knowledge to participate. The Direction phase consisted of organizing the students in pairs (management) and presenting the task of the activity. During this phase, teachers organized the pair or triads making sure that every single student had a partner to interact. While partners were assigned for a specific period of time (about 1 month), there were times when students were absent and the teachers had to quickly reorganize the students to make sure all students had a chance to share with someone. During this phase, the task of the TPS (i.e., the actual question students had to discuss) was also explained and presented. The third phase, the Pair-Talk phase, occurred after the task was given to the pairs. The students physically turned to one another and faced each other and were expected to share their answers to the posed question. The final phase, the Sharing phase, occurred when students were invited to share their discussions with the whole group. In both classrooms the primary mode of sharing was oral or oral with some teacher writing of key words phrases on the board.

Twenty-one TPS events were observed for Sra. Esperanza, sixteen during her Morning Message and five during Literacy. The difference can be explained by the organization of the literacy block. Typically, the students would engage in an independent rotation of their centers after a brief explanation or reminder of the centers, or a review of the general literacy theme they had been studying. The teacher engaged almost exclusively with the guided reading group during this time. While spontaneous peer talk occurred in the centers, they had not been organized to require collaboration or talk and were therefore excluded from analysis. Thirty-three TPS events were identified in the ELD classes. When the ELD taught the same lesson twice (i.e., first with group A and then the same lesson or activity with Group B), the TPS events were counted separately since it involved a different group of students.

FINDINGS

Teachers structured and facilitated peer interaction in different ways once they had elected to implement a paired activity during their whole group instruction. Different roles emerged: they prepared student to negotiate the activity and the content of the TPS, they ensured access to the language of the TPS, and they encouraged extended student talk. Each role is illustrated with examples in the sections below.

Helping Students Negotiate the Activity and Content

The presence of L2 learners and students from diverse socioeconomically, cultural, and linguistic backgrounds prompted teachers to use strategies to make their instruction more comprehensible. Examples of how teachers provided comprehensible input included building on and referencing prior learning, providing relevant content information and using nonverbal and visual supports (such as gestures, pictures, and drawings). The following excerpt is taken from a Morning Message on November 18, 2009 in Sra. Esperanza's class. The original excerpt in Spanish is provided first, following by a translation in English. The social studies unit focused on the Pilgrims and a guest speaker, Master Cooke, who had visited the class the day prior. Master Cooke was a Pilgrim arriving in Plymouth, Massachusetts. He talked about his travels and differences in language and customs. The following occurs after the class has read the morning message together (written on chart paper).

Excerpt 1 MM Spanish (11.18.09)

1. *Sra. Esperanza:*Ahora la pregunta que les hice fue ¿Qué aprendiste del

2. Master Cooke? El Master Cooke fue el peregrino que vino ayer y yo podría hacer

3. una lista de cien cosas que aprendí, pero yo quiero que le cuentes a tu pareja tres

4. (*mostrando tres dedos*) cosas que aprendiste, entonces vas a decirle a tu pareja, la

5. pregunta primera vas a ser a tu pareja es ¿Qué aprendiste del Master Cooke? Y tu

6. pareja te va a contestar: aprendí... que los peregrinos... que los Wampanoags ... tres

7. cosas (muestra tres dedos), pero una pregunta ¿debo de decir mis tres cosas de

8. inmediato y mi pareja se queda ahí esperando o podríamos turnarnos?

9. *Students (all)*: Turnarnos.

10. *Sra. Esperanza:* Digo una cosa, mi pareja me cuenta otra cosa, cuento una

11. cosa, mi pareja me cuenta otra cosa, le cuento la tercera cosa y mi pareja me

12. cuenta la tercera cosa. La única persona que no puede hacer, contar tres cosas es

13. Elizabeth que tristemente no estuvo ayer, pero los demás sí tres cosas sí tenemos

14. tiempo para más de tres cosas pueden seguir ¿ok?

15. Primero hacen la pregunta, ¿Qué aprendiste del Master Cooke?

16. (student turn to one another and begin talking)

English Translation

1. *Sra. Esperanza*: Now the question I asked was, what did you learn from Master

2. Cooke? Master Cooke was the pilgrim that came yesterday and I could make a list of

3. a hundred things that I learned from him, but I want you to tell your partner three

4. things (*shows three fingers*) you learned, so you will tell your partner, the first

5. question you will ask your partner is, what did you learn from Master Cooke? And

6. your partner will answer: I learned ... that the pilgrims ... that the Wampanoags...

7. three things (*showing three fingers*), but I have a question, should I tell my three

8. things all at once and then my partner has to wait? Or should we take turns?

9. *Students (together)*: Take turns

10. *Sra. Esperanza*: I say one thing, my partner says another thing, I tell one thing, my

11. partner tells another thing, I tell my partner the third thing and then my partner tells

12. me the third thing. The only person that cannot tell three things is Elizabeth who was

13. not here yesterday, but everybody else should tell three things. If we have some time

14. for more, you can continue, ok? First, you ask the question, what did you learn from

15. Master Cooke?

16. (students turn to one another and begin talking)

In the excerpt above, Sra. Esperanza begins by activating students' prior knowledge, reminding them of the visitor (line 2—"*El Master Cooke fue el peregrino que vino ayer*"). This strategy of tapping into prior knowledge was used in both classrooms. Mrs. Moore often used the paired activity to achieve this purpose, for example, by asking students to tell their partner something they had learned or remembered about a specific topic or event. Sra. Esperanza also explicitly references the expected behaviors of the pair work. In lines 7 through 12, she reminds students to take turns and share one idea at a time. Students are clear on what it means to "do TPS." During one observation in the ELD classroom, Mrs. Moore specifically role-played with one of the students what good partner work looked like, such as making eye contact, taking turns, listening to your partner, and showing the teacher when you are ready. The Direction Phase is initiated in lines 1 and 2 when Sra. Esperanza explicitly poses the question, the task for students to perform ("*Ahora la preguntaque les hice fue¿Qué aprendiste del Master Cooke?*") and reiterates the same question later on (line 5). Both times, the question is supported by a nonverbal signal (increasing comprehensible input) to indicate she wants them to list three things they learned.

Providing Access to Language

Linguistic scaffolding responded to differences in students' language production levels in the language of instruction as well as diversity in background knowledge. Vocabulary building and review was an integral component of the TPS events. This occurred primarily during the Preparation phase. In these cases, vocabulary was selected by the teachers as part of the topic of discussion and focused on key concepts related to the unit, for example, "solid," "the past," "matter." Vocabulary building strategies were consistently accompanied by strategies to ensure comprehensible input. For example, when discussing what families need, Mrs. Moore put picture of a house (for shelter), a shirt (for clothing), and a plate with food (for food) on an easel with the label underneath. Vocabulary was also clarified during the Pair-Talk and Sharing phases. In the latter case, explanations were prompted by something the teachers overheard the student say. This happened as the lesson on Master Cook in Sra. Esperanza continued. As the pairs begin to discuss their answers, Sra. Esperanza sits down on the floor and joins one of the pairs.

Excerpt 2MM Spanish (11.18.09)

1. *Sra. Esperanza:(interactuando con un grupo de estudiantes, sentada en el suelo con*

2. *los estudiantes)* entre los peregrinos y los Wampanoags y lo más chistoso, cuéntale

3. del pelaje del castor (*a un estudiante*) ¿sabes lo que es un castor? (*a toda la clase*) Un

4. castor es un animal, el castor si estás buscando la palabra, el castor es el animal que

5. usa sus dientes así (*mostrando sus dientes*) y es mas marrón (*usando sus manos*)…

6. usa sus dientes así, se llama un castor, el pelaje del castor fue lo que usaron los

7. peregrinos para, ¡perdón! los Wampanoags para algo chistoso.

8. *(Students continue to talk among one another. The following interaction takes place*

9. *with one of the pair during this Pair Talk Phase.)*

10. *Sra. Esperanza:* ¿Qué comía qué? Comidas duras ¿Te acuerdas que tenía ese

11. pan que era tan duro y toco la mesa así y sonó, sonó como si fuera un tambor?

12. ¿Te acuerdas?

13. *Sra. Esperanza: (interactuando con otro grupo de estudiantes)* Quiero que

14. cuenten también sobre la comida de los peregrinos, sobre la ropa de los niñas y las

15. 15 niños… (*a todo el grupo*)sigan, sigan…la comida, la ropa, el viaje, los animales, el

16. olor que los peregrinos estaban comentando que había (pausa) su familia ¿dónde dejo

17. su familia? (*a un estudiante*) Cuéntales una cosa que aprendiste de los peregrinos ¿ya

18. terminaron? ¿Me pueden mostrar que terminaron? ¿Me pueden-mostrarque

19. terminaronasí? (*tocandosucabeza*)

English Translation Spanish Excerpt 2

1. *Sra. Esperanza*: (*interacting with a group of students, sitting on the floor with the*

2. *students*) between the pilgrims and the Wampanoags and you can talk about the funny

3. thing about the fur of the beaver (*to one student*) Do you know what a beaver is? (*to*

4. *the entire class*) A beaver is an animal, if you are looking for the word, a beaver is an

5. animal that has teeth like that (shows front teeth) and it is brown (uses her hands)…

6. has front teeth, it is a beaver, the fur of the beaver was used by the pilgrims to (*makes*

7. *a face, puts her hand in front of her mouth*) I mean the Wampanoags for something

8. funny

9. (*Students continue to talk among one another. The following interaction takes place with one of the pair during this Pair Talk Phase.*)

10. *Sra. Esperanza:* What did they eat? Hard foods. Do you remember that they had that

11. bread that was so hard that when it touched the table it sounded like a drum? Do you

12. remember?

13. *Sra. Esperanza:* (*interacting with another group of students*) I also want you to talk

14. about the foods of the pilgrims, the clothing of the boys and the girls… (*to the entire*

15. *class*) continue, continue… the foods, the trip, the animals, the smell the pilgrims were

16. talking about (pause) the family, where was the family? (*to a student*). Talk about one

17. thing you learned from the pilgrims, do you finish? Can you show me that you finish?

18. Can you show me that you finish like this? (*touches her head*)

Excerpt 2 illustrates that Sra. Esperanza as an active participant continues to use multiple scaffolding strategies during the Pair-Talk phase. She sits down on the floor with the students and engages with specific student pairs to encourage their talking (see also below). In lines 1 through 7, she responds to students' need for vocabulary development. While interacting with one pair of students, she realizes that other students might also be struggling with the meaning of the word "*castor*" (beaver). In response, she addresses the entire class and explains what "castor" means, using verbal (descriptive language) and nonverbal (drawing) means to make input comprehensible. She also uses body and hand gestures to represent the size of the beaver and the beaver's front teeth. Neither teacher used translation into the other language as a strategy. In addition to using drawings and pictures, Sra. Esperanza continues to make her content comprehensible by reminding the students of important content and the background knowledge they have to facilitate their discussion (lines 10-12: "*¿te acuerdas que tenía ese pan que era tan duro...? ¿te acuerdas?*").

In addition to vocabulary, the TPS task is accompanied by the specific scaffolding of grammatical structures. Returning to Excerpt 1, we can see that Sra. Esperanza explicitly models the question to be answered during the pair-talk phase (Excerpt 1, line 5—"*¿Qué aprendiste del Master Cooke?*"), and possible ways to answer (line 6—Aprendí). This modeling occurs orally and is reinforced by referencing the question and answer written on the Morning Message chart. Such grammatical structures were introduced and modeled during the Direction Phase and provided the question-answer stems for the student to use for their interaction. This strategy recognizes that students at the beginning levels of language proficiency may not be able to generate all the language needed for an activity independently. The use of such question and answer stems was consistently used in the Spanish class. Another example from a different observation during Morning Message is the following:

Sra. Esperanza: "vas a decirle a tu pareja a _____ (makes mmm sound) le gusta computación, no vas a decir 'a mi le gusta' ¿cierto? ni 'a ti le gusta', vas a decir 'a Andrea le gusta la clase de computación'" [*you are going to tell your partner _____ (makes mmm sound) likes computer class, you are not going to say 'I like', right? Or 'you like', you are going to say 'Andrea likes computer class'*]

[handwritten margin notes: question/answer stems, explicit direction, modeling behavior, modeling expectations reviewed]

In this case, Sra. Esperanza teacher models the correct phrase she wants the students to use when asking their partner (*"Vas a decir ..."*). She also contrasts it with other phrases in order to explicitly draw students' attention to the use of the third person pronoun for this TPS event and not the first or second person pronoun.

Mrs. Moore used the same strategies for structuring her TPS events and for providing comprehensible input. Like Sra. Esperanza, she verbally and nonverbally reinforced the expected behaviors during the pair-talk phase and encouraged individual students to talk more by prompting them through questions. One difference between the two classes was in terms of the kind of linguistic scaffolding that took place. While both teachers paid attention to vocabulary definition and clarification, the provision of language structures varied. In the following excerpt, Mrs. Moore role-plays the activity and what she expects students to do during the pair-talk phase. The lesson is part of the same social studies unit. The students have been learning about the Wampanoags and the pilgrims and are comparing the lives of these peoples to their own lives today.

Excerpt 3 Social Studies ELD (11.19.09)

1. *Mrs. Moore*: So, today we're going to be looking at some pictures ... luckily, Ana and

2. Robert are ready to go ... we're going to be looking at some pictures of some Pilgrims

3. and Wampanoag. When you and your partner get a picture, your job is going to be to

4. find out.... Who is this? And your job is also going to be to find out.... What are they

5. doing? Let's practice saying those questions.

6. Students: (Collectively repeat after teacher) "Who is this?"..."What are they doing?"

7. *Mrs. Moore*: So if I, for example, looked at this picture that we saw from the book

8. with Mrs. Taylor.... I might say to my partner..."Who is this?" ...What do you think

9. they might say?

10. (one student gives an answer, unintelligible)

11. *Mrs. Moore*: So you answered my question..."What are they doing?" .... Right? If I

12.   said "What are they doing?" And then if I said…"Who is this…?"

13.   Robert: "The Wampanoag"

14.   (Teacher leans over toward Robert to look at the picture with him)

15.   *Mrs. Moore*: I think it's the Wampanoag's too.

16.   So Robert and I have talked about, who they are, and what they're doing, we can put

17.   our hands on our heads to show that we're ready. Alright…any questions? Let's see,

18.   we're going to have to use our brains, some of these are a little bit tricky. …(Teacher

19.   hands out pictures) Put the picture in between you…on one leg of each partner. "Who

20.   is this?"…and…"What are they doing?" You can start…

21.   *Students talk with their partner as they receive a picture.*

22.   *Mrs. Moore*: ok everybody ok…Let's put your pictures right down on the floor…and

23.   let's have Jack and Robert share with us first…so when it's your turn to share, you

24.   can lift your picture up and show it to us.

In this excerpt, we see that Mrs. Moore uses similar strategies for content and task scaffolding as those used by Sra. Esperanza, that is, uses of visuals (pictures) to prompt language, connects with prior knowledge (reference to Mrs. Taylor's book, lines 7-8), and scaffolds expected behaviors during TPS, in this case what to do when the partners are done talking (lines 16-17). In terms of linguistic scaffolding, Mrs. Moore extensively models the questions she wants students to ask during pair-talk. She does this first by stating the two questions ("you are going to find out who is this … what are they doing") (lines 4-5) and asking the student to chorally repeat the two questions. She then acts out a partner exchange with Robert as a model for the other pairs prior to the pair-talk phase, using the two questions (lines 11-15) and clarifying what information each question asks for. Finally, as she hands out the pictures, she once more repeats the two questions that she wants the students to answer in pair-talk (lines 19-20). This is different than the pattern observed in Spanish. As explained above, Sra. Esperanza modeled question-answer patterns that structured the interaction between the partners both orally (lines 5-6) and in writing. In English, Mrs. Moore specifically provided language models for the questions she wanted students to ask but not for the responses.

Encouraging Extended Student Talk

Teachers encouraged students to use as much language as they could and stretching their output. This was accomplished by enthusiastically responding to students' efforts, by explicitly eliciting an answer or a more extended answer than the one given. Sra. Esperanza used this strategy particularly during the pair-share phase when she would join the students on the rug and engage in conversations with specific partners. In Excerpt 2, she encourages on-going talk (line 15-17) for all pairs and provides specific suggestions for individual pairs (lines 13-15) or students (lines 17-19) for sharing information. During the Sharing Phase, Mrs. Moore used questioning to prompt for multiple responses, for example, 'Do you have something else?' or 'Do you have something to add?' She asked follow-up questions that extended students' thinking as well as language use (e.g., by asking students to explain their answers).

Teachers Roles During TPS

In summary, the analysis identified four roles during the TPS events. First, as a facilitator of the TPS activity itself, the teachers implemented TPS frequently and developed specific verbal and nonverbal routines that characterized an activity as a TPS event, which they reviewed regularly as part of the event. This included cuing the TPS events through linguistic routines that were consistent across the two languages (e.g., "turn to your partner" or "tell your partner"). The second role focused on using a range of verbal (repetition, vocabulary building) and nonverbal (the use of gestures, drawings, pictures) strategies for making instruction comprehensible (Waqui, 2006). The third role focused on mediating the language demands associated with the TPS events. Since it is common in TWI programs that the gap in language proficiency between native speakers and L2 learners is and remains wider in Spanish than in English due to differences in exposure to the languages outside of school (de Jong & Howard, 2009), different teacher behaviors were observed. Sra. Esperanza's modeling of possible answers responded to the presence of students with less productive fluency in Spanish. In order for these students to participate in the TPS, a linguistic scaffold was needed that would provide them with both a question and an answer format. In Mrs. Moore's classroom, all the students were at higher proficiency levels. She therefore modeled questions and encouraged them to generate their answers more independently without a modeled linguistic structure. Finally, the teachers were instrumental in encouraging students to use the target language through interactions with individual or pairs of students. These four roles were linked to the different phases of the TPS events and involved multiple strategies (see Figure 11.1).

Role: Ensuring Understanding of the Activity	*Role: Ensuring Access to Content*
Strategies Observed:	Strategies Observed:
• Routines • Verbal and non-verbal reinforcement of behavior expectations Main TPS Phase: Direction Phase	• Non-verbal scaffolding (comprehensible input) • Building on prior learning Main TPS Phase: Preparation Phase
Role: Mediating Access to Language	*Role: Encouraging Language Use*
Strategies Observed:	Strategies Observed:
1. Vocabulary teaching 2. Modeling of grammatical structures (question/response stems) Main TPS Phase: Preparation, Pair-Talk, Sharing Phase	• Individual prompting • Enthusiastic response • Questioning strategies Main TPS Phase: Pair-Talk and Sharing Phase

Figure 11.1.   Teacher roles and scaffolding strategies for each of the TPS phases.

DISCUSSION AND IMPLICATIONS

This study was concerned with how classroom teachers facilitate peer interaction, with a particular interest in the interaction of native and non-speakers of the language of instruction. The analysis focused on a specific recurring interactive event in two first grade two-way immersion classrooms, a partner activity similar to the cooperative activity Think-Pair-Share. During the TPS events observed (21 in Spanish, 33 in English), the teachers posed a question that students then discussed with their partner (Think-Pair) and subsequently shared out with the whole group (Share). The TPS events typically consisted of a Preparation phase, a Direction phase, a Pair-Talk phase and an (often optional) Sharing phase. A unique feature of this study was the presence of second language and native speakers of the languages of instruction, or target languages (Spanish and English).

The presence of less fluent language speakers was purposefully mediated through specific strategies which were observed during the opening phases (Preparation and Direction) of the TPS events. The type of scaffolding that happened during this phase tended to be characterized by more teacher-centered instruction, especially when the teachers thought students had little familiarity with the topic (cf. the pilgrim TPS event describe above, Spanish Excerpt 1). The teachers modeled language structures and built vocabulary (both linguistic scaffolding strategies), made content comprehensible through the use of gestures, drawings, and other visuals (content scaffolding), and used verbal and non-verbal cues to reinforce the norms for interaction during the TPS activity itself (task scaffolding).

These "fronted" scaffolding strategies mediated potential sources for interactional inequities that might otherwise have arisen during the Pair-Share phase. As noted by other scholars, students with limited language proficiency are often excluded from participating in small group work (e.g., Valdés, 2001). By scaffolding content as well as language, the teachers in this study provided native and nonnative speakers from diverse backgrounds the knowledge and skills to respond to the assigned TPS question and talk about it with their partner. This kind of extended teacher-fronting was also observed, for instance, in a study of a primary teacher working with students from a rural and working class backgrounds. McIntyre, Kyle, and Moore (2006) describe how the teacher encouraged rich dialogue and extensive student talk but also engaged in extended teacher talk particularly when introducing unfamiliar concepts or skills. McIntyre et al. conclude, "teachers need to be 'frontal' at times to demonstrate, explain, and define in order to lead students to complex literary academic understandings" (p. 59). Similarly, the TWI teachers' way of structuring their interactions with the students during the Prepara-tion and Direction Phases afforded students access to the instructional activity, including those at lower language proficiency levels.

Interactional patterns shifted once students engaged in the Pair-Talk and Sharing Phases. During these phases, the teachers became facilitators and encouragers of *student* language use (Hall, 2010). This role shift was often accompanied by a physical change, such as joining the students on the floor (cf. Spanish Excerpt 2). Teachers encouraged student talk dur-ing the Pair-Talk phase by being a cheerleader ("go on," "continue!"), by suggesting additional topics to discuss if they saw that a particular pair seemed having difficulty generating talk, and by asking genuine ques-tions when interacting with individual pairs (Spanish Excerpt 2). During the Sharing Phase, teachers also focused on eliciting students' responses, strategically used questioning as a way to invite students to explain or to expand on what they had said (cf. English Excerpt).

In short, the TWI teachers used various strategies to engage in multi-ple macroscaffolding (teacher fronted) and microscaffolding (student-centered) strategies to facilitate peer interaction during TPS events (Sharpe, 2006). Both types of scaffolding appeared necessary to equitably mediate the linguistic, cultural, and academic diversity in the classroom. This finding supports McIntyre et al. (2006), who caution to not concep-tualize dialogic and teacher-fronted teaching as mutually exclusive. Rather, this study points to the possibility that effective fronted teacher-student interaction can achieve greater equity during subsequent activi-ties that require student-student interaction.

This study has important implications for further research and for practice. From the perspective of implementing CL activities in the class-room, this study affirms the key role that teachers play in selecting and implementing CL. The findings of the study suggest that it is important to capture the multiplicity of scaffolding strategies and roles for teachers as they may shift during instruction. The findings also highlight that teachers must not only model expected social behaviors (what does it mean to be cooperative) or cognitive behaviors (the kind of thinking to take place), but also the language needed to facilitate both the social and the academic purposes of CL activities. Moreover, in linguistically hetero-geneous classrooms, teachers need to balance the use of macro- and microscaffolding in order to allow all students to participate, engage in, and take advantage of the kind interaction and language use encouraged by the cooperative learning activity. There is a need, therefore, for a nuanced approach to the role of teacher-student interactions in relation-ship to peer interaction that incorporates, among others, student charac-teristics and purpose.

REFERENCES

Angelova, M., Gunarwarneda, D., & Volk, D. (2006). Peer teaching and learning: Co-constructing language in a dual language first grade. *Language and Education, 20*(3), 173-190.

Cazden, C. B. (2001). *Classroom discourse. The language of teaching and learning.* Portsmouth, NH: Heinemann.

Cohen, E. G. (1994). Restructuring the classroom: Conditions for productive small groups. *Review of Educational Research, 64*(1), 1-35.

Cohen, E. G., & Lotan, R. A. (1985). Teacher as supervisor of complex technology. *Theory into Practice, 24*(2), 78-84.

Cohen, E. G., & Lotan, R. A. (1997). *Working for equity in heterogeneous classrooms: Sociological theory in practice.* New York, NY: Teachers College Press.

de Jong, E. J. (2006). Integrated bilingual education: An alternative approach. *Bilingual Research Journal, 30*(1), 23-44.

de Jong, E. J., & Howard, E. R. (2009). Integration in two-way immersion education: Equalising linguistic benefits for all students. *International Journal of Bilingual Education and Bilingualism, 12*(1), 81-99.

Gibbons, P. (2002). *Scaffolding language, scaffolding learning.* Portmouth, NH: Heinemann.

Gillies, R. M., Ashaman, A. F., & Terwel, J. (2007). *The teacher's role in implementing cooperative learning in the classroom.* New York, NY: Springer.

Gillies, R. M., & Boyle, M. (2005). Teacher's scaffolding behaviours during cooperative learning. *Asian-Pacific Journal of Teacher Education, 33*(3), 243-259.

Hall, J. K. (2010). Interaction as method and result of language learning. *Language Teaching, 43*(2), 202-215.

Hammond, J., & Gibbons, P. (2005). Putting scaffolding to work: The contribution of scaffolding in articulating ESL education. *Prospect, 20*(1), 6-30.

Jacob, E., Rottenberg, L., Patrick, S., & Wheeler, E. (1996). Cooperative learning: Context and opportunities for acquiring academic English. *TESOL Quarterly, 30*(2), 253-280.

Johnson, M. (2004). *A philosophy of second language acquisition.* New Haven, CT: Yale University.

Johnson, D., & Johnson, F. (2003). *Joining together: Group theory and group skills* (8th ed.). Boston, MA: Ally & Bacon.

Kagan, S. (1986). Cooperative learning and sociocultural factors in schooling In C. F. Leyba (Ed.), *Beyond language: Social and sociocultural factors in schooling language minority students* (pp. 231-298). Los Angeles: Evaluation, Dissemination and Assessment Center, California State University.

Lantolf, J. P. (2000). *Sociocultural theory and second language learning.* Oxford, England: Oxford University Press.

Long, M. H., & Porter, P. A. (1985). Group work, interlanguage talk, and second language acquisition *TESOL Quarterly, 19*(2), 207-228.

Lotan, R. A. (2006). Teaching teachers to build equitable classrooms. *Theory into Practice, 45*(1), 32-39.

Mackey, A. (2007). *Conversational interaction in second language acquisition. A series of empirical studies*. Oxford, England: Oxford University Press.

Martin-Beltran, M. (2006). *Opportunities for language exchange among language minority and language majority speakers* (Unpublished Dissertation) Stanford University.

McGroarty, M. (1989). The benefits of cooperative learning arrangements in second language. *NABE Journal, 13*(2), 127-143.

McIntyre, E., Kyle, D. W., & Moore, G. H. (2006). A primary-grade teacher's guidance toward small-group dialogue. *Reading Research Quarterly, 41*(1), 36-65.

Meloth, M., & Deering, P. D. (1999). The role of teacher in promoting cognitive processing during collaborative learning. In O'Donnell & A. King (Eds.), *Cognitive perspectives on peer learning* (pp. 253-256). Mahwah, NJ: Lawrence Erlbaum.

Montague, N. S., & Meza-Zaragosa, E. (1999). Elicited response in the pre-kindergarten setting with a dual-language program: Good or bad idea? *Bilingual Research Journal, 23*(2-3), 289-296.

Naughton, D. (2006). Cooperative strategy training and oral interaction: Enhancing small group communication in the language classroom. *Modern Language Journal, 90*(2), 169-184.

Peregoy, S. F., & Boyle, O. F. (1999). Multiple embedded scaffolds: Support for English speakers in a Two-Way Spanish Immersion Kindergarten. *Bilingual Research Journal, 23*(2), 135-146.

Pica, T., Lincoln-Porter, F., Paninos, D., & Linnell, J. (1996). Language learner's interactions: How does it address the input, output, and feedback needs of L2 learners. *TESOL Quarterly, 30*(1), 59-84.

Potowski, K. (2004). Student Spanish use and investment in a dual immersion classroom: Implications for second language acquisition and heritage language maintenance. *The Modern Language Journal, 88*(1), 75-101.

Rubinstein-Avila, E. (2003). Negotiating power and redefining literacy expertise: Buddy reading in a dual-immersion programme. *Journal of Research in Reading, 26*(1), 83-97.

Sharpe, T. (2006). 'Unpacking' scaffolding': Identifying discourse and multimodel strategies that support learning. *Language and Education, 20*(3), 211-231.

Slavin, R. E. (1985). Cooperative learning: Applying contact theory in desegregated schools. *Journal of Social Issues, 41*(3), 45-62.

Swain, M. (1995). Three functions of output in second language learning. In G. Cook & B. Seidlhofer (Eds.), *Principles and practice in applied linguistics: Studies in honour of H.G. Woodson* (pp. 125-144). Oxford, England: Oxford University Press.

Swain, M., Brooks, L., & Tocalli-Beller, A. (2002). Peer-peer dialogue as a means of second language learning. *Annual Review of Applied Linguistics, 22*, 171-185.

Valdés, G. (2001). *Learning and not learning English*. New York, NY: Teachers College Press.

Waqui, A. (2006). Scaffolding instruction for English language learners: A conceptual framework. *International Journal of Bilingual Education and Bilingualism, 9*(2), 159-180.

Webb, N. M., Franke, M. L., Tondra, D., Chang, A. G., Freund, D., Shein, P., et al. (2009). "Explain to your partner": teachers' instructional practices and students' dialogue in small groups. *Cambridge Journal of Education, 39*(1), 49-70.

Wiltse, L. (2006). "Like pulling teeth": Oral discourse practices in a culturally diverse language arts classroom. *The Canadian Modern Language Review, 63*(2), 199-223.

CHAPTER 12

AN ESL INSTRUCTOR'S STRATEGIC TEACHING IN A COLLABORATIVE LEARNING COMMUNITY

Eun-Jeong Kim

ESL learners who strive to achieve communicative competence should develop not only linguistic competence but also discourse and strategic competence. Unless they are fully exposed to an L2 environment, learners will greatly benefit if they can receive strategic support from their teacher in classroom. In this chapter, I examined a veteran ESL teacher's instructional scaffolding of learners' communicative interaction in a speaking and listening class at an ESL institute. I collected the data through classroom observation, interviews, field-notes, and class artifacts. Findings indicated that the teacher successfully mediated students' communicative interaction by constructing a collaborative learning climate where students work in groups interdependently and engage in strategic learning such as focused listening and higher order thinking.

Teachers' Roles in Second Language Learning:
Classroom Applications of Sociocultural Theory, pp. 213–229
Copyright © 2012 by Information Age Publishing
All rights of reproduction in any form reserved.

Learning is social. Young children learn their mother tongue by observing their caretakers and interacting with them. ESL students learn a second language in a similar fashion. However, in order to acquire communicative competence, they will need to receive systematic instruction unless they are fully exposed to an L2 environment. In this regard, the classroom functions as an essential venue for ESL learners. In a communicative classroom, learners are expected to learn about not only linguistic knowledge but also discourse and strategic skills. Given the complexity of learning an L2, learners will need a great deal of support from their teacher. Few will argue how critical and influential the role of teachers is to their students. In particular, ESL learners might need closer guidance of their teacher as they are apparently not fully functional nor emotionally secure in interacting with native speakers of the target language.

In a scaffolded classroom, the teacher mediates students' learning by providing calibrated, contingent assistance and having them explore learning interactively with their teacher and peers. In such interactive classrooms, students learn social skills and develop linguistic means to argue, to reason, to disagree and to discuss (Barnes & Todd, 1995). However, many classroom teachers might be concerned about whether they can provide such quality instruction as they may not know how to. In this respect, the illustration of a veteran teacher's instructional scaffolding practice can inform classroom teachers, teacher educators and researchers what scaffolded instruction is and what it entails in their daily instructional practice. It would be particularly useful if an illustration is focused on the ways in which a teacher scaffolds students' learning in whole class settings.

The purpose of this book chapter is to describe an ESL teacher's instructional scaffolding practice in a speaking and listening class. Through this case study, I will introduce in what ways the teacher mediated his students to develop communicative competence—more specifically academic strategies—in a whole-class format, and what students learned through their teacher's scaffolded instruction.

INSTRUCTIONAL SCAFFOLDING

Instructional scaffolding is a metaphorical term originating from sociocultural theory. While defined in various terms, van Lier (1996) calls it "pedagogic scaffolding" and defines it as "a multilayered teaching strategy consisting of episodes, sequences of actions, and interactions which are partly planned and partly improvised" (p. 199).

As the context of learning varies from situation to situation, major features of instructional scaffolding can differ. However, among commonly quoted features of instructional scaffolding (e.g., Palincsar, 1986; Wood, Brunner, & Ross, 1976), those put forth by Langer and Applebee (1986)—ownership, appropriateness, support, collaboration, and internalization[1]—appear to be most encompassing, incorporating both macroscaffolding (e.g., organizational framework of the instructional context) and microscaffolding (e.g., moment-to-moment discursive scaffolding). Unless it is in a dyad or small group setting, the teacher might have difficulty in providing individualized scaffolding. In a daily situation in which many teachers deal with a large number of students, it would be more effective to assist learners on the basis of the organizational framework for collaborative learning. Hogan and Pressley (1997) suggest, "the teacher's role in large class is not so much to execute a set of specific strategies, but rather to organize the learning environment to establish an underlying culture that centers around thinking together with students" (p. 88).

In the classroom, the teacher or a more capable peer tends to provide scaffolding to the learner (Applebee & Langer, 1983; Barnes, 1995). However, recent research studies indicate that peers with equal or less cognitive ability are able to scaffold learners as well (De Guerrero & Villamil, 2000; Kewley, 1998; Lantolf & Thorne, 2006; Wollman-Bonilla & Werchadlo, 1999). The effectiveness of peer scaffolding is succinctly summarized by Lantolf and Pavlenko (1995): "Individuals, none of whom qualifies as an expert can often come together in a collaborative posture and jointly construct a ZPD in which each person contributes something to, and takes something away from interaction" (p. 16). In a communicative classroom, peer scaffolding can be an effective medium for instructional intervention as learners often engage in group work.

In brief, the review of the literature in instructional scaffolding indicates that teachers in a communicative classroom will greatly benefit if they become familiar with how to mediate students' communicative competence in a whole class format. First, while teachers can minimize scaffolding students' learning individually, students are likely to learn the desired behavior more easily as they will be able to frequently observe their teacher's strategic instruction in public. Second, teachers will offer students an input and output rich classroom setting where learners will have to work together for a common goal.

Two research questions were developed as follows: (1) In what ways does the teacher's instruction promote students' communicative interaction?; and, (2) What do students learn as a result of scaffolded instruction?

METHODOLOGY

This book chapter is part of my doctoral dissertation study that I conducted in an ESL institute affiliated with a university in Western New York, United States (Kim, 2003). I observed a speaking and listening class for one school semester. The purpose of this chapter is to describe classroom interaction in a careful and holistic manner (Creswell, 2007; Johnson, 1992). In this study, the case was bounded (Stake, 2000) by the instructional scaffolding practices of the ESL teacher in this class. Classroom activities largely consisted of idiom comprehension, role-plays, individual and group presentations.

The goal of the class was to help students improve their speaking and listening skills. The class met two hours per session from Monday through Friday. Mike (pseudonym) was a veteran ESL teacher in his early 30s with a master's degree in TESOL. I came to know Mike through my pilot study. He had a high reputation among his colleagues and students for his teaching. When I contacted the teacher, he willingly consented to participate in the study. As I was able to observe a great number of scaffolding features in his teaching during the pilot study, I asked him to participate in my dissertation study as well and he agreed. Mike was called the 'master teacher' in this institute, being innovative and hard-working. Therefore, he consulted regularly with new teachers in the institute and regarded teaching as his given vocation. In this class there were 15 students, mostly in their early 20s, and their proficiency level was low-advanced. While the majority came from Korea and Japan, the rest were from Burundi, Brazil, Congo, and Ukraine.

Classroom observation was the primary data collection method, and all of the class discussions were audiotaped and transcribed. The focus of my observation was on the teacher's discourse pattern and scaffolding behaviors. During the class observation, I took field notes. Furthermore, I observed some students to examine if any learning took place as a result of scaffolded instruction. Interviews were conducted with the teacher and the students three times; once each during the beginning, middle, and end of the semester. I then collected artifacts from the teacher and the students (i.e., the class syllabus, handouts, and students' homework) as a supplementary data source.

Data analysis was done on an ongoing basis, and after identifying recurring patterns of the teacher's discourse I analyzed them based on the five criteria of effective instruction (Langer & Applebee, 1986). In the meantime, in order to triangulate the data, I referred to interview transcripts and field-notes. After the analysis of the teachers' scaffolding practices, internalization of the students was examined. Internalization was defined as students' self-directed learning without the teacher's scaffolded assistance. In the analysis of internalization, I first sought to identify the particular strategies the teachers used to scaffold learners' communicative competence, and then, examined if the students used these strategies during class. Last, upon completion of the analysis, I reviewed the entire transcript for the final revision.

In order to validate the data, I followed Maxwell's (1996) suggestions: I employed the triangulation methods, using multiple data sources such as class observation, field-notes, interviews, and artifacts. Then I conducted member-checks by asking colleagues to review my interim-data analysis.

FINDINGS

Mike mediated students' communicative interaction by creating a collaborative learning community where students worked interdependently in groups and co-constructed learning with their teacher and classmates. In the collaborative ethos, the teacher apprenticed students to acquire communicative competence—in particular strategic listening and higher order thinking so as to prepare them for college entrance in America.

Creating a Collaborative Learning Community

When one was walking into the classroom there was an air of liveliness. Students were actively engaged in group work—sometimes debating over an issue and other times working on a comprehension activity. One day they squatted on the floor to match a series of scrambled strips of a persuasive speech. Students, as such, worked collaboratively in small and big groups most of the class time, changing partners from one activity to the other; therefore, they knew each other well. While students worked in groups, Mike observed them carefully so that he could assess whether they worked harmoniously and, if not, he pondered how to group them better for the next activity. Once he paired an academically weak student with a strong one. He then found out that it was normally a strong student who got the job done. Next time, the teacher matched a strong student with a strong one. Moreover, when he observed that some students had personality conflicts during group work he tried not to group them again. This way Mike put forth a great deal of effort to construct a collaborative learning community so students could maximize their learning opportunities by learning from one another.

Mike ensured that every student was engaged. When students were not involved in seat work they often performed role-plays or gave individual and group presentations. He assigned those who did not present a listen-

taking time for appropriat groupings for collaboration btwn peers

ing task with specific questions they should complete. This was "to make sure that everyone is listening and paying attention." As soon as a presentation was over, Mike asked students what they had listened to. The following excerpt illustrates a typical way the teacher ran a whole class review session. After one group completed a role-play, Mike asked students what idioms they heard in what context.

Example 1 (T: Teacher)

01   T: Wow, that was very nice, you guys. Good job. All right, Suho, any idioms that you have heard?

02   Suho: Make sure.

03   T: Who used it and how?

04   Suho: Make sure [inaudible]

05   T: Make sure what?

06   Suho: I can't remember.

07   T: You can't remember that. Did anyone hear that one?

08   Issa: Make sure.

09   T: I didn't get that one either.

10   Anna: Make sure you take the bull on the horns.

11   T: Make sure you take the bull by the horns. Good. Asante. Did you get anything?

After complimenting the presenting group, the teacher started to ask Suho, a student, "any idioms that you have heard?" (01). When he provided a very brief response "Make sure," Mike solicited more detailed information by inquiring "Who used it and how" (03). Yet, Suho did not remember in what context it was used. The teacher did not remember either and then solicited the other students' participation by asking "Did anyone hear that one?" (07). For the invitation, Anna came up with a detailed utterance, yet as it was somewhat incorrect (*take the bull on the horns*), Mike recast it and then moved on to the next question. While the teacher wanted students to learn idioms in a meaningful context, he maximized their participation by aligning himself as colearner, as indicated in his statement "I didn't get that one either" and avoiding explicit corrective feedback for students' incorrect utterance (10). The teacher, as demonstrated in the excerpt, aptly interspersed group activity with individual work so as to make certain that each student was accountable for both collaborative and individual work.

While Mike structured most class activities to be collaborative by having students work together in groups, he also tried to make classroom learning and teaching genuinely collaborative by making boundaries between the teacher and students fluid. For classroom activities, the teacher was not hesitant of aligning himself as a colearner and positioning students as coteachers. Therefore, knowledge was co-constructed rather than transmitted from the teacher to learners.

In one instance during a class about persuasive speech, a student asked Mike what persuasive means. He, instead of providing an answer right away, invited another student to explain the meaning to his peers. This way, classroom discourse was jointly created by the teacher and students.

Example 2 [italics added]

01   Issa: What is persuasive?

02   T: Persuasive? Chul, can you explain what persuasive means?

03   Chul: Uhmn. To change opinion.

04   T: Who? [wait] the speaker, the people?

05   Asante: Audience

06   T: To convince. Yeah, you have to convince your *audience* to *change* their *opinion* about something or to have the same opinion that you have. To persuade them to have the same opinion that you have.

For Issa's question, the teacher directed it to Chul, who, he thought, would be able to give an answer. When Chul provided a somewhat partial definition (03), the teacher scaffolded his answer to be more elaborate: first, Mike asked "who" and when there was no answer, he simplified the task by offering Chul an option "the speaker, the people." While observing this, when there was no immediate response by Chul, another student Asante took over the turn and said "audience" (05). Then, finally, the teacher provided a detailed definition of persuasive speech, incorporating all of the participating students' responses (refer to the italicized utterance in 06). From these pieces of dialogue, we can learn that the teacher was skillful at eliciting students' participation as well as at constructing collaborative discourse. Students likewise appeared to feel a sense of ownership as they were treated as knowledgeable beings and their thoughts and opinions were valued by their teacher.

The following episode illustrates another example of co-constructive instruction. After completing idiom comprehension activities, Mike engaged students in an impromptu role-play without any prior notice.

This was to help students "to stand on their own feet." Here, he created the directions together with students.

Example 3

01   T: The next thing that I wanna do is kind of difficult, but I wanna do it anyway. Uhm, take 5 minutes, just review ch. 1 idioms, ch. 7 idioms, and ch. 8 idioms. Just 5 minutes. That's all you would get. Just review them.

02   Issa: Will we take a test?

03   T: No, I'm not gonna give you a test. It's gonna be much more difficult than the test but it will be fun ... okay, everybody ready? I would like Tomoko, Youri, Chul, and Issa to stand in front of the room. I know it is very very difficult. Don't look. It is difficult to do it. It is just fun. So, you can relax. Uh, everybody, just tell me, where are they? Let's create a place. Where are they? It could be any place in the world. Anything, any place. Who are they? Maybe in a bathroom. That could be in the desert. Anything. Where are they?

04   Anna: *Tops*

05   T: They are at *Tops*.

06   Ss: [laugh]

07   T: Anything else?

08   Tamer: Zoo

09   T: Zoo?

10   Hiro: Mike's house.

11   T: At Mike's house. Okay, that's good. They are at Mike's house. Uhm, who are they? They are no longer Tomoko, Youri, Chul and Issa. Who are they? Who is Issa?

12   Yasu: [inaudible]

13   T: Who is Tomoko?

14   Heechun: Mother.

15   T: Who's Youri?

16   Hiro: Wife.

17   T: Wife of whom?

18   Ss: Mike. [laugh]

...

19   T: Youri is Mike's wife, and Chul is a neighbor. All right, you guys. Ready? You have no time to prepare. I have 5 idioms up here.

Okay, you know where you are. You are at Mike's house. You know who you are. When I show you the idiom, you must begin to act. You must use all 5 idioms. When you use all 5 idioms, you can sit down, and the next group will come. If you use #1 idiom, Youri will use #2. Okay, ready? Begin.

In the beginning Mike asked students to review the idioms they had learned earlier without telling them what they were about to do. The students were quite curious, but nervous as well because the teacher told them it would be very difficult but fun. While students were reviewing the idioms, Mike wrote down five idioms on the folding board secretly so that students would not be able to see them and started to give instructions.

Mike asked four students—Tomoko, Youri, Chul, and Issa—to stand in front of the classroom and suggested the rest to create the scene together. As soon as he modeled possible places for the scene (03), students listed a number of places. It sounded interesting because all the places they named did not come from a textbook or a remote place but from their neighborhood: *Tops* (a supermarket), *zoo* (a zoo downtown), and their teacher *Mike's house*. When the class decided the teacher's house as the setting, they assigned respective roles to the four students. In so doing, the class burst into laughter as the four students would act out as their teacher Mike, Mike's wife, mother, and neighbor. When each presenter was assigned a role, the teacher summarized the scene and the role of each character, stressing that each student uses a different idiom. The students then started to act out.

The students who were watching this role-play were all amused at seeing their peers play as their teacher and his family members. The acting students also enjoyed the play. In the beginning they looked somewhat nervous, not knowing how to start the lines. However, they soon became calm, acting out smoothly and were full of smiles when they finished. They would not have been able to perform as successfully as they did had they not been given practice opportunities by their teacher for both planned and impromptu speech before. The students seemed to appreciate this. Chul mentioned "I think Mike asked us to do the impromptu role-play to give us a practice opportunity."

Through this activity, the teacher assisted students in moving into a higher intermental plane by having them try out role plays instantaneously. In other words, once Mike felt that students were accustomed to rehearsed role-plays, he had them act out spontaneously in groups. Later on, Mike engaged students in impromptu debate in pairs as he facilitated students' task-taking by having them perform a challenging task collaboratively rather than individually until they were ready for independent performance. In this carefully crafted co-constructive learning climate, students also learned to relate school knowledge to their lived experience. Their learning, therefore, became purposeful and motivating.

Strategic Teaching to Promote Learners' Academic Competence

A majority of students in this class wanted to pursue higher education in American universities. Therefore, Mike paid special attention to improving students' academic competence. In this chapter, among a number of strategies that Mike tried to foster for his students, I will confine the discussion to strategic listening and higher order thinking.

Mike involved students in a series of listening activities. In doing so, he skillfully used various resources at hand. In particular, Mike turned students' role plays and presentations into listening materials. The listening activity, therefore, not only motivated students but also offered them ownership of their learning. While the original purpose of the activity was to have students attend to their classmates' performance, it helped them to become strategic listeners as they were given specific questions to work on for each listening activity. To illustrate, for role-plays, students were asked to find main ideas as well as to identify which idioms were used by whom in what context (refer to Example 1). In order to perform this task, students had to use both skimming and scanning strategies. Thus, while carrying out the task, students were busy listening to their classmates' presentations and taking notes of the gist and specifics. This way, the teacher apprenticed students to acquire academic abilities—strategic listening and note-taking—which are requisite skills at college.

In addition to these follow-up listening activities after students' presentations, Mike arranged an exclusive video-viewing session once a week. In these sessions, students watched a video called *Crossroads Café*, worked on worksheet with a set of comprehension questions, and reviewed it altogether later on. They enjoyed watching this series as it was full of interesting cross-cultural episodes immigrants encounter in the United States. However, since this series was noted by various accents and idiomatic usage, students found listening challenging. During interviews, students unanimously told me, "It is very difficult." Hence, the teacher tried to make the task manageable by having students work in three phases: first, individually; second, in pair, and lastly, as a whole class. He also graded the difficulty of questions in the worksheet by ranging them from simple true/false and multiple-questions to open-ended ones. Some of these questions engaged students in a higher level of learning since they were given a number of wh-questions (e.g., what, how, why) as well as were asked to "describe," "predict" or "express" their opinions. These were the questions that demand learners' active cognitive processing such as activating background knowledge, synthesizing information and making statements logical or persuasive.

With the *Crossroads Café* series, by challenging students with openended questions, the teacher apprenticed them to build higher order thinking. In the post-viewing activity below, Mike asked students to 'describe' the conversation in the movie. Because the students had low-advanced proficiency, it must have been demanding for them to describe something without having a transcript to refer to.

Example 4

01   T: ... Customer, very good. Does anybody want to describe with some detail the conversation between Jess and his wife? Who wants to try? Yasu, do you want to try?

02   Yasu: Yeah.

03   T: Okay, let's hear. Don't read to me. Just remember the conversation. Try to describe to me the whole, you know, she came home from work, right?

04   Yasu: Yeah.

05   T: Okay, continue.

06   Yasu: She gave some gift, no, watch to Jess, Jess?

07   T: Jess.

08   ss: [laugh]

09   Yasu: But he said they cannot afford to buy the watch. Maybe expensive. So, [pause]

10   Youri: Uh, she says his birthday [pause][laugh]

11.   T: Not his birthday.

12   Youri: it is not his birthday but she said, just I love you.

13   T: Uh-hum.

14   Youri: But Jess couldn't understand how, because they, they couldn't afford buy.

15   T: Perfect. That's exactly, wonderful. No.8, Minji.

In this episode, Mike asked students, "Does anybody want to describe with some detail the conversation between Jess and his wife?" (01). Since it may be a hard question, the teacher opened the floor to the whole class, "Who wants to try?" Then he asked Yasu, "Do you want to try?" In this way, the teacher gave the student room to opt out in case he was not ready to give an answer. When Yasu said "yeah," Mike gave him a specific command, "Don't read to me ... Try to describe to me the whole" (03). Then, to scaffold his response, the teacher gave a cue, "she came home from work, right." In the ensuing turns, it was evident that, as the teacher instructed, Yasu did not read his notes but constructed his utterances (06 and 09). When he got stuck, as indicated by his unconfident tone and pause (06 and 09), Youri, his partner, chimed in and completed the description (l0, 12 and 14). Although it was challenging, through active collaboration between the teacher and students, Yasu and Youri success-fully performed the task. Through this conversational interaction, we can see that learning is social; Mike closely monitored students' utterances and made timely intervention when they were in trouble (e.g., 06, 10). When students received immediate feedback from their teacher, they felt reassured and constructed correct responses.

The teacher furthermore engaged students in higher order thinking by asking them wh-questions consistently. While some wh-questions elicited simple factual information, Mike often made his questions open-ended by asking students "what do you think" or "why." The following excerpt illus-trates a typical way Mike asked wh-questions and elicited students' sub-stantive responses.

Example 5 [bold emphasis added]

01   T: Okay, Tae, picture no. 3. **What do you think** is going to happen?

02   Tae: Nobody is there.

03   Ss: [laugh]

04   T: Yes. **Why** (do) you think no one is there?

05   Tae: Uhm

06   T: **Why** is nobody there?

07   Chul:[inaudible]

   ...

08   Chul: It is

09   Hiro: midnight?

10.   Ss: [laugh]

11   T: Okay. Nobody is there **because** it is midnight. Anna, picture no. 4, **what do you think** is gonna happen?

12   Anna: Brashov invites some musician to café.

13   T: **Why** does he invite them?

14   Anna: to a party.

15   T: Okay. Suho, picture no. 5?

16   Suho: Oh, one of the customers is looking for Mr. Brashov **because** this customer wants to see him.

17   T: Perfect, very nice.

For the teacher's question, "What do you think is going to happen" (01), Tae responded, "Nobody is there" (02). So as to make the response more elaborate, Mike continued to ask her, "*Why* you think no one is there?" (04). When Tae was unsure of the answer, as indicated in her filler "uhm" (05), the teacher made the question simpler "Why is nobody there?" Seeing that Tae struggles to produce an utterance, Chul intervened and started to utter "It is" and Hiro cautiously added "midnight" in an interrogative form. The students were quite collaborative with harmonious turn-taking (05-09). The teacher then aptly affirmed their utterances by summarizing what they said. The ensuing turns were similarly patterned as the earlier ones (01-10) in that the teacher prompted Anna to be more elaborative in her explanation. It is notable that by the time the teacher asked Suho a question, he produced the desired response without the teacher's intervention (16).

Students worked on the same thematic activity *Crossroad Café* about three weeks later. The teacher ran the activity in the same format as before; however, the way students responded was quite contrastive. All of them substantiated their statements with the 'because' clause without the teacher's prompting.

Example 6 [bold emphasis added]

1   T: Okay, Tae, let's go over this together. First one, Asante and Tae. Let's hear it.

2   Asante: Henry has to work hard **because** Rosa is absent today.

3.   T: Okay, but I think Katharine is absent.

4   Asante: Uh, Katherine have to work hard **because**, uh, Henry, Henry has to work hard **because** Katherine is absent today.

5   T: Yes, good. No. 2 Yasu and Minji

6   Yasu: Henry, Henry and customer who was from India, we have argument **because of** [inaudible].

7   T: Wow, very good. Nice. No., Tamer and Youri.

...

8   T: And finally, no. 6, Tomoko and Anna?

9   Tomoko: Rosa takes a manager, manager position **because** everybody change the work place.

10   T: Good. Rosa takes the manager position because everybody changes the work place.

In this episode, contrast to Example 5, the teacher did not ask "why" to the students as all of them supported their claim with the conjunctive "because." By observing the communicative interaction between the teacher and peers, students appropriated the use of "because" when they elaborated a claim. It is also worth noting that even though every student used the "because" clause, they did not seem to use it mechanically. As in the earlier example, students evidently constructed sentences as their utterances contained a number of errors, self-correction, and repetition (04, 06, 09). We therefore can understand that the students used the causal conjunctive in a meaningful context. This way, internalization took place in a collaborative social setting.

DISCUSSION AND IMPLICATIONS

Mike carefully crafted a collaborative learning climate through a number of arrangements. First, he designed most activities to be performed in groups. Students therefore learned how to work with other people in various grouping formats, harnessing their communication and interpersonal skills. As demonstrated in a number of transcripts (Examples 2 and 4), students became good at taking turns harmoniously and mediating when their classmates were in trouble during group or whole-class activities. While group work tended to be the norm in class activities, the teacher also managed to have individual accountability in place by assigning students a listening activity during presentations or having them perform individual presentations. Based on this structural formatting of collaborative learning through group work, Mike tried to instill a collaborative spirit by treating students as knowledge-sources and shifting his position between the teacher and colearner. Therefore, there was active interaction among class members and knowledge was co-constructed.

In this collaborative instructional environment, in order to apprentice students to acquire skills that they would need when they go to college, Mike assigned students intensive listening tasks regularly, which made them vigorously employ skimming and scanning strategies. This automatically inducted students to build a habit of taking notes and become focused when they listen to the other speakers or media. At the end of the semester, Youri, a student who complained that the listening activity was very difficult, commented "*Crossroads Café* helps me listen and watch TV or radio. Now I understand more than 90%."

Furthermore, the teacher strategically inculcated students to become higher order thinkers by asking them open-ended questions such as "why do you think" or "can you describe." In order to answer these questions, students had to learn how to regurgitate what they knew and organize it coherently. In particular, students, who tended to provide a brief response to the teacher's question, were able to respond substantively by using the causative conjunctive marker 'because'.

Overall, in a collaborative learning climate, the teacher took special care to meet students' needs and gave instruction in reference to them (Nunan, 1999). Students, therefore, found learning purposeful and engaging, and under their teacher's guided practice, became strategic learners, appropriating such key skills as listening intently, taking notes, and elaborating their views, which could be essential when they go to college.

In this chapter, I illustrated an ESL teacher's instructional scaffolding practice in promoting learners' communicative competence in a collaborative learning climate. The study will hopefully bring classroom practitioners, in particular inexperienced ones, insights into what elements to consider in lesson planning, and in what context to provide strategic assistance in what sequence. Sharpe (2008) holds that "Teacher awareness of the function of specific teacher talk strategies and their potential for supporting student conceptual development will assist teachers in both planning lessons and acting responsively in teacher-student interactions" (p. 132).

When one examines the teacher's instructional scaffolding practice, it may appear like a common instructional strategy. However, orchestrating respective components of instructional scaffolding harmoniously is very challenging. Hogan and Pressley's (1997) claim echoes this: "Taken alone, each component of a scaffolding sequence is a familiar instructional strategy but using them in combination results in more than the sum of the parts" (p. 84). Instructional scaffolding as such takes many years of experience and dedication of the teacher. This resonates with my own teaching. Even though I researched instructional scaffolding, I feel there is still a great amount I need to learn in order to improve my pedagogic practice. I would therefore like to end this chapter by quoting a number of researchers who stress that teachers can have their performance assisted (Gallimore & Tharp, 1990; Hardman & Mroz, 1999) by engaging in reflective teaching, practicing microteaching, or joining a teacher support group.

NOTE

1. **Ownership:** The task has a clear purpose. The learners are given the room to have something of their own to say.
   Appropriateness: The task is given at the learners' ZPD.

Support: The task is structured around a model of appropriate approaches and leads to a natural sequencee of thought and language.
Collaboration: The teacher does not reject what the learners have accomplished. Instead, he or she responds to the learners' work through modeling, telling, extending, questioning, rephrasing and praising. The teacher works as collaborator not as evaluator.
Internalization: Scaffolding is gradually withdrawn as the patterns are internalized.

REFERENCES

Applebee, A., & Langer, J. (1983). Instructional scaffolding: Reading and writing as natural language activities. *Language Arts 60(2)*, 168-175.

Barnes, D. (1995). Talking and learning in classrooms: An introduction. *Primary Voices K-6, 3*(1), 2-7.

Barnes, D., & Todd, F. (1995). *Communication and learning revisited: Making meaning through talk*. Portsmouth, NH: Heinemann.

Creswell, J. (2007). *Qualitative inquiry and research design: Choosing among five traditions*. Thousand Oaks, CA: SAGE.

De Guerrero, M., & Villamil, O. (2000). Activating the ZPD: Mutual scaffolding in L2 peer revision. *The Modern Language Journal, 84*(1), 51-68.

Kim, E. -J. (2003). *The influence of two ESL teachers' instructional scaffolding on students' communicative interaction*. (Unpublished doctoral dissertation), State University of New York at Buffalo, New York.

Gallimore, R., & Tharp, R. (1990). Teaching mind in society: Teaching, schooling, and literate discourse. In L. Moll (Ed.), *Vygotsky and education: Instructional implications and applications of sociohistorical psychology* (pp. 175-205). New York, NY: Cambridge University Press.

Hardman, F., & Mroz, M. (1999). Post-16 English teaching: From recitation to discussion. *Educational Review, 51*(3), 283-293.

Hogan, K., & Pressley, M. (1997). Scaffolding scientific competencies within classroom communities of inquiry. In K Hogan & M. Presley (Eds.), *Scaffolding student learning: Instructional approaches and issues*, (pp. 74-107). Cambridge, MA: Brookline Books.

//Johnson, D. (1992). *Approaches to research in second language learning*. New York, NY: Longman.

Kewley, L. (1998). Peer collaboration versus teacher-directed instruction: How two methodologies engage students in the learning process. *Journal of Research in Childhood Education, 13*(1), 27-32.

Langer, J., & Applebee, A. (1986). Reading and writing instruction: Toward a theory of teaching and learning. In E. Rothkopf (Ed.), *Review of Research in Education, 13*, 171-194.

Lantolf, J., & Pavlenko, J. (1995). Sociocultural theory and second language acquisition. *Annual Review of Applied Linguistics, 15*, 108-124.

Lantolf., J., & Thorne, S. (2006). *Sociocultural theory and the genesis of second language development*. Oxford, England: Oxford University Press

Maxwell, J. (1996). *Qualitative research design*. Thousand Oaks, CA: SAGE.

Nunan, D. (1999). *Second language teaching & learning*. Boston, Mass: Heine & Heine.

Palincsar, A. (1986). The role of dialogue in providing scaffolded instruction. *Educational Psychologist, 21*(1&2), 73-98.

Sharpe, T. (2008). How can teacher talk support learning? *Linguistics and Education, 19*, 132-148.

Stake, R. (2000). Case studies. In N. Denzin & Y. Lincoln (eds.), *Handbook of qualitative research*, (pp. 236-247). Thousand Oaks, CA: SAGE.

van Lier, L. (1996). *Interaction in the language curriculum: Awareness, autonomy and authenticity*. London: Longman

Wood, D., Brunner, J. S., & Ross, G.(1976). The role of tutoring in problem solving. *Journal of Child Psychology & Psychiatry, 17*, 89-100.

Wollman-Bonilla, J. E., & Werchadlo, B. (1999). Teacher and peer roles in scaffolding first graders' response to literature. *The Reading Teacher, 52*(6), 598-607.

CHAPTER 13

TEACHERS' ROLES AND MEDIATING STRATEGIES OF LEARNERS' ENGAGEMENT IN THE L2 CLASSROOM

Jennifer R. Smiley and Marta Antón

Classroom interaction is of interest to sociocultural theory because learning originates in the dialogue that occurs between teacher and learners and among learners. This chapter reports on a case study of teachers' roles enacted through discourse in L2 Spanish high school classes in the United States. Following ethnographic techniques, we investigate what teachers' roles are apparent in the interaction and how the teacher enacts his roles through discursive strategies. Relating roles to the semiotics of mediation, four teacher's roles emerge as relevant: providing linguistic models, providing assistance, creating a participatory environment, and creating a sense of community. The study suggests that teachers should devote attention to how their roles are expressed through language in the classroom.

"We are always doing something, even when we don't do anything"

—A. G., Spanish teacher

Teachers' Roles in Second Language Learning:
Classroom Applications of Sociocultural Theory, pp. 231–248
Copyright © 2012 by Information Age Publishing
All rights of reproduction in any form reserved.

When Mr. G walked into his Spanish Level 4 class, he noticed that some students seemed to be dressed for a special occasion. He remarked on it asking what the occasion was (*¿cuál es la ocasión?*). The conversation that followed engaged five different students explaining, in the L2, that there was a game that day against another school and where the other school was located. Then, all the students walked around greeting each other in the L2. Meanwhile, the teacher joked with some of the students about a picture of a famous Spanish football player that one of the students had. Then he talked about signing up for extracurricular trips to Mexico and Peru. After 87 turns, the teacher started giving directions for students to write an original song in Spanish. Some may think that up to this point teacher and students were not doing much. It is quite common in Mr. G's classes to engage in conversations about topics that seem to be unrelated to the Spanish class. However, all interaction in Mr. G's class is part of a deliberate plan to act as a linguistic model, a guide and partner in the learning communities he creates through discourse in his classrooms.

Interaction between teachers and learners and among learners is of utmost interest to sociocultural theory (SCT) because the genesis of learning in that context is encapsulated in the dialogic exchanges that take place in the classroom. This is a case study of discourse between teacher and learners in two high school L2 Spanish classrooms. Adding to previous sociocultural research on L2 classroom interaction (Adair Hauck & Donato, 1994; Antón, 1999; Donato & Adair Hauck, 1992; Hall & Verplaetse, 2000), the study seeks to understand whether the teacher's perceived roles as a linguistic model, guide, and partner in the learning community are observable in the interaction, and how teachers' roles are realized through discursive strategies.

SOCIOCULTURAL PERSPECTIVE ON LANGUAGE LEARNING AND CLASSROOM INTERACTION

A growing number of sociocultural studies have analyzed classroom discourse between teachers/tutors and learners. In sociocultural theory, learning is viewed as a process of cognitive and social transformation that takes place in a collaborative social context. The theory is concerned with the relationship between language and mind, and is based on the ideas of the Russian psychologist L. S. Vygotsky (1978, 1987). In Vygotsky's view, human action is mediated by technical and psychological tools or signs, such as language. The concept of mediation and how mediation is realized by language in the classroom setting is central to our study of the teacher's role as an agent of mediation in the process of learning. This study pays attention to the learning space created through dialogue in the classroom. In sociocultural terms, a novice (L2 learner) learns under the guidance of an expert (teacher) who provides support in the completion of the task (Radziszewska & Rogoff, 1991; Wertsch, Minick, & Arns, 1984). Teaching may be viewed as assisting performance through the Zone of Proximal Development (ZPD) (Tharp & Gallimore, 1988), where one's behavior is supported by objects in the environment (object-regulation) or another person (other-regulation) until learners are able to function independently (self-regulation). Thus, the ZPD constitutes "a potential for learning that is created in the interaction between participants in particular settings" (Wells, 1998, p. 345).

In the ZPD, the expert (teacher or another peer) offers scaffolded assistance to the learner in carrying out new components of the task which the learner would not be able to complete without assistance (Rogoff & Gardner, 1984). In order to investigate how mediation is enacted through dialogue by this teacher, we adopt the metaphor of scaffolding (Wood, Bruner, & Ross 1976). During scaffolded interaction, the expert controls the elements of the task that are above the learner's ability, thus allowing the learner to focus on those elements of the task that are within his or her capacity. Although the link between scaffolding and the concept of ZPD has been questioned (Lantolf & Thorne, 2006), the metaphor of scaffolding is useful in analyzing L2 learning situations. The scaffolded help that the expert provides the novice is characterized by six functions that interact dynamically, as experts assess the situation and determine the type and degree of assistance needed (Wood et al., 1976, p. 98):

1. **Recruitment**—enlisting the learner's interest in the task.
2. **Reduction in degrees of freedom**—simplifying the task.
3. **Direction maintenance**—keeping the learner motivated and in pursuit of the goal
4. **Marking critical features**—highlighting certain relevant features and pointing out discrepancies between what has been produced and the ideal solution,
5. **Frustration control**—reducing stress and frustration during problem solving, and
6. **Demonstration**—modeling an idealized form of the act to be performed by completing the act or by explicating the learner's partial solution.

As we will discuss later on, our teacher's perceived roles align closely with these functions, as one would expect when teachers see their main role as that of mediating learning. A main focus of the study is precisely how these functions are semiotically realized during the interaction.

Several studies have analyzed teachers assisting learners through scaffolded interaction in order to mediate second language learning. For instance, Aljaafreh and Lantolf (1994) showed how negotiation of corrective feedback during tutorial sessions promotes learning. Donato and Adair-Hauck (1992) and Adair-Hauck and Donato (1994) analyzed how formal explanations can be co-constructed by teacher and learners through a negotiation process. Antón (1999) studied negotiation and scaffolding during formal instruction and feedback events while McCormick and Donato (2000) focused on the strategic use of teachers' questions for scaffolding purposes. At advanced levels of L2 instruction, Donato and Brooks (2004) studied the discursive structure of class discussion in an L2 Spanish literature course. Hall (2004) and Toth (2004, 2008) also showed that attention to discourse cohesiveness in the classroom is essential to engage students in complex thinking and to foster language learning. The present study of interaction in L2 Spanish classrooms builds on previous research by focusing on teachers' roles and how they manifest themselves through the teacher's intentional use of language in relation to the concept of mediation and the scaffolding functions discussed above.

RESEARCH QUESTIONS

The central research questions for the study ask what teachers' roles are apparent in the interaction that takes place in this classroom, whether the teacher's stated roles are indeed observable in the interaction, and how the teacher enacts his roles through the use of discursive strategies. The latter question is intrinsically related to the functions of scaffolding and the semiotics of mediation.

METHOD OF STUDY

Participants

This particular teacher was selected for the study because he had developed a reputation as a master teacher, evidenced by state-level teaching awards and students' success in Spanish competitions. At the time of the study, he had been teaching Spanish in high school for 13 years and he had also taught college classes for 7 years. He had a well-articulated methodology, presented at teachers' conferences and other professional gatherings, which was guided by his determination to teach exclusively in the target language and to increase students' responsibility for their own learning. The teacher believed that language is acquired more efficiently when interpersonal relations are established and maintained in the classroom through the target language. A sense of community was fostered in the classroom and beyond the classroom with trips to target language countries and service to the local Latino community. The teacher saw his role in the classroom as a language model, as a partner in the learning process (through the joy and suffering involved in the process), and as a guide who held high expectations for the learners. He had planned variations in his teaching methodology according to learner's level, ranging from more predictability and direction with beginning learners to more independence and increased learners' contribution to class discussions from advanced-level students.

The teacher's philosophy and pedagogical principles aligned well with sociocultural theory, particularly with respect to the importance of interaction in a social context, the role of language as object and medium of learning (L2), and the need to be attentive to learner's needs and skills in order to assist them and lead them towards self-regulation.

Thirty-one students participated in the study (twenty students in Level 2 and eleven in Level 4). Classes met daily for 45 minutes. All of the students were English-speaking learners of Spanish at a small private high school in an urban area of the Midwestern United States. The school has a high graduating rate (over 90%) and a high percentage of college-acceptance (95%).

Data Collection and Analysis

A case study was an appropriate methodology to understand how the teacher's roles were enacted through classroom discourse. We hypothesized that this teacher's discursive practices would be helpful to other teachers who wish to use assisting language and increase student participation in their L2 classrooms.

One of the authors attended a Level 2 and a Level 4 Spanish class once a week for a semester. Both classes were taught by the same instructor. Following ethnographic techniques (Antón, 1996; Spradley, 1980), the researcher observed lessons and took field notes during her observations. In addition, lessons were videotaped once a month throughout the semester. Videotaped lessons were then transcribed for language and other paralinguistic cues (gestures, silence, etc.) following Psathas' (1995) method of transcription. The analysis presented here is based on the first and second lesson for each level (four lessons). It was assumed that during these first lessons the teacher would establish his roles through his use of language. The detailed analysis of classroom discourse at the beginning of the academic year allows us to see how learners reciprocate the mediated assistance offered by the instructor and, thus, how cultural patterns of classroom interaction emerge.

Analysis of data was conducted using a mixed-method approach. Descriptive quantification of L2 use and teacher vs. students' turns provided contextual background for the qualitative analysis of selected episodes. Lesson transcripts were coded for verbal and nonverbal strategies in the discourse. As it is common practice in sociocultural studies of classroom interaction (Donato & Adair-Hauck, 1992; Hall & Verplaetse, 2000), microgenetic analysis of selected episodes from second and fourth-level students was conducted. In this chapter we focus on our qualitative analysis. The description of the interaction and the discussion of selected episodes are guided by our main research question; how the teacher enacts his roles through discursive strategies.

RESULTS

In order to provide an overall picture of participation patterns in these classrooms, we briefly summarize the results from our descriptive quantification of classroom talk (for a detailed account see Smiley, 2010). First, the target language was used almost exclusively by teacher and learners. Second, the higher proportion of learners' turns at both levels indicates that the teacher successfully engaged learners in interacting in the target language, although teacher's turns are longer than learners' turns. The final point that we can gather from quantifying the interaction is that there is a considerable decrease of teacher participation in Level 4. These pieces of evidence are consistent with the teacher's explicit goals of exclusive target language use and increased learners' participation. We now move to the discussion of the teacher's roles that were apparent in our observation and the discursive mechanisms used by the teacher to enact his roles.

Four major teacher's roles emerged out of the classroom observations: providing linguistic models, providing assistance, creating a participatory environment, and creating a sense of community.

Providing Linguistic Models

The teacher believed that having something to say and being able to express it in the L2 started by imitating good models (teacher and other students). Hence, conversing in the L2 about any topic that held the students' interest was a mechanism to provide appropriate L2 models. Demonstrating how language is used enables learners with the linguistic tools and processes needed to express themselves in the L2. In an illustrative episode, the teacher modeled the task students were about to perform, which involved stating three things they were passionate about doing. He started by asking students what they thought he was passionate about (*¿Qué es mi pasión?*). Several students offered different responses: Spanish, dancing, Mrs. G (the teacher's wife). He prodded students to continue offering suggestions with a question that helped maintain students' motivation to keep with the task (what else?) and four more students reciprocated with more suggestions (singing, basketball, us). Once the teacher had elicited several ideas and the L2 lexicon necessary to express these ideas, he directed the students to talk about things they were passionate about and provided several L2 examples for students to imitate: *Mi pasión es comer. Yo como hamburguesas todos los días ... Mi pasión es hablar español. Mis amigos y yo hablamos en la casa, por el teléfono celular ...* (I am passionate about eating. I eat hamburgers every day ... I am passionate about speaking Spanish. My friends and I speak Spanish at home, on our cell phones...). When students actually started writing their own sentences, fifty turns after the episode started, they had been provided with an abundance of linguistic models and ideas to accomplish their task.

Assisting With Language Problems

The teacher's role as mediator of learning was enacted differently according to the amount and type of assistance required by the task. The following episode illustrates how the teacher scaffolded the interaction while providing assistance on L2 grammar usage. In Episode 1, after returning graded exams, the teacher responded to a student's question regarding how to substitute a noun phrase for an object pronoun and where to place the pronoun.

Episode 1 (Level 2)

01   T:...Número u:no, dice así, tengo ((extends arms)) la ropa más bonita ((slows speech on each word)) en mi tienda...(3s) la ropa más bonita ((slows speech on each word)) ((extends arms)) Whooosh! ((quickly puts arms together and hold up one finger))...(3s), es una cosa cuando hablamos de pro:nombres. No repetimos más bonita. No repetimos la ropa. Todo es ((extends arms)) la ropa más bonita Whoooosh! ((quickly puts arms together and holds up one finger)), es la... (3s) viene ese la. La otra cosa es te:ngo, tengo es un verbo: conjugado...(3s) Entonces, no es posible ((puts thumb and index finger together)) poner la al final...(4s) No

se dice te:ngo la. Es <u>la::</u> te:ngo....(4s) A ver, con número dos, hablando de la pregunta más específica, eh, <u>más</u>, o digo, muchas personas compran bolsas de cuero ((extends arms)), bolsas de cuero Whoooosh! ((quickly puts arms together and holds up one finger)) es sólo una cosa, <u>las</u>. Y simplemente: <u>repetimos</u> el verbo co:mpran...(3s) <u>La:s</u> compran.

02   S1: las compran em

03   T: ¿es lo que tienes tú? ((looks at student))

04   S1: ¿qué?

05   T: ¿es lo que tienes ((points to student)) en tu papel?

06   S1: em, no, uh, dijo muchas personas comprarla

(Translation)

01   T:...Number one, it says, I have ((extends arms)) <u>the cutest clothes</u> ((slows speech on each word)) in my store...(3s) <u>the cutest clothes</u> ((slows speech on each word)) ((extends arms)) Whooosh! ((quickly puts arms together and hold up one finger))...(3s), it's <u>one</u> <u>thing</u> when we speak of <u>pronouns</u>. <u>We don't repeat</u> the cutest. We don't repeat clothes. Everything is ((extends arms)) the cutest clothes Whoooosh! ((quickly puts arms together and holds up one finger)), <u>it's them</u>... (3s) you get them. The other thing is <u>I have</u>, I have is a conjugated verb...(3s) So, it's not possible ((puts thumb and index finger together)) <u>to put them</u> at the end...(4s) One does not say 'I have them.' It's <u>them</u> I have ....(4s) Let's see, with number two, speaking of a specific question, uh, <u>more</u>, or I say, many people buy leather bags ((extends arms)), leather bags Whoooosh! ((quickly puts arms together and hold up one finger)) is only one thing, <u>them</u>. And simply <u>we repeat</u> the verb they buy...(3s) <u>They buy them</u>.

02   S1: They buy them, em

03   T: Is that what you have? ((looks at student))

04   S1: what?

05   T: Is that what you have ((points at student)) in your paper?

06   S1: em, no, uh, I said [wrong verb form] many people to buy them

The teacher assisted these lower-level learners in understanding his grammatical explanation through a variety of discursive strategies displayed in this episode. Several functions of scaffolding (Wood et al., 1976) are realized in the discourse: modeling, simplifying, and highlighting critical features. The teacher highlighted important words in his explanation by pronouncing them with emphasis (*poner la*) and elongating vowels (*número u:no*). He simplified the language by speaking slowly and using repetition (*la ropa más bonita...la ropa más bonita*) in order to draw the learners' attention to key words (Duff, 2000). He also made use of gestures and sounds to add a visual component to his explanation. In addition, definitions (*tengo es un verbo: conjugado*) and explanation of incorrect forms (*No se dice te:ngo la*) aided comprehension of the explanation. Of particular interest is the teacher's use of pauses (...) which appeared before key words pronounced with emphasis and after key concepts (*no es posible poner la al final...*). It seems that pauses played a strategic cognitive function of calling attention to what is coming next and allowing time for reflection on what had just been said. As Schegloff (2001) has noted, silence "is as fully fledged an event in the conversation as any utterance, and as consequential for the ensuing talk" (p. 239). Following the explanation, the student who had asked the question about pronoun placement repeated the correct form "*las compran*" as if signaling her understanding. When the teacher asked if that was the answer she had in the test, she replied negatively adding that she had used the wrong form "*comprarla.*" In this episode we see the teacher mediating learning through the use of discourse that addresses several functions of scaffolding. The wide variety of discursive strategies used aimed at giving very direct assistance. The teacher checked, through questioning, if the explanation had been appropriated. Learner' s reciprocity to the mediation (Poehner, 2008), repeating the correct form and contrasting it with her previous incorrect answer, marked that the teacher's mediation had been successful.

The next episode, also from Level 2, illustrates how the teacher performed his mediating role by engaging learners in a grammatical discussion. In this case, the teacher estimated the level of assistance learners needed to continue with the activity. He judged that the answer requested was within the learners' capabilities and, thus, his attention turned to getting the learners involved in the activity. What we want to highlight here is how the teacher recruited student participation while maintaining the interaction in the target language.

Episode 2 (Level 2)

01   T: ...Ok. ¿Cuáles son las terminaciones en <u>A-R</u>, de los verbos, de las terminaciones en el presente en los verbos que terminan en A-R? ((pauses and looks at students)) <u>Las</u> terminaciones ((pauses and looks at students)) ¿Saben qué son las terminaciones ((writes 'las terminaciones' on the board))? ((pauses)) Terminaciones, ((pauses)) ter-mi-na ((talks slow and underlines 'termina' on board)), <u>el final</u> ((motions hand down and looks at students))?

((pauses and looks at students)) <u>Esta</u> parte ((points to –AR)), está al final del verbo ((motions hand down again)) ((looks at students)) Las terminaciones, ¿qué son?.....(6s) ((still looking at students)) °<u>Ah</u> sí, saben eso°, sí, a ver, ((looks at students))

02   S1: o

03   T: ((writes 'yo –o'))

(Translation)

01   T: ...Ok. What are the verb endings of <u>A-R</u>, verbs, the endings in the present in the verbs that end in A-R? ((pauses and looks at students)) <u>The</u> endings ((pauses and looks at students)) Do you guys know what the endings are ((writes 'the endings' on the board))? ((pauses)) Endings, ((pauses)) en-dings ((talks slow and underlines 'endings' on board)), <u>the end</u> ((motions hand down and looks at students))? ((pauses and looks at students)) <u>This</u> part ((points to –AR)), it's at the end of the verb ((motions hand down again)) ((looks at students)) The endings, What are they?.....(6s) ((still looking at students)) °<u>Ah</u> yes, you all know this°, yes, let's see, ((looks at students))

02   02 S1: o

03   03 T: ((writes 'I –o'))

This episode started with a rhetorical question that recruited the learners' interest in the grammatical explanation. When there was no response, the teacher used several assisting strategies. He simplified the question by focusing on the key concept, *las terminaciones*, by repeating the word with emphasis, writing it on the board, highlighting the meaning (*termina*), offering a synonym (*el final*), and finally, pointing at the relevant portion of the word, reassuring the students that they knew the answer (*sí, saben eso*) and inviting them to answer (*sí, a ver*). Significantly, the last two phrases were uttered in a low voice, which reinforced the intention of the teacher to give voice to the learners. Eight pauses are interspersed in the teacher's turn, combined with gazing at the learners. These pauses played a key role in signaling that the teacher was not willing to provide an answer himself and that the learners' active participation was expected for the continuation of the interaction. At this point, one learner provided an answer and then several others contributed to the discussion. With these lower-level learners we see the teacher extending his hand, as it were, with words that encourage learners to become involved in the class activity and reinforce the sense of learning community. Using several scaffolding functions (recruiting interest, simplifying, marking critical features, and maintaining the direction of the task), he offered assistance to students with a wide variety of discursive strategies that mediated the learners' understanding of the question and encouraged their participation in the class. The teacher's assisting role in Episode 2 is markedly different from the previous episode in that the teacher evaluated what assistance was needed and provided (Episode 1) or withdrew (Episode 2) direct answers accordingly.

Creating a Participatory Environment

Increasing learners' participation, especially among advanced learners, was an explicit role for the teacher which was evident in the interaction. Level 4 classes consisted mostly of discussions of literary works, newspaper readings, and cultural topics. In the following episode, Episode 3, teacher and students were discussing a literary play that the students had read, *La Celestina*. At this point in the interaction the teacher was trying to lead students to use the modern word for 'act' and to define the word. Questioning and humor are the main strategies deployed here during an episode that developed in a relaxed atmosphere and with considerable student participation.

Episode 3 (Level 4)

01   T: ...¿Qué más sabemos? ((holds hand out and looks at students))... (4s)

02   S1: °¿sobre qué?°

03   T: La Celestina, lo que supuestamente leyero:n anoche...(4s) ((looks at students))

04   S2: Tiene dieciséis (°autos°)

05   T: ((walks to get megaphone and puts it to his ear))

06   S1: Tiene dieciséis °autos°

07   S2: no triente uno

08   T: ((still holds megaphone to his ear and looks at S1))....(4s)

09   S1: Pues, original tiene dieciséis autos

10   T: ¿Dieciséis autos? ¿Qué són? ((crosses arms and looks at student))

11   S1: em no sé cómo, autos

12   T: ¿Es una colección de carros?

13   S1: ¡No::::!

14   SS: ((students laugh))

15   S1: No se cómo explicarlo.

16   T: hmmmm[

17   S1: [cuándo (como, em) cuentas °pequeñas°

18   T: ¿Dices <u>autos o actos</u>?

19   S1: Autos, auctos

20   T: ((looks at student))=

21   S3: =o carros

22   T: ((looks at S3)) Sí, es como la colección de Jay Leno

23   SS: ((students laugh))

24   T: ((looks back to S1)) .....(4s) Entonces, ¿esta obra de teatro tiene un <u>garaje</u> grande?

25   S1: Sí

26   T: ¿Es eso? ((arms still crossed)) o todo:, toda la obra tiene, dura en, un garaje

27   S4: ¡Sí!.

28   T: Ah-ha. ¿autos? ¿Qué son autos?... (3s)

29   S2: [[los partes de, no sé]]

30   T: [[(((puts hands together and moves them the left))]]. ¿Partes de qué? ((holds hands out))

31   S1: [[de obra]]

32   S2: [[cuenta]]

33   T: Huh

34   S5: ¿capítulos de °obra °?

35   T: <u>Capí:tulos</u> de una obra de teatro ((has a confused look on his face))

36   S1: ¿Cómo?

37   T: ((walks to board to write)) Ah-ha. ((writes 'actos' on board))

(Translation)

01   T: ...What else do we know? ((holds hand out and looks at students))... (4s)

02   S1: °about what?°

03   T: La Celestina, what you were supposed to read last night...(4s) ((looks at students))

04   S2: It has sixteen acts (*autos*)

05   T: ((walks to get megaphone and puts it to his ear))

06   S1: It has sixteen acts (*autos*)

07   S2: no thirty-one

08   T: ((still holds megaphone to his ear and looks at S1))....(4s)

09   S1: Well, the original has sixteen acts (*autos*)

10   T: Sixteen *autos*? What are they? ((crosses arms and looks at student))

11   S1: em I don't know, like, *autos*

12   T: Is it a collection of cars?

13   S1: ¡No::::!

14   SS: ((students laugh))

15   S1: I don't know how to explain it

16   T: hmmmm[

17   S1: [when (like, em) °short stories° [incorrect words]

18   T: Do you mean *autos* or *actos*?

19   S1: Autos, auctos

20   T: ((looks at student))=

21   S3: =or cars

22   T: ((looks at S3)) Yes, it is like Jay Leno's collection

23   SS: ((students laugh))

24   T: ((looks back to S1)) .....(4s) then, this play has a big garage?

25   S1: Yes

26   T: Is that it? ((arms still crossed)) or the whole, the whole play has, takes place in a garage?

27   S4: Yes!

28   T: Ah-ha, *autos*? What are *autos*?... (3s)

29   S2: [[parts of, I don't know]]

30   T: [[(((puts hands together and moves them left))]] Parts of what? ((holds hands out))

31   S1: [[of a play]]

32   S2: [[story]]

33   T: Huh

34   S5: chapters of a °play °?

35   T: Chapters of a play ((has a confused look on his face))

36   S1: What?

37   T: ((walks to board to write)) Ah-ha. ((writes 'actos' on board))

What is relevant here is how the teacher mediated the discussion leading the students to define the word *autos*, which means "acts" but also "cars." The word appeared first in turn 4, uttered by S2. In eliciting a reconsideration of the word, the teacher used gesturing first (turns 5 and

8), emphasis (10), questioning (10, 18 and 28), humor (turns 12-26) and pauses (1, 3, 8, 24, 28). Some of the teacher's turns are simple expressions of clarification (16, 33). Five students voluntarily became involved in the definition. Some followed the teacher's lead in language play with the double meaning of the word *autos* (21, 25, 27). The teacher minimized his intervention with short turns, silences and a variety of strategies that communicated his expectation that students provide answers and rely on each other when they do not know how to express an idea. These strategies successfully recruited the participation of several learners in the interaction without being prompted by the teacher.

We see a certain degree of self-regulation in learners' self-correction (7) and in learners' correction of each other's answers, as in turn 9. There is evidence of learners' independence as well in their use of humor, as in 21 where S3 appropriated the teacher's use of language play with the words *autos/carros* leading to three subsequent teacher's turns using humor. Humor helps establish a relaxed and cooperative atmosphere that increases oral participation (Consolo, 2000). In this classroom, humor is a key strategy to decrease frustration, to engage student participation and to maintain a sense of community. Not only did learners often respond to the teacher's humorous remarks with laughter, but they frequently created humorous remarks themselves following the teacher's model. While the interaction in these episodes follows the prototypical IRF pattern, Level 4 learners show some degree of autonomous behavior by asking questions, assisting and instructing each other, and joking with each other in the L2 (van Lier, 2008). The teacher's mediation here is intentionally more focused on his role as guide and participant in the community than on being a linguistic model. Assistance is less direct and his role is minimized. Several of the strategies used here (gestures, clarification requests, humor, and silence) seem beneficial to promote agentive behavior increasing participation.

Creating Community

Lesson transcripts showed that the teacher had successfully created a sense of community (one of the stated goals of his philosophy). A good amount of time at the beginning of each lesson and throughout the lesson period was spent conversing in L2 with students about their life (school games, school friendships, their jobs and other topics of interests to them) in a relaxed classroom atmosphere. For instance, in a Level 2 class, the teacher started the class by greeting individually each student in the target language (*Buenas tardes*) at the same time that he would slap hands with each of them in a cordial greeting. Then, students walked around greeting each other. This routine at the beginning of class reinforced a sense of community and the value the teacher placed on interacting with each individual student and on interaction among students. Conversing about students' lives and interest was an effective way of eliciting their participation. An example of this is the long conversation ensuing the teacher's questions *¿qué hay? ¿qué pasó hoy?* (what's going on? what happened today?) during a Level 2 class period. After one student responded indicating that they had a game against another school, the teacher was able to engage the participation of 17 other students during 85 turns with a few prodding questions (where? do we have a good team? how many sports do we have here?) leading them to list sports and clubs they could engage in at school.

Humor emerged as an important mechanism to create a sense of community as well. The teacher constantly made humorous remarks and students laughed often, sometimes engaging in the jocose discourse. As an illustration of this point, during an episode in which teacher and students were negotiating the meaning of the lexical item *ruido* (noise), the teacher asked if students knew what an airport was (*¿saben qué es un aeropuerto?*), to which one student responded singing an elongated negative word. This caused general laughter among the rest of the students.

The sense of community was also fostered by activities outside the classroom, which included short group trips to Spanish-speaking countries and service to the local Latino community. These activities were sometimes topics of conversation in the classroom. During one of the class periods under study, for instance, the teacher discussed travel plans for two trips, one to Mexico and one to Peru, with the students. By including students' lives and interests as topics of interaction, and by using discursive mechanisms such as referential questions, humor, and gesturing, the teacher enacted his stated roles as a language model (since all the interaction was in L2) and as participant in the classroom community.

DISCUSSION AND IMPLICATIONS

In his teaching philosophy, Mr. G articulated his role in the classroom as that of a linguistic model and guide-participant in the learning community. Classroom observations showed that, indeed, these roles were observable in his interaction with the learners. Four main roles were apparent in the teacher's language: providing a linguistic model, providing assistance, creating a participatory environment, and creating a sense of community. In sociocultural terms, the teacher's role was to mediate learning by performing several subroles with the overall goal of providing learners with scaffolded help as needed: modeling language, maintaining interest, simplifying the language or task, highlighting relevant features, controlling frustration through humor, and so on.

Looking at teacher-learner interaction from a sociocultural perspective, we can improve our understanding of how the teacher's roles are conveyed by discursive moves and their effect on learners' discourse. We have illustrated the use of a variety of discursive strategies, ranging from very explicit assistance (explanation, repetition, emphasis, etc.) to more indirect assisting strategies such as clarification requests and silence. The teacher's talk communicated his expectation that learners should be highly participatory in the interaction and that the role of the teacher should be reduced when he estimated that explicit assistance was not necessary, as was often the case with advanced learners. Although we are not claiming that Level 4 learners achieved self-regulation, there are qualitative and quantitative differences in the teacher's discourse that provide evidence of more involvement in the interaction by Level 4 learners and less need of direct assisting strategies, such as repetition, linguistic simplification, and gesturing. Instead, silence, questioning and humor are common strategies with more advanced students. The creation of a sense of community emerged as an important teacher's role, which was achieved in several ways. Devoting class time to converse with learners about their activities and interests, at the same time that the teacher shared his life stories as well, was a discursive mechanism that fostered a sense of community. Humor was also a strategy deployed by the teacher, and appropriated by the learners, that worked well to create a relaxed and participatory environment.

This study identifies the strategies used by this teacher to promote learners' engagement in the L2. This should be useful to teachers reflecting on how to plan discourse in the classroom in order to express their roles. Intentional and responsive use of classroom language is important in learners' development. From a pedagogical standpoint, this study provides language teachers and supervisors with a better understanding of teachers' roles and how roles are semiotically conveyed by discursive strategies. In particular, we have illustrated how a sociocultural perspective on the teacher's role as mediator of learning, who assists in the learning process, is evidenced by the language used. We propose that it is important for FL/L2 teachers to include in their lesson planning consideration of the language to be used and the discursive strategies that may be most helpful in performing their roles. Teachers should have a plan for realizing their teaching philosophy through words in the classroom. To this effect, videotaping and analyzing their lessons is a helpful heuristic to become aware of how they are interacting with their learners. A sociocultural view of learning calls for teachers to be aware of the degree of assistance needed by the learners, and to use language in a way that will encourage learners to be involved and to move towards assuming more responsibility for their learning.

REFERENCES

Adair-Hauck, B., & Donato, R. (1994). Foreign language explanations within the zone of proximal development. *The Canadian Modern Language Review, 50*, 532-557.

Aljaafreh, A., & Lantolf, J.(1994). Negative feedback as regulation and second language learning in the zone of proximal development. *Modern Language Journal, 78*, 465-483.

Antón, M. (1996). Using ethnographic techniques in classroom observation: A study of success in a foreign language class. *Foreign Language Annals, 29*, 551-561.

Antón, M. (1999). The discourse of a learner-centered classroom: Sociocultural perspectives on teacher-learner interaction in the second-language classroom. *Modern Language Journal, 83*, 303-318.

Consolo, D. A. (2000). Teachers' action and student oral participation in classroom interaction. In J. K. Hall & L. S. Verplaetse (Eds.), *Second and foreign language learning through classroom interaction* (pp. 91-108). Mahwah, NJ: Lawrence Erlbaum Associates.

Donato, R., & Adair-Hauck, B. (1992). Discourse perspectives on formal instruction. *Language Awareness, 1*(2), 73-89.

Donato, R., & F. Brooks. (2004). Literary discussions and advanced speaking functions: Researching the(dis)connections. *Foreign Language Annals 37*, 183–199.

Duff, P. (2000). Repetition in foreign language classroom interaction. In J. K. Hall & L. S. Verplaetse (Eds.), *Second and foreign language learning through classroom interaction* (pp. 109-138). Mahwah, NJ: Lawrence Erlbaum Associates.

Hall, J. K. (2004). "Practicing speaking" in Spanish: Lessons from a high school foreign language classroom. In D. Boxer, & A. D. Cohen (Eds.), *Studying speaking to inform second language learning* (pp. 68-87). Clevedon, England: Multilingual Matters.

Hall, J. K., & Verplaetse, L. S. (2000). *Second and foreign language learning through classroom interaction*. Mahwah, NJ: Lawrence Erlbaum.

Lantolf, J., &Thorne, S. (2006). *Sociocultural theory and the genesis of second language development*. Oxford, England: Oxford University Press.

McCormick, D. E., & Donato, R. (2000). Teacher questions as scaffolded assistance in an ESL classroom. In J. K. Hall & L.S. Verplaetse (Eds.), *Second and foreign language learning through classroom interaction* (pp. 183-201). Mahwah, NJ: Lawrence Erlbaum Associates.

Poehner, M. (2008). Both sides of the conversation: The interplay between mediation and learner reciprocity in dynamic assessment. In J. Lantolf & M. Poehner (Eds.), *Sociocultural theory and the teaching of second languages* (pp. 33-56). London: Equinox.

Psathas, G. (1995). *Conversation analysis: The study of talk-in-interaction*. Thousand Oaks, CA: SAGE.

Radziszewska, B., & Rogoff, B. (1991). Children's guided participation in planning imaginary errands with skilled adult or peer partners. *Developmental Psychology, 27*, 381-397.

Rogoff, B., & Gardner, W. (1984). Adult guidance of cognitive development. In B. Rogoff & J. Lave (Eds.), *Everyday cognition: Its development in social context* (pp. 95-116). Cambridge, MA: Harvard University Press.

Schegloff, E. (2001). Discourse and interactional achievement III: The omnirelevance of action. In D. Schiffrin, D. Tannen & H. Hamilton (Eds.), *The handbook of discourse analysis* (pp. 229-249). Malden, MA: Blackwell.

Smiley, J. (2010). *El discurso del profesor en el aula: Recursos discursivos para el uso de la lengua meta a distintos niveles de dominio lingüístico* [Teacher discourse in the classroom: Discursive mechanisms for L1 use at different levels of proficiency] (Unpublished Master's thesis). Indiana University-Purdue University, Indianapolis.

Spradley, J. (1980). *Participant observation*. New York, NY: Holt, Rinehart and Winston.

Tharp, R., & Gallimore, R. (1988). *Rousing minds to life: Teaching, learning and schooling in social context*. Cambridge, England: Cambridge University Press.

Toth, P. (2004). When grammar instruction undermines cohesion in L2 Spanish classroom discourse. *Modern Language Journal, 88*, 14-30.

Toth, P. D. (2008). Teacher- and learner-led discourse in a task-based grammar instruction: Providing procedural assistance for L2 morphosyntactic development. *Language Learning, 58*(2), 237-283.

van Lier, L. (2008). Agency in the classroom. In J. Lantolf & M. Poehner (Eds.), *Sociocultural theory and the teaching of second languages* (pp. 163-186). London: Equinox.

Vygotsky, L. S. (1978). *Mind in society: The development of higher psychological processes*. Cambridge, MA: Harvard University Press.

Vygotsky, L. S. (1987). *The Collected Works of L. S. Vygotsky*. New York: Plenum Press.

Wells, G. (1998). Using L1 to master L2: A response to Antón & DiCamilla's Socio-cognitive functions of L1 collaborative interaction in the L2 classroom'. *Canadian Modern Language Review, 54*, 343-353.

Wertsch, J. V., Minick, N., & Arns, F. J. (1984). The creation of context in joint problem-solving. In B. Rogoff & J. Lave (Eds.), *Everyday cognition: Its development in social context* (pp. 151-171). Cambridge, MA: Harvard University Press.

Wood, D., Bruner, J. S., & Ross, G. (1976). The role of tutoring in problem solving. *Journal of Child Psychology & Psychiatry, 17*, 89-100.

CHAPTER 14

SECOND GRADE ESL LITERACY SUCCESS IN A U.S. MAINSTREAM CLASSROOM

Amma K. Akrofi, Carole Janisch, Amira Zebidi, and Karla Lewis

The purpose of this study was to examine one teacher's social interactional roles that fostered effective literacy learning in an ESL-inclusion second grade classroom. Interactions between the teacher and her students were documented but with special focus on one ELL. The study was undergirded by the sociocultural and activity theories and predicated on a revelatory single-case study design. Multiple qualitative methods and inductive procedures were utilized for data collection and analysis, respectively. Two teacher roles were identified: (1) the teacher as a team-builder and, (2) the teacher as a team captain. From the data analysis, the authors concluded that the teacher's facilitation of learning through peer-collaboration enabled the ELL to make strides and, ultimately, become a more capable peer.

*Mrs. Lewis tells her second graders that a guest reader will come to the class today to read chapters 15 and 16 of **Charlotte's Web**. Then she calls Jacques (pseudonym), an English Language Learner (ELL), to work one-on-one with her. [Jacque takes on the task at hand and accomplishes it successfully.] Mrs. Lewis: Great job! You're done. [He goes to pick a book and excitedly joins the reading group at the back of the classroom. He first flips through several books like **Too Many Pumpkins** and studies the pictures before settling down to read **Highlights**.]*

Teachers' Roles in Second Language Learning:
Classroom Applications of Sociocultural Theory, pp. 249–265
Copyright © 2012 by Information Age Publishing
All rights of reproduction in any form reserved.

249

This excerpt provides a snapshot of the typical daily teacher-student interactions in one second grade classroom. Mrs. Lewis' classroom is one where students rarely, if ever, are without teacher- (or other adult-) student interactions during learning: Guests come to interact with the children and the teacher continuously engages in dialogues with them to support their development. Additionally, children's peers in the reading group are always available for interactions/conversations about books and reading.

In Vygotsky's view of learning, literacy experiences begin with social interaction and move to internalized independent functioning through mediation of signs or mental tools (Dixon-Krauss, 1996). Mental functions, examples of which are classroom reading and writing, are advanced through the prompts and interactions with the teacher and as a means for children to move to independent functioning and learning. According to Combs (1996), the ultimate goal for a teacher is to provide learning assistance through interactions that will enable children to "move from other-regulated to self-regulated reading and writing" (p. 26). Mrs. Lewis, the fourth author, exemplifies the theory into practice for Jacques, the focal ELL in this study.

BACKGROUND

Several semesters during the past 3 years, the first author has taught an ELL undergraduate course. A major expectation of this Foundations of Reading for ELLs course is for preservice teachers to read, discuss, and produce group responses to research articles from journals such as *The Reading Teacher*. While the articles suggest diverse instructional strategies for enhancing ELL reading proficiency, the authors overwhelmingly paint a dismal picture of ELL literacy development: Few report success stories. Clear and convincing evidence that mainstream teachers and/or English as a Second Language (ESL) specialists use strategies successful with this population of learners is not available. Thus, after doing the readings, the pre-service teachers express some trepidation about how hard their chosen career—teaching English language learners—is going to be; they wonder in their response papers whether they will be up to the task facing them as prospective ESL teachers.

In the aforementioned course, the article readings and responses precede the teacher candidates' 2-day classroom observations in elementary schools that are considered "main ESL campuses" in the local school district. During those field experiences, a magical transformation of perceptions occurs because the preservice teachers are provided with an opportunity to meet and interact with ELLs who are dissimilar from those they had been reading about in the articles, that is, successful ELLs who, in the preservice teachers' words, are:

> On the same level as the majority of mainstream students. If she [mainstream teacher] had not told me when I first walked in who the ELLs were, I would have never known. The only way I could have ever known is that the rest of the students were Caucasian and Mexican and the ELLs were different ethnic groups. (A preservice teacher's reflective paper. Fall, 2009)

Seemingly, those are the ELLs who have been left out of the literature on English language learning in American public school mainstream classrooms. We believe that it is important for the literature to more accurately reflect the diversity of learners in that rapidly growing population of students, especially for the benefit of preservice teachers striving to get an unbiased view of their potential students so they can better prepare for their future career. This chapter seeks to capture the successes of Jacques and offer a counter example to the dismal picture usually painted of ELL's learning development. To that end, the purpose of the study was to examine one teacher's social interactions that fostered effective literacy learning for one ELL. The following research question framed the study: What teacher roles in terms of social interactions are supportive of ELL literacy learning in an ESL-inclusion second grade classroom? We chose to document verbal and nonverbal interactions between the teacher and all her students but with special focus on one student, Jacques.

THEORETICAL FRAMEWORK

Vygotsky's (1978) sociocultural theory holds that because a child's development is too complex to be isolated, dissected, and studied in discrete units, it should be studied first in the social or cultural and linguistic context, i.e., between the child and other people or at the *interpsychological* level, and then in the historical context, that is, inside the child or at the *intrapsychological* level (Dixon-Krauss, 1996). Interactions within social environments such as peer groups and school contexts are the most important drivers of children's cognitive development (Lantolf & Thorne, 2006). Another core component of the sociocultural theory is the notion of the zone of proximal development (ZPD) which explains that "both development achieved and developmental potential" (p. 206) depend on scaffolds or adult-child interactions and assisted performance (Wood, Bruner, & Ross, 1976). Such interactions provide opportunities for children to create or approximate language modeled after adult forms.

Applications of this theory to children's language and literacy development have been explained in terms of how more capable others' availability for dialogue with children greatly influences the latter's language acquisition (Ruddell & Ruddell, 1994). Dixon-Krauss (1996) contends that for Vygotsky, the classroom instructional context is the most appropriate setting for studying children's literacy learning and cognitive development. Dixon-Krauss' interpretation of the theory reflects Moll's (1990) proposition that Vygotsky views formal instruction in writing and grammar, for instance, as refocusing attention *from* the content *to* the means of communication. That is, a teacher may direct children's attention to word meanings, definitions, and "the systematic relationships among [words] that constitute an organized system of knowledge" (p. 10). All of these, Moll explained, give children the capacity to manipulate the symbolic system of the language as well as provide a "foundation for the development of conscious awareness of important aspects of speech and language" (p. 10).

The study was also undergirded by activity theory (e.g., Scribner, 1987) which is described as an integration of social practice and psychological process "conceptualized as *activities*" (p. 20) which, in turn, serve "to fulfill distinctive motives" (p. 20). Even more compelling is researchers' extension of activity theory into *activity settings*, which are analytical constructs that identify "when collaborative interactions, intersubjectivity, and assisted performance occur ... (or) when *teaching* occurs" (Gallimore & Tharp, 1990, p. 189) between children and more capable others. The concept has three essential components (Tharp, 1993). First is the setting, that is, the external, environmental, and objective features of the occasion, such as the whole class settings, small groups, learning centers, and teacher-student conferences. The second component of an activity setting is made up of the cognitive, motoric, and/or verbal actions of the child in collaboration with more capable others which provide the child with opportunities to learn through strategies like modeling, joint production, and apprenticeship (Gallimore & Goldenberg, 1993). In the third component of an activity setting, the *activity* and *setting* intertwine with *participants' experiences*, *intentions*, and *meanings* and together they comprise the reality of life and learning (Tharp, 1993). These three components guided our data analysis.

RELATED LITERATURE

Success is not an attribute that is often associated with the ELL in the U.S. mainstream classroom. Findings indicate that not only do ELLs lag behind their mainstream public school counterparts, but the achievement gap is unlikely to close in the near future (Strickland & Alvermann, 2004). Skill areas where gaps have been documented include phonological awareness (Helman, 2005), word recognition (Helman & Burns, 2008), spelling (Cañado, 2005), fluency (Wilhelm, Contreras, & Mohr, 2004), vocabulary and comprehension (Hickman, Pollard-Durodola, & Vaughn, 2004; Manyak, 2008; Ranker, 2009), and academic language, particularly the forms and structures of scientific and other academic texts (Avalos, Plasencia, Chavez, & Rascon, 2007). Earlier evidence of such gaps resulted, for the most part, in the implementation of programs like the dual language program (Calderon, & Minaya-Rowe, 2003; Collier & Thomas, 2004) and the Structured English Immersion program (Krashen, Rolstad, & MacSwan, 2007; Ramirez, Yuen, & Ramey, 1991).

Apart from program level solutions to the existing gap, several practices relative to (1) classroom organizational structures, (2) instructional methods/approaches, and (3) instructional strategies have been suggested. The classroom organizational structures include learner-centered instruction (Manyak, 2008), creating communities of learners to foster peer scaffolding (Krashen, 2003), and a host of multifaceted and multipurposed literacy practices (Pérez, 2004). Suggestions of instructional methods/approaches comprise the use of teacher read-alouds to enhance vocabulary and comprehension development (Hickman et. al., 2004), shared reading (Holdaway, 1980; Parkes, 2000), and discussion-based instruction to encourage ESL participatory talk in mainstream classrooms (Yoon, 2007). Last, the instructional strategies consist of extended writing and reading practices, purposeful uses of texts, opportunities to use the new language in open-ended and communicative ways (Fu, 2003; Gutiérrez, 1992; Ranker, 2009), the Language Experience Approach (Stauffer, 1970), and the Reciprocal Teaching Strategy (Palincsar & Brown, 1986). These instructional modifications notwithstanding, the impression that ELLs are struggling learners who have difficulties catching up with their mainstream counterparts still remains, an impression backed by results of large scale testing and quantitative research findings (e.g., Helman, 2005). This persistent notion is not dissimilar to other deficit views of minority student learning (Delpit, 1988). Therefore, our interest was to examine one teacher's social interactions with students that resulted in triumphs in ESL literacy learning in a mainstream classroom.

RESEARCH METHODS

Mrs. Lewis' school was selected because it is designated as an ESL campus, the larger of two such campuses in the school district. A Caucasian teacher-researcher with more than 20 years of teaching experience, Mrs. Lewis had eight ELLs of varying English proficiency levels in her classroom. We used a revelatory single-case study design (Yin, 1994) to aid our exploration of classroom literacy interactions between Mrs. Lewis and her students but with a focus on Jacques, an ELL from the Philippines who speaks Tagalog as his first language. Jacques' mother, a nurse, who had been in the U.S. with her family for eight months at the start of the study, told Mrs. Lewis that before coming to the United States, Jacques had learned initial English from the Cartoon Network in the Philippines, played lots of video games, and could retell in English what was on each game (e.g., the Greek goddess Athena).

According to Yin (1994), a revelatory case provides an investigator an opportunity to examine "a phenomenon previously inaccessible to scientific investigation" (p. 40). We paid particular attention to Jacques because, in addition to being an extroverted learner, he was making improvements in his literacy learning, a phenomenon seldom reflected in the literature. He was at the intermediate proficiency level. ("Intermediate" is defined by Chen & Mora-Flores (2006) as ELLs who are nonbeginners and are able to use more complex sentences in their speech and writing.) His performance on a formative classroom assessment test administered to primary students, showed his impressive progress in literacy throughout the academic year. For example, although his graphophonemic knowledge level was Still Developing (SD) at the beginning of the year, his scores climbed to Developed (D) by the end of the year. In the same way, his fluency and reading comprehension proficiency went from SD at the beginning of the year to D at the end.

Data Collection

Data was collected in Mrs. Lewis' classroom for one hour and forty-five minutes daily during a two-week period for a total of 23 literacy lessons. The following multiple methods—observations, interviews, and artifacts—were used. Literacy lessons were observed and detailed field notes were taken. Brief informal interviews were conducted with Mrs. Lewis to seek information on the participant's background and clarifications on, or explanations of, various literacy activities and student directions. The interviews followed the observations and were recorded as field notes. Artifacts consisted of photocopies of Jacques' instructional and assessment materials, his journal entries, and all his writings over the 2-week period. Short descriptive notes were written for each artifact.

We followed Wolcott's (1973) "time and motion" observation data collection procedure in which he recorded what his subject did, where he went, and with whom he interacted at 60-second intervals (Gall, Gall, & Borg, 2005). In this study, we modified the procedure to a "setting, action, and operation" technique. We recorded teacher directions, comments and questions (actions), participant activities and interactions (operations), and the microsettings (including time settings).

Data Analysis

Vygotsky's sociocultural theory framed the analysis of the literacy interactions. Additionally, Gallimore and Goldenberg's (1993) activity settings procedures were used to analyze the data because of their theoretical sensitivity to the sociocultural theory. Gallimore and Goldenberg proposed that the following elements are germane to operationalizing activity settings in empirical research: (1) the personnel present during the activity, (2) salient cultural values, (3) the operations and task demands of the activity, (4) the scripts for conduct that govern the participants' actions, and (5) the purposes or motives of the participants. In order to analyze occasions when collaborative interactions occurred between Mrs. Lewis and Jacques and his peers, we compressed the five elements to fit our "actions, operations, and settings" data collection procedure: #1 and #4 were ensconced in our "actions" and "setting" elements and #2, #3, and #5 were captured in our "operations" elements. Inductive procedures (Strauss & Corbin, 1990) were then used for detailed analysis.

Open manual coding was preceded by each researcher's reading and rereadings of the observation field notes taken during the first two days of data collection. Individual coding of those field notes relative to "actions, operations, and settings" followed. Subsequently, all researchers met to discuss the coding schemes for those field notes and after a consensus on the scheme had been reached, each researcher coded the remaining field notes. The same procedure of coding and meeting to compare, revise, and update the scheme (Miles & Huberman, 1994) was carried out for the interview transcripts and notes on the artifacts. A third case study meeting was held in order to merge similar codes and subcodes into categories, following our modified operational elements of activity settings.

FINDINGS

We used two metaphors to capture what we saw as the characteristics of the teacher roles in the classroom where social interactions learning was promoted: (1) The Teacher as a Team-Builder, and (2) The Teacher as a Team Captain. All the findings relate directly or indirectly to Jacques. He was a part of the "team" and benefitted from membership and Mrs. Lewis' "team management."

The Teacher as a Team-Builder

The team-builder knows her members, is technically competent, makes strategic decisions about team organization and management, and frequently consults with members while at the same time providing them with the leeway to communicate and support each other. Furthermore, the team-builder works on the sidelines while the team ultimately "carries on" with its projects. A successfully completed project always calls for a celebration which builds a team spirit.

A key strategic decision Mrs. Lewis made in her classroom related to the type of seating arrangement that enhanced cooperative learning. Students were grouped by fours with their desks clustered to form a working unit with assignment of diverse tasks (e.g., Books Distributor, Locker Monitor, and Supplies Sergeant). Another example of the teacher's team-building acumen was her provision of frequent encouragement and peer consultation and collaboration among the unit members as well as the non-unit members. Mrs. Lewis knew what she wanted as a learning outcome and provided the scaffolding to ensure that outcome. She worked with the students to create sample products (e.g., a poem) and, thereafter, guided them to engage in reciprocal peer interactions to create individual work. The following chain of verbal exchanges is illustrative and shows interactions between Mrs. Lewis, Jacques, and the rest of the class.

Mrs. Lewis: We're going to do a diamante. If you went to Mrs. Knotts yesterday, you might think you know how to do it. But we're going to do it differently. I'm going to do one with "girl" at the top. (For "girl," she made a connection to Fern, a character in *Charlotte's Web*, their read-aloud novel.) I'm doing Fern. Nobody else is to do Fern. Two adjectives I'm going to write about Fern are "sweet" and "caring." (She erased "caring" and substituted "tomboyish.") "Tomboy" is the noun but if you put "-ish" after it, you get an adjective. Now, the next word is a participle.

Jacques:	What's a participle?
Mrs. Lewis:	That's what I'm going to explain. Participles have "-ing" after them. So the next words I'm going to put are "-ing" words: "caring," "loving," "listening." Now the next words are nouns. She was a "sister," "daughter."
Jacques:	Babysitter.
Another Student:	Piggysitter.
Mrs. Lewis:	Ha, ha! Okay. Piggysitter. Nice. Now the next one is another set of participles. So let's put three more words: "working." (Students suggested and she wrote

	"feeding," and "sharing.") You see, there's a lot you could use. Now, the next one?
Another Student:	Adjective.
Mrs. Lewis:	Great. You got it. Now two more adjectives.
Several Students:	"Pretty?"
Mrs. Lewis:	Well, I don't remember anywhere in the book where they said she was pretty. But if you think so, let's write "pretty." Another word? …"Dirty"… Now the last word…. It's her name. Fern.
Jacques:	Can we write about anybody?
Mrs. Lewis:	Anybody that's in the book. (She used a sheet of paper to demonstrate how to shape their diamante poem, like a diamond shape). It's got to turn out like a diamond shape. Otherwise, it's not a diamante.
Another Student:	It's gonna be hard.
Mrs. Lewis:	Why is it gonna be hard? You all helped me to write this one on the board. Now, you can do one with another character. Just focus on the words and the shape. If you get stuck, you can ask your partner…. Remember, pick someone else, a different character. I can't wait for you to share this. (The following is the sample diamante she left on the board. She showed this sample because, before she stepped to the sidelines to let the students carry on, she wanted to ensure that they had access to a mentor text to guide their writing.)

Providing mentor text through shared write [handwritten annotation]

Girl	noun
Sweet, tomboyish	adjective, adjective
Caring, loving, listening	participle, participle, participle
Sister, daughter, piggysitter, niece	noun, noun, noun, noun
Working, feeding, sharing	participle, participle, participle
Pretty, dirty	adjective, adjective
Fern	noun

Mrs. Lewis' sample diamante text was a catalyst for the students' writing because after the class finished reading it aloud, Jacques got ready to write his diamante. He folded a sheet of paper then unfolded it as the teacher had shown them. He wrote "Spider" in the center of his paper, then "small" as his first adjective.

Providing the mentor text also enabled Mrs. Lewis to "stand back" at her table and encourage the students to take charge of their literacy learning tasks by consulting their within- and across-group members as they wrote their poems. However, even as she stood back, she constantly provided support and monitored the work of the students in an ongoing manner. For example, Jacques wanted to write "sweet" as his next adjective but he accepted a classmate's suggestion of "clever." He then went to the teacher and asked her how to spell "clever." He loudly repeated the teacher's spelling when he proceeded to add the word to his poem. After that, he checked his summary book for more ideas on words that might work, and said, "I don't know what else." His nearby classmate suggested that he add participle words, to which he retorted: "Drinking is a participle." After that he consulted his summary book again, read the phrase "it helped Wilbur!" to his classmate, which made the classmate suggest that he write "helping." Jacque wrote "helping" and then said to his classmate: "I need one more." He added "making."

He then went to show his work to the teacher again and was advised thus: "It has to look like a diamond shape. If it doesn't, you'll have to redo it." He went back to his desk to consult again with his classmate about what a noun is, wrote "pretty," excitedly said "it's Wilbur's friend," and also wrote "friend." He went back to the teacher a third time to show her what he had written so far but she said: "'Pretty' isn't a noun. You can't use 'pretty.'" While returning to his desk, he muttered to himself: "I can't use pretty!" He pulled out his summary book, heard the teacher say "'door' is a good one," and smiled to himself. He erased "pretty," wrote "door," and then added "web." He showed his work once more to the teacher who excitedly said: "That's a good one, good for you!" He returned to his desk, said "One more," then wrote "watching."

Spider

Small, clever

Drinking, helping, making

Door [initially "pretty"], friend, web,

Watching,

Next, he showed his poem to his classmate again, consulted with her for a while, and added "farm," "watching," and then "spinning:"

Spider

Small, clever

Drinking, helping, making

Door, friend, web, farm

Watching, spinning,

At this point, one of Jacques' desk-mates read his diamante and volunteered to assist Jacques to finish his poem.

Desk-mate: Erase "small" and write "tricky."
   Jacques: How do you spell "tricky"?
Desk-mate: "t-r-i-c-k-y." You need to put a comma.
   Jacques: Why?
Desk-mate: Because you are making a list. Now write "Charlotte" as
              your last noun. "Charlotte, C-h-a-r-l-o-t-t-e."

The above illustration is a typical and classic example of how Mrs. Lewis provided individual support while at the same time nurturing peer support.

The following is a final chain of events highlighting Mrs. Lewis' role as a team-builder who stepped to the sidelines and let her students consult each other and carry on. Jacques took his finished diamante to show Mrs. Lewis. She praised him for his excellent work, asked him to choose a celebration skit so the whole class could celebrate his success. Jacques proudly chose "Saturday Night Fever" [Ah, ah, ah, ah, you did a good job! You did a good job!]. The entire class engaged in the chant. After that, Mrs. Lewis asked him to help others who had not yet finished: "Go and help somebody. Remember you cannot help anybody who has a spider." He chose a classmate who was also an ELL and was working on "Goose." Jacques informed him that adjectives are easy and suggested "quacky." He further suggested "sitting" as a participle, "farm" as a noun, and said excitedly: "You are so close." The classmate wanted Jacques to tell him the goose's proper name. He happened not to know so a subsequent chain of verbal interactions formed culminating in Jacques asking Mrs. Lewis to help and she suggesting: "Just put Mrs. Goose." Soon, Mrs. Lewis approved the diamante of the ELL Jacques had helped. This student then read his poem aloud to the class, selected a celebratory skit, and then performed it with the whole class.

The social interaction in the classroom appeared as "team work" which contributed to successes in Jacques' language use and his creation of a diamante and, also interestingly, his ability to emerge in the class as a "more capable other." Mrs. Lewis was able to promote the teacher-student and peer-peer chain interactions through constant reminders like "Go round and help others after I check your work" and "If you get stuck, you can ask your partner." Moreover, Mrs. Lewis provided suggestions to move the task to completion ("Just put Mrs. Goose") and encouragement. ("That's a good one, good for you.")

The Teacher as a Captain of the Team

A team functions better when there is a team captain who is monitoring how the players are performing and suggesting ways to improve that performance. The captain can guide the team with expert eyes and ears, constantly asking probing questions, providing cues and prompts, and in general, overseeing the entire endeavor. Mrs. Lewis, the captain, kept lessons brisk and students busy. Additionally, she used a barrage of questions to generate language output. First, the actions and activities directed by the teacher were fast-paced, affording little chance for students to be off-task. She maintained briskness with phrases like "Keep busy" and constant reminders to students to finish current tasks so they could move on to the next. She frequently announced the next activity, set time limits for tasks, and counted to 10 to get students ready for the next endeavor. In Mrs. Lewis' classroom, even Break Time did not exactly mean they could cease working.

Mrs. Lewis: Bell for break. That means you can take your snacks but you can also continue with your summaries and pictures. If you have finished your summary, you can continue writing your acrostic poem. Also, if you have finished your *Charlotte's Web* summaries, you may redo your Minute Math worksheet if you got any of that wrong, or finish your handwriting practice if that is incomplete.

To that directive, Jacques continued to work on his *Charlotte's Web* summaries, copying two chapters he had missed the previous day from his peer's summary book. Mrs. Lewis continued with the Break Time instructions.

Mrs. Lewis: If you have finished your *Charlotte's Web*, acrostic poem, and Minute Math worksheet, you may go outside for break with Coach Hancock. (That is, they were to go for P.E. or other supervised activities; not exactly what one would call free time.)

Second, Mrs. Lewis capitalized on questioning to generate language output. Built into her read-aloud lessons were questions for various purposes: prediction ("Before Breakfast." What does the chapter heading tell you?" Student response: "Morning."), critical thinking ("In this story, we always have a problem and a solution. In chapter two, the problem is that the pig is to be sold. What was the solution?" Student response: "The pig had to go to Mrs. Zukermann's farm."), evaluation ("Do you agree? If you agree, thumbs up. It's okay to disagree. If you don't agree, give me a thumbs down."), personal connection ("How many of you have some kind of a pet?" Jacques raised his hand and answered: "Mine's a fish." The teacher allowed other students to take turns and talk about their pets.), inferential comprehension ("What's important in the middle? What does she do?" A student answered: "Fern had to convince her father not to kill the pig. Going to take care of it."), and literal comprehension ("What happened at the end?" Student response: "She names her Wilbur."). A majority of the literal level questions focused on new vocabulary and concept-building while the other question types were on plot development, characterization, theme, setting, along with main and supporting ideas. Ideas and sentences for chapter summaries on *Charlotte's Web* were all generated through questioning. Additionally, efforts were made to confirm, clarify, suggest alternative answers, respond to student questions and extend student responses, and acknowledge "smart" answers and provide praise. She also gave students the benefit of the doubt with statements like "Well, I don't remember anywhere in the book where they say she was pretty. But if you think so, let's write pretty." The generous questioning helped to strengthen comprehension for all students, both mainstream and ELL.

DISCUSSION

The two characterizations of this classroom teacher portrayed diverse levels of social interactions with, and assisted performance for, students on an individual, small group, and whole class basis, thus propelling them toward their developmental potential (Wood et. al., 1976). Teacher scaffolding and questioning in the interactions were veritable building blocks "for the development of conscious awareness of important aspects of speech and language" (Moll, 1990, p.10).

The findings revealed the teacher's facilitation of learning through peer-collaboration (Vygotsky, 1978). The teacher's provision of prompts, her constant checking and rechecking of their work to monitor how they advanced toward their ZPD (Lantolf & Thorne, 2006), and the celebrated sharing of accomplishments enabled the focal ELL to make strides and, ultimately, become a more capable peer. This is an encouraging finding because it shows that ELLs strive to forge ahead in some mainstream classrooms where social interaction undergirded learning activities, notably the case in this study. A few studies (e.g., Yoon, 2007) have described teacher approaches and instructional styles that foster ELL engagement and engender their participation in literacy lessons. However, research in this area has so far provided less descriptive evidence of an ELL interacting and flourishing in a sociocultural classroom setting.

The findings give credence to Moll's (1990) assertion that language classrooms that reflect a sociocultural predisposition tend to promote an enabling environment for learning key aspects of language. In this case, through a chain of direct and indirect prompts, the teacher assisted the ELLs in her class (including Jacques) to understand distinctions between different parts of speech and an appreciation of why each grammatical category can fit only one slot of the texts they were constructing.

Finally, and extremely interesting, is the supporting role played by more capable peers in this teacher's classroom. Their eager and ready assistance for Jacques obviously aided his ability to resolve spelling and diction challenges (Ruddell & Ruddell, 1994). This validates Yoon's (2007) finding that teachers' positive engagement with ELLs has a backwash effect on mainstream students' engagement with ELLs. But even more eye-opening is the fact that Jacques was, in turn, able to assist other ELL peers with unrelenting confidence. This is a new finding and requires further research.

IMPLICATIONS

No Child Left Behind (NCLB) requires ELLs to make Adequate Yearly Progress (AYP) to meet state requirements (Abedi, 2000). Meeting the requirements is not without challenges as amply documented in the literature, but this study indicates that frequent teacher and peer interactions and scaffolding enable some ELLs to stand even with their mainstream classmates in literacy learning. One obvious implication is that classrooms that do not display these attributes may not provide an enabling and nurturing environment for unleashing ELLs' literacy learning potential. To help forestall this, it is important for teacher educators to be attentive to strategies like cooperative learning strategies (e.g., Stevens, Slavin, & Famish, 1991) in their methods courses.

As teacher educators, we are often reminded by our preservice teachers of their desire for hands-on practical experiences from their teacher preparation course work. As borne out by this study, a solid theoretical grounding to undergird what we do in the classroom to promote student learning also seems necessary. Within the milieu of the sociocultural theory, the dynamic, responsive interactions in this one classroom enabled an ELL learner to experience success. Further studies involving multiple participants and classrooms will help to extend this finding.

To conclude, in the same way that ELLs' challenges are identified and examined with a view to strengthening their literacy and academic learning, their successes should be equally showcased so as to boost their morale and minimize the negative and "deficit" shroud that is usually cast over this amazing group of learners. This study is significant because it is among the first few qualitative case studies that present the flip side of the ELL's literacy learning coin—the successes of an ELL. This view is a necessary addition to the literature in order to form an accurate picture of preservice teachers' future students.

REFERENCES

Abedi, J. (2000). *Confounding of students' performance and their language background variables.* ERIC Number ED449250.

Avalos, M. A., Plasencia, A., Chavez, C., & Rascón, J. (2007). Modified guided reading: Gateway to English as second language and literacy learning. *The Reading Teacher, 61*(4), 318– 329.

Calderon, M. E., & Minaya-Rowe, L. (2003). Designing and implementing two-way bilingual programs: A step-by-step guide for administrators, teachers, and parents. Thousand Oaks, CA: Corwin Press.

Cañado, M. L. P. (2005). English and Spanish spelling: Are they really different? *The Reading Teacher, 58,* 522-530.

Chen, L., & Mora-Flores, E. (2006). *Balanced Literacy for English Language Learners, K-2.* Portsmouth, NH: Heinemann.

Collier, V. P., & Thomas, W. P. (2004). The Astounding Effectiveness of Dual Language Education for All. *NABE Journal of Research and Practice, 2,* 1-20.

Combs, M. (1996). Emerging readers and writers. In L. Dixon-Krauss (Ed.), *Vygotsky in the classroom* (pp. 25-41). White Plains, NY: Longman.

Delpit, L. D. (1988). The silenced dialogue: Power and pedagogy in educating other people's children. *Harvard Educational Review, 58,* 280-298.

Dixon-Krauss, L. (1996). *Vygotsky in the classroom: Mediated literacy instruction and assessment.* New York, NY: Longman.

Fu, D. (2003). *An island of English: Teaching ESL in Chinatown.* Portsmouth, NH: Heinemann.

Gall, J. P.,(W. R. (2005). *Applying educational research: A practical guide* (5th ed.). Boston, MA: Pearson Allyn & Bacon

Gallimore, R., & Goldenberg, C. (1993). Activity settings of early literacy: Home and school factors in children's emergent literacy. In A. E. Forman, N. Minick, & C. A. Stone (Eds.), *Contexts for learning: Sociocultural dynamics in children's development* (pp. 269-282). New York, NY: Oxford University Press.

Gallimore, R., & Tharp, R.(1990). Teaching mind in society: Teaching, schooling, and literate discourse. In L. C. Moll (Ed.), *Vygotsky and education* (pp. 175-202). Cambridge: Cambridge University Press.

Gutiérrez, K. (1992). A comparison of instructional contexts in writing process classrooms with Latino children. *Education and Urban Society, 24*(2), 244–262.

Helman, L. A. (2005). Using literacy assessment results to improve teaching for English-language learners. *The Reading Teacher, 58,* 668-677.

Helman, L. A., & Burns, M. K. (2008). What does oral language have to do with it? Helping young English-Language Learners acquire a sight word vocabulary. *The Reading Teacher, 62*, 14-19.

Hickman, P., Pollard-Durodola, S., & Vaughn, S. (2004). Storybook reading: Improving vocabulary and comprehension for English-language learners. *The Reading Teacher, 57*, 720-730.

Holdaway, D. (1980). *Independence in reading: A handbook on individualized procedures*. Gosford, Australia: Ashton Scholastic.

Krashen, S. (2003). *Explorations in language acquisition and use*. Portsmouth, NH: Heinemann.

Krashen, S., Rolstad, K., & MacSwan, J. (2007). *Review of "Research Summary and Bibliography for Structured English Immersion Programs" of the Arizona English Language Learners Task Force*. Takoma Park, MD: Institute for Language and Education Policy. Retrieved from www.elladvocates.org/documents/AZ/Krashen_Rolstad_MacSwan_review.pdf

Lantolf, J., & Thorne, S. (2006). *Sociocultural theory and the sociogenesis of second language development*. Oxford, England: Oxford University Press.

LeCompte, M. D., & Preissle, J. (1993). *Ethnography and qualitative design in educational research* (2nd ed.), San Diego, CA: Academic Press.

Manyak, P. C. (2008). What's your news? Portraits of a rich language and literacy activity for English-language learners. *The Reading Teacher, 61*, 450-458.

Miles, M. B., Huberman, A. M. (1994). *Qualitative data analysis: An expanded sourcebook* (2nd ed.). Thousand Oaks, CA: SAGE.

Moll, L. C. (1990). *Vygotsky and education: Educational implications and applications of educational psychology*. L. C. Moll (Ed.), New York, NY: Cambridge University Press.

Palincsar, A. S., & Brown, A. L. (1986). Interactive teaching to promote independent learning from text. *The Reading Teacher, 39*, 771-777.

Parkes, B. (2000). *Read it again! Revisiting shared reading*. Portland, ME: Stenhouse.

Pérez, B. (2004). *Becoming biliterate: A study of two-way bilingual immersion education*. Mahwah, NJ: Erlbaum.

Ramirez, J. D., Yuen, S. D., & Ramey, D. R. (1991). *Final report: Longitudinal study of structured immersion strategy, early-exit, and late-exit transitional bilingual education programs for language-minority children*. San Mateo, CA: Aguirre International.

Ranker, J. (2009). Learning nonfiction in an ESL class: the interaction of situated practice and teacher scaffolding in a genre study. *The Reading Teacher, 62*(7), 580-589.

Ruddell, R. B., & Ruddell, M. R. (1994). Language acquisition and literacy processes. In R. B. Ruddell, M. R. Ruddell, & H. Singer (Eds.), *Theoretical models and processes of reading* (pp. 83-103). Newark, DA: International Reading Association.

Scribner, S. (1987). Introduction. In D. A. Wagner (Ed.), *The future of literacy in a changing in a changing world*. Oxford, England: Pergamon Press.

Stauffer, R. G. (1970). *The language experience approach to the teaching of reading*. New York: Harper & Row.

Stevens, R. J., Slavin, R. E., & Famish, A. M. (1991). The Effects of Cooperative Learning and Direct Instruction in Reading Comprehension Strategies on Main Idea Identification. *Journal of Educational Psychology*, 83(1), 8-16.

Strauss, A., & Corbin, J. (1990). *Basics of qualitative research: Grounded theory procedures and techniques*. Newbury Park, CA: SAGE.

Strickland, D. S., & Alvermann, D. E. (2004). *Bridging the literacy achievement gap grades* (Eds.), (pp. 4-12). New York, NY: Teachers College Press.

Tharp, R. (1993). Institutional and social context of educational practice and reform. In E. A. Forman, N. Minick, & C. A Stone (Eds.), *Contexts for learning: Sociocultural dynamics in children's development* (pp. 269-282). New York, NY: Oxford University Press.

Vygotsky, L. (1978). *Mind in society: The development of higher psychological processes*. (M. Cole, V. John-Steiner, S. Scribner, & E. Souberman, Eds). Cambridge, MA: Harvard University Press.

Wilhelm, R. W., Contreras, G., & Mohr, K. A. J. (2004, April), *Barriers or frontiers: A bi-national investigation of Spanish-speaking immigrant students' school experience*. Paper presented at the Annual Convention of the American Educational Research Association, San Diego, CA.

Wolcott, H. (1973). *The man in the principal's office*. New York, NY: Holt, Rinehart & Winston.

Wood, D., Bruner, J., & Ross, G. (1976). The role of tutoring in problem-solving. *Journal of Child Psychology and Psychiatry, 17*, 89-100.

Yin, R. K. (1994). *Case study research: Design and methods* (2nd ed.). Thousand Oaks, CA: SAGE.

Yoon, B. (2007). Offering and limiting opportunities: Teachers' roles and approaches to English-language learners' participation in literacy activities. *The Reading Teacher, 61*, 216-225.

ABOUT THE CONTRIBUTORS

EDITOR BIOS

Bogum Yoon is an associate professor of literacy education in the Graduate School of Education at the State University of New York at Binghamton. She has worked in the field of language and literacy as a teacher educator in South Korea and the United States. Her current research interests include teacher education for English language learners, adolescent immigrants, critical literacy, and multicultural education. Her most recent articles were published in *American Educational Research Journal, Journal of Adolescent and Adult Literacy, and the Reading Teacher.*

Hoe Kyeung Kim is an associate professor of TESOL at Cleveland State University, Ohio. She has published articles in peer-reviewed journals including *Foreign Language Annals, Computer Assisted Language Learning, International Journal of E-Learning,* and *CALICO Journal* and several book chapters. Her research interests include teacher education, sociocultural theory, second language acquisition, educational technology, and culture and identity.

AUTHOR BIOS

Maureen P. Boyd is an assistant professor in the Department of Learning and Instruction in the Graduate School of Education at the University at Buffalo. Her research examines patterns of classroom talk to better understand the role and impact of teacher questioning and follow up, and the likely context in which engaged, elaborated student utterances and exploratory exchanges will occur. Her articles have been published in *Elementary School Journal, Language and Education, Journal of Literacy Research, Research in the Teaching of English and the Reading Teacher*. She recently completed her first book, Real talk in elementary classrooms: Effective oral language practice, coauthored with Lee Galda, and published by Guilford Press.

José David Herazo is an associate professor in English as a Foreign Language (EFL) in the School of Education at Universidad de Córdoba at Montería (Colombia). He has worked as a teacher educator and secondary school teacher in Colombia and is currently a PhD student under a Fulbright scholarship at the University of Pittsburgh, PA (United States). He has worked as author and editor for Greenwich ELT (Colombia) and has presented at various international conferences. His research interests include school applications of systemic functional linguistics (SFL), EFL teaching and learning from a sociocultural perspective, and EFL policy in Colombia.

Richard Donato is chair of the Department of Instruction and Learning at the University of Pittsburgh and holds joint appointments in the Departments of French and Italian and Linguistics. His research interests include early foreign language learning, sociocultural theory, discourse analysis, and teacher education. His research on foreign language education earned him the American Council on the Teaching of Foreign Languages/Modern Language Journal Paul Pimsleur award (1997 and 2006), the Northeast Conference Freeman Award (2004), and the French Institute of Washington Award (2003). He is the coauthor of the book *A Tale of Two Schools: Developing Sustainable Early Language Programs*.

Lara J. Handsfield is associate professor of literacy and elementary education at Illinois State University. A former bilingual teacher, Lara's research centers on literacy instruction in culturally and linguistically diverse classrooms, teachers' negotiations of multiple political and pedagogical demands in their teaching, and implications for student and teacher identities. She recently guest edited an issue of *Theory into Practice* on new and critical perspectives on comprehension strategy instruction, and has published her research in a variety of professional and academic journals, including the *Reading Research Quarterly, Language Arts*, the *Journal of Literacy Research, Harvard Educational Review*, and *Research in the Teaching of English*.

Alessandro Rosborough is an assistant professor of teaching English language learners in the McKay School of Education at Brigham Young University. He teaches in the area of second language learning and dual-language immersion. He has multiple years of experience working with minorities and ELLs in urban and rural school districts and adult ESL programs. His current research interests include application of sociocultural theory to second language learning/teaching, gesture and second language learning in elementary and secondary settings, and meaning-making through an ecosocial perspective. His interest lies in the interrelationship between gesture, identity, and discourse, in second language learning.

Kristy Beers Fägersten is an assistant professor of English linguistics at Södertörn University in Stockholm, Sweden. Her teaching responsibilities include a variety of courses in general and applied linguistics, as well as specific TESOL courses for Södertörn University's Teacher Education Program. Dr. Beers Fägersten's research interests include discourse and conversation analysis, and she has published a number of articles on code-switching, multimodality, and classroom discourse, including face-to-face and net-based interaction. Dr. Beers Fägersten's current research is concerned with the promotion of communicative competence in the Swedish EFL classroom.

Melinda Martin-Beltrán is an assistant professor of Language, Literacy, Culture and Social Inquiry in the College of Education at the University of Maryland, College Park. She has worked as a bilingual and ESOL teacher in the United States and Latin America. Her research focuses on classroom interaction and discourse, two-way language exchange, educational equity for language minority students, sociocultural perspectives on language learning, and preparing teachers for culturally and linguistically diverse classrooms. She has published articles in journals such as *Linguistics and Education, English Teaching: Practice and Critique, International Journal of Inclusive Education,* and the *Modern Language Journal.*

Soyoung Lee is a full-time lecturer at the English Program Office at EwhaWomans University in Seoul. She has taught at several schools in Korea at the university level from 1994. She holds a PhD in English Literature and film and has published in this field along with books using film in English teaching and teaching writing to Korean students (*Write Now*). Being brought up in both America and Korea, she is interested in the role of culture in the English as a Foreign Language classroom

Paula M. Carbone is an assistant professor of clinical education in the Rossier School of Education at the University of Southern California. She received her PhD in education from the University of California, Los Angeles, in 2009. Her previous experience as a secondary teacher in low-performing urban schools prompted her research on literacy interventions. She investigates teacher development in the use of theoretically informed methodologies and pedagogies that build on the sophisticated knowledge and literate behaviors students from nondominant backgrounds bring to the classroom, focusing on the bicultural and bilingual students from Generation 1.3

Joyce Bezdicek is an assistant professor in early childhood education and ESL/bilingual education at Millikin University in Decatur, IL. She was a Title VII Fellow in bilingual/ESL education and obtained her PhD from the University of Illinois in 2008. Previously, she was an early childhood teacher in Japan, the Canary Islands, and the United States. In the US, she taught English language learners (ELLs) in a multilingual/multicultural preschool setting and was the coordinator of a preschool program that served ELLs. She has given national, state, and local presentations on teachers and their work with ELLs.

Georgia Earnest García holds the rank of professor in the Language and Literacy Division in the Department of Curriculum and Instruction at the University of Illinois at Urbana-Champaign. She teaches courses in bilingual and ESL education and second-language literacy. Her current research focuses on teacher education issues related to English learners and the literacy development, instruction, and assessment of bilingual students. She was a member of the National Literacy Panel for Language Minority Children and Youth, and has published in the *American Educational Research Journal*, *Reading Research Quarterly*, and *Anthropology & Education Quarterly*, among others.

Ester J. de Jong is associate professor of ESOL/bilingual education in the School of Teaching and Learning at the University of Florida in Gainesville, Florida. Her research interests include: integrated, linguistically diverse, classroom settings, language policy, and dual language education. She also works in the area of mainstream (standard curriculum) teacher preparation for bilingual learners. Her book, *Foundations of Multilingualism in Education: From Principles to Practice* (Caslon Publishing), focuses on working with multilingual children in K-12 schools. Her work has been published in the *Bilingual Research Journal*, the *International Journal of Bilingualism* and *Bilingual Education, Language Policy, Language and Education*.

Eun-Jeong Kim is an assistant professor of English education at Gyeong-sang National University in Korea. She earned her PhD in Foreign and Second Language Education from the University at Buffalo, the State University of New York. She also serves as vice dean of internal and external cooperation. She is engaged in preservice and in-service teacher development. Her current research interests include teacher development, classroom research, and critical pedagogy.

Jennifer Smiley has recently completed her Master's of arts in the Teaching of Spanish from Indiana University-Purdue University at Indianapolis. She is currently teaching L2 English in Madrid, Spain. She has taught L2 English and Spanish in the United States. Her research interests include classroom interaction, second language acquisition and sociocultural theory.

Marta Antón is an associate professor of Spanish at Indiana University-Purdue University Indianapolis and Research Fellow at the Indiana Center for Intercultural Communication. She is also an examiner for Diploma de Español como Lengua Extranjera. She has taught L2 English and Spanish in Spain and in the United States. Her research interests include classroom interaction, sociocultural theory, dynamic assessment and Spanish sociolinguistics. Recent publications have appeared in *Estudios de Lingüística, Foreign Language Annals, International Journal of Applied Linguistics, Language Teaching,* and *Revista Española de Lingüística Aplicada.*

Amma K. Akrofi is an associate professor of Language & Literacy in the Department of Curriculum and Instruction, Texas Tech University. She has taught ESL courses in Sierra Leone and Ghana. Her research interests include issues confronting English learners who live in linguistic contexts where English is not a first language, ESL literacy in American mainstream classrooms, immigrant and low-SES parents' involvement in children's reading development, and reader response to children's literature. Journals that have published her recent articles are *Reading Psychology, Literacy Research & Instruction,* and *Childhood Education.*

Carole Janisch is an associate professor in the Language & Literacy Program in the College of Education at Texas Tech University. Her graduate teaching within the program centers on foundations of reading, writing pedagogy, classroom based assessment measures, and writing across the graduate program. Her writing and research interests stem from the course content. She is particularly interested in reading, writing, and assessment as applied to examining effective classroom literacy practices across the grade levels.

Amira Zebidi is a doctoral candidate in educational psychology at Texas Tech University and a visiting student researcher in the School of Education at the University of Michigan at Ann Arbor. Her graduate experiences include Fulbright foreign language teaching assistant of Arabic at Pacific University in Oregon, graduate part-time instructor of French at Texas Tech University, and graduate assistant at Texas Tech University. Her current research interests include research self-efficacy, research anxiety, and thesis/dissertation self-efficacy among graduate students.

Karla Lewis is a veteran teacher of 30 years in Texas public schools with experience ranging from kindergarten to junior high. She is a doctoral candidate in the Language & Literacy Program in the College of Education at Texas Tech University. She has focused on the use of portfolios as assessment with elementary-aged students in her own classroom and throughout her graduate research. She is also interested in literacy—reading, writing, and speaking—across her content area teaching.

CPSIA information can be obtained at www.ICGtesting.com
Printed in the USA
BVOW06s2141140815

413450BV00004B/58/P

9 781617 358470